INTERMISSION

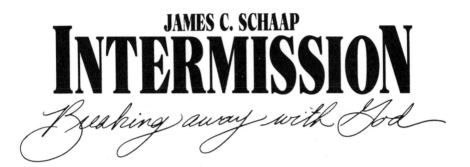

JAMES C. SCHAAP
INTERMISSION
Breaking away with God

Board of Publications of the Christian Reformed Church
Grand Rapids, Michigan

The Education Department is
grateful to Mr. Terry Treman of
Grand Rapids, Michigan, for his
photography that appears on the
cover and in the text.

Library of Congress Cataloging in Publication Data

Schaap, James C., 1948–
    Intermission: breaking away with God.

    1. Youth—Prayer-books and devotions—English.
I. Title.
BV4850.S32   1984   242'.63   85-4156
ISBN 0-930265-06-8

CONTENTS

PREFACE

Most books are meant to be read *alone*. This one's meant to be read *with*.

First, with your Bible. Before you read the "story" for each day, please take time to first read the Bible passage it's based on. If you make a habit of doing this, by the time you've finished this book you'll have read through 180 important Bible passages from Genesis to Revelation.

Second, with your family. Of course it's OK to read this book by yourself, whenever you find a few quiet minutes in your busy day. But try reading it with your family too—maybe around the table after you've eaten together. Why? Well, for one thing your family will probably enjoy hearing the stories in the book. And they might have some interesting things to say, things that will help you get more out of the readings.

Third, with the author. Jim Schaap, a teacher at Dordt College, wrote this book. Sitting in the basement office of his Sioux Center, Iowa, home, Jim read each Scripture passage, thought about it for awhile, and then wrote down the stories and thoughts the passage triggered in his mind—remembrances from his own school days, experiences of young people, things he's heard and read. Reading Jim's book will help you see—in a fresh, interesting way—what the Bible says. And you'll get to know and like Jim as you read.

I hope you'll enjoy this book and learn a lot from it.

Harvey A. Smit
Director of Education

1

THE ONLY CREATOR

Prayer:

Thank you,

God, for

creating

everything in

the world we

live in. Thank

you for flowers

and trees, for

the subway and

the sandbox

and basketball.

Help me to use

it well, all of it,

because it was

and still is your

creation.

Amen.

Read Genesis 1:1–13

Basketball has always been an exciting sport, but it used to be much slower than it is today. Years ago, a good team could win a game by scoring no more than a dozen points. In those days kids learned to shoot by holding the ball between their hands, then snapping it up toward the basket with their wrists. It was called a "set shot," and it was terribly slow.

Then along came players like Bob Cousy, a lightning-quick guard who played professionally for Boston back in the days when the Celtics won championships as if there were no competition. Cousy wasn't very big, so he figured he didn't have much of a chance to get those "set shots" off against the tall guys who were starting to dominate the league. He figured he needed a different way to shoot. So Cousy put one hand behind the ball, jumped up as high as he could, and at the very peak of his jump, released the ball with his fingertips. Cousy, and others of his time, created the shot every kid today knows as the "jump shot."

The jump shot changed the game of basketball. Instead of having to stop and set, then get a hand on either side of the ball and launch it toward the bucket, a player could run, jump, and shoot in almost one motion. Suddenly twelve points were barely enough to get a lousy team through one quarter of a basketball game. And it all happened because guys like Cousy created a new shot.

Because Cousy came up with something absolutely unknown before, it's easy to think of him as a "creator." The creation of the jump shot changed the game of basketball.

Of course, all kinds of people are "creators." Writers create stories. Painters create impressions on canvas or storefronts or even subway walls. Technicians create new programs for computers. Kids create backyard games out of mud and sand and junk from the garage.

But no human, not even Bob Cousy, can create out of nothing as God did. Cousy already had a ball—he inherited it from Dr. James Naismith, the creator of the game of basketball. Cousy already knew how to jump and how to play the game. What Cousy and writers and backyard kids have in common is material. What they do is reshape, retell, or rework what is already there.

Not God the Creator. He made everything under the sun—and even the sun itself—out of nothing. Every single thing. Before God said the Word, there was nothing. The whole world was more blank than a computer screen, more blank than anything we can imagine.

And when God finished his creation, he sat back and looked it over, and "he saw that it was good." If you can, try to picture him looking around and smiling one broad smile, even bigger than the biggest smile ever smiled by the greatest coach on record.

2

GOD'S INCREDIBLE CREATURES

Read Genesis 1:14–25

The Soviets claim to have an elephant that talks. His name is Batir, and reportedly, he can speak as many as twenty different phrases. He can even ask, "Have you watered the elephant?" The thirteen-year-old elephant is kept in Karaganda Zoo in Kazakhstan, a rather remote republic of the USSR. According to the Soviet news organization, Tass, because Batir was raised by humans and never knew other elephants, he simply began mimicking human speech.

Since Americans are generally skeptical about Soviet claims, well-known US zookeepers pooh-pooh the story of Batir, saying that a talking elephant is "extremely unlikely." They are willing to admit, however, that elephants are among the most intelligent mammals.

Other animals speak, of course. Lots of people have parakeets that talk. Some folks claim that big black crows can talk too—if you split their tongues. And we all know that parrots talk. The ones in the old pirate stories even picked up cuss words from their swaggering pirate masters.

We used to visit a pet store where the manager kept a parrot on a perch above a sign that urged customers to speak to Polly. All kinds of people—grandmothers and kindergartners and college kids in T-shirts—would stand there and beg the bird to let out a few words. "Hello," they'd say; "Polly want a cracker?" And the big green parrot would stand there on his perch, wink a time or two, and watch the gawkers as if they were too silly for words. "Braaawwk," he'd say, "ice cream"—or something that made little sense—and those folks would walk away grinning, as if their day had been made by the talking parrot.

Of course, there is something noteworthy in hearing actual words drop from the fat beak of a parrot. And it would be quite surprising to hear an elephant ask for water. But the real wonder in all of animal vocabulary is the remarkable variation in these creatures God has made. At the very beginning of time, when God created feathered and finned wonders "after their own kind," he didn't stop creating. Growth and development keep changing things in his world. If you don't believe it, just visit a nineteenth-century house sometime and look at the length of the beds: we're much taller than our great-grandparents were. And, like us, all the living things God created continue to develop and change. His world is full of surprises.

So what if the Soviets have an elephant that talks? A friend of ours has a big brown hound that smiles. And every one of them—every weeping coyote, every lovesick humpback, every big-shot talking parrot—is just a part of God's museum of natural wonders.

3

THE STING OF RESPON- SIBILITY

Read Genesis 1:26–31

I never thought of myself as a king, but when I was in the fourth grade, my teacher decided I would make a good one. She gave me the part of the king in our class play. Those of us who were lucky enough to get parts were given thick old red books. Today I can't remember the play, but I will never forget the book.

Being in a play means having to memorize lines. That's part of an actor's responsibility. So each of us took the beat-up red book home to study.

As I was walking home that night, clutching my red book, I noticed that some of the guys had a baseball game going. I put the book down somewhere, picked up my glove, and played for hours. When I went home, I was sweating hard, probably remembering some fancy fielding play at third base.

But I had forgotten the book.

That night, I remembered. I snuck out of the house, went back to the diamond, and searched through dandelions that grew like wires at the bottom of the backstop. I followed the baselines toward third and first. But the book wasn't there.

All night long I tried to figure out where I had left that red book. I imagined it covered with heavy dew—curling up like the swoop of a fish hook. I imagined finding it dirty, warped, and ruined. But, even though I got up early and looked everywhere I could think of, I didn't find the book.

That day in school, while the teacher wasn't looking, I snuck another old red book out of the cupboards in the back of the room. Later, when we practiced, I pretended nothing was wrong. No one except me knew that somewhere outside, in the middle of the rain that fell all afternoon, was a crummy red book, filling up with water like a sponge.

I never found the book. And my teacher never discovered that one book didn't make it back to the stack of rejects in the back of the room. I escaped.

But that red book stays in my memory even today. I'm not telling you this story to warn you about taking care of your things. I'm telling you about the book because I've never been able to wash it out of my mind—even though no one ever caught me.

When God told people to be fruitful and multiply, to replenish the earth and subdue it, he called us to the very special role of governing, of ruling, of taking responsibility. We must respond to him in ways unlike the animals, even the talking elephants.

When we fail to be responsible with the world he has given us, we have been created to know that we have failed. That's why I can't forget about the red book. Human beings, unlike anything else in God's marvelous creation, know very well that they are God's people and that they must be responsible to him.

In some ways we have it tougher than the animals. But in one very important way we have it much better: we know God and we feel his love.

4

SUNDAY SENSE

Read Genesis 2:1–3

Sundays are often toughest on kids. Not so many years ago, kids couldn't even go outside on Sunday—except to church, of course. Some parents insisted that their children spend even the sweetest and warmest Sunday afternoons sleeping or, at best, reading.

Usually, these parents set other rules that were just as rough on themselves—men shaved on Saturday night, women peeled Sunday dinner potatoes the evening before, and no one worked in the garden after church. Ma's scissors stayed in the drawer, kids' bicycles stayed in the garage, Dad's fishing gear stayed in the basement. It's no wonder that in those days, just like today, kids figured they were suffering.

Rules aren't quite as strict these days, but people still observe Sunday. And people still *need* Sunday. Adults who work all week look forward to Sunday. Even for those who don't go to church or believe in God, Sunday is special. On Sunday there's no factory work, no more letters to type, no students waiting to take spelling tests, no office full of patients. For a lot of people, Sunday is still a day of rest.

That's the way God planned it, of course. "God blessed the seventh day and hallowed it," the Bible says. It's hard to think of God sitting back, sweaty and hot from the earth's first, long six-day work week, but that's what he did. God the Creator not only took the whole day off but also blessed that day. God hallowed Sunday or, as another translation words it, he "sanctified" that day—he made it holy.

So today, just like yesterday, there are two reasons parents generally like Sunday more than their kids do. First, they need the rest. Kids have to understand that parents really enjoy taking a nap on a quiet Sunday afternoon. But Christian parents also love Sunday because Sunday is the day the Lord specially blessed, commanding his people to "remember the sabbath day, to keep it holy." Making Sunday different becomes a matter of obeying God himself.

All of us—parents and kids—are commanded to remember that Sunday is "the Lord's Day." Even today some of us don't play Little League, some don't go to amusement parks, and some don't watch TV on Sunday. Even today some bicycles stay in the garage.

That we remember to obey God and "remember the sabbath" is more important than what we do or don't do on Sunday. But when Sunday turns into an everyday, we're not obeying the God that made the sabbath—the Creator that fashioned every one of us.

God expects our obedience, even if it keeps us from the park and our parents from the office.

5

NAMES AND WORDS

Prayer:

Lord, you gave us the power to learn about your creation. Help us to rule it to your glory. Amen.

Read Genesis 2:15–25

What does your last name mean?

My name, *Schaap*, means "sheep" in Dutch; and while neither I nor any of my relatives go around bleating or chewing grass or growing wool coats, there's a perfectly understandable reason why I carry such a tag. My immigrant ancestors came from a North Sea island named Terschelling, just off the coast of the Netherlands. Years ago, when nobody knew anything about tourists, people on that island made their living by raising sheep. Today, I am told, the place is a resort. But long ago, my great-great-great (and then some) grandparents were named on the basis of what they did for a living.

Lots of other names have similar sources. Names like Baker and Taylor come from obvious occupations. Zimmerman, a German name, means carpenter—though most of those who bear that name today probably don't know the difference between a ripsaw and a crosscut.

God gave Adam an immense responsibility when he told him to name everything from a water lily to a water buffalo. It was a task given only to humans, because only human beings are able to discriminate the way Adam had to. Way back then, long before science books, Adam had to note the differences between moths and butterflies, between horses and zebras. And he had to come up with a separate tag for each member of the whole menagerie. Think of the records he must have had to keep—here a box elder, there a birch; here a field mouse, there a pack rat.

Of course, Adam didn't name every single species of toad and cabbage plant that we know of today. We've already seen how God made the world safe for talking elephants. Things develop and change. But by commanding Adam to name every living thing, God gave people incredible power over his creation. Only people keep the books. The field of science includes biology, chemistry, geology, physiology, anatomy, paleontology, and a whole encyclopedia full of other "studyologies"—and every one of them is based upon the kind of discrimination Adam had to practice on that first day in God's garden classroom.

What's in a name? Plenty, if you can be the namer. As Adam's heirs, we inherit his responsibility. The Creator wants us to know his world.

What's in a name? Plenty, if you're named in the family of Christ. Just think of what it means to be named a Christian.

6

ADAM AND EVE IN THE BUFF

Read Genesis 3:1–7

When our kids were younger, we took them to *The Fox and Hound*, a feature-length Disney cartoon, at a neighborhood theater. They loved it, of course. And the next week, when we drove past the theater, they begged to go in again, thinking whatever was playing had to be as delightful as the show they had seen the week before. The new week's marquee poster featured two naked people—male and female, of course—with tree branches hanging down at the perfect angles to hide what the law demands must be hidden. I don't remember the movie—it must have been something about passion in the South Sea Islands, or something like that.

"They got a different movie this week," my wife told the kids. "This one isn't for kids." Then she looked at me and snickered, as parents will do sometimes.

But my daughter wasn't ready to give up: "It is too," she said. "This week it's Adam and Eve."

The movie was a far cry from Adam and Eve, I'm sure. But we didn't even try to explain that to her. We figured we'd wait until she got to grade school, at least . . .

It isn't all that unusual today for actors and actresses to take off their clothes in movies or even on stage. But it used to be. In all the plays William Shakespeare ever wrote, only one character ever appears without clothes. The character is King Lear, a man who can't face the responsibilities given him by the people. When he comes before the audience, his nakedness is meant to show how pitifully broken he is and how ugly he has become.

That's the kind of nakedness Adam and Eve felt before God after the first bad bite of the apple. Before the Lord God Almighty, their Creator, the one who had promised so much and asked so little, they were naked and full of sin. And they knew it. Oh, how they knew it. They could feel their stomachs curl with guilt.

And we feel it too, even today.

7

CAUSE AND EFFECT

Read Genesis 3:8–21

It was done. Eden's glory was suddenly thrown into darkness by Adam and Eve's disobedience. Everything changed.

Adam and Eve hightailed it into the bush when they heard God coming around again. Adam, in a very shaky voice, told God they were hiding because they were naked.

"Who told you you were naked?" God asked. "You've eaten from that tree, haven't you?" He didn't even give Adam time to answer the first question; in a second he had the whole business cased.

That reminds me of my father. When I was a little boy, my parents didn't want their kids dancing. They thought dancing was sinful. Some parents still think so today.

But kids are disobedient sometimes. Often, when my parents were out for the night, my older sisters would have some kids over. The year was about 1960 or so, and a new kind of dance—a silly thing called "the twist"—was very popular.

Almost anybody can do the twist. Even kids who've never been to a real dance can learn in no time flat. So, with the stereo blasting, the kids would start in dancing. I know—I was young, but I was watching. The living room shook with wiggling bodies.

Now my father knew that a whole floor full of kids, shaking to the same beat, would be tough on the house he had built with his own hands. All that jumping around had a way of drawing the nail heads out of the walls and floor. A couple nights of twisting, and the whole living room was full of hairline cracks where the nails were pushing out.

My father took one look at those ugly nail heads bursting out from the paint, and he knew right away that my sisters had been dancing. He didn't even have to ask. For him, the protruding nails were the effect, and dancing was the cause. Just that simple.

It was just that simple for God too. He saw that Adam and Eve were feeling ashamed, and he knew that shame comes from doing something wrong. The only wrong Adam and Eve could have done in that beautiful garden was to eat of the forbidden tree. It was simple cause and effect. Shame was the effect—something like the protruding nails in my parents' living room. The cause was disobedience.

That's not the end of cause and effect in this passage. God himself addressed each of the characters—Adam, Eve, and the serpent—and he told them very clearly how each of them would suffer (effect) for what they'd done (cause).

That's not the end of it either. Because Adam and Eve are our own ancestors, we share in their disobedience and their curse. Be(cause) of their sin, we all are affected—even a bunch of kids in 1960, kids who thought twisting was fun.

Maybe it was. But they did disobey, didn't they? So did I. So do you. So does everyone. That's the effect of sin.

8

THE FIRST MURDER

Prayer:

Lord, when we

see how fast

Cain committed

murder, we feel

how strong sin

is. Help us to

stay strong

against the

power of sin

and unbelief.

Help us always

to obey.

Amen.

Read Genesis 4:1–16

Not many years ago a popular play was made into what became a very popular movie: *Elephant Man.* The movie portrayed the life of a man whose face was so horribly disfigured that it took people's breath away. His was the kind of face you see in old, Saturday afternoon horror movies.

Cain was humanity's first murderer. God punished him by marking him for the rest of his days on earth. That's awful. We don't really know what kind of mark God put on Cain, but let your imagination wander—maybe it was a big red *x* right smack in the middle of his forehead. Whatever it was, we know everyone could see it. That means it was big and, likely as not, ugly.

I used to think of Cain as a kind of "elephant man," someone so horribly disfigured that he really couldn't put his feet up and rest anywhere on earth. I used to think that big *x* made this a real horror story.

I don't anymore. Other parts of this story of the first murder scare me more than an ugly face. Look at the story again, and you'll see what I mean.

Here's the horror: Cain wasn't what you'd call a really bad guy. That's right. He farmed—like his father, Adam. Apparently, he did well on the farm, so he must have worked hard. He was probably a good farmer.

Cain was even quite religious. After all, he could have just skipped bringing offerings to God if he wanted to. But he didn't skip—he brought offerings regularly, just as his brother Abel did. Cain was no fire-breathing villain.

What did God think of Cain? Look at verse 5: " . . . on Cain and his offering he did not look with favor." Why not?

God knew something we don't. We see someone who went through the right motions, but God saw a fake—a real fake. So he warned Cain to "do what is right" (v. 7). He warned him that right outside his door sin itself was crouching, waiting to have him for lunch. God knew that Cain didn't really love him.

Cain killed his own brother. Because he couldn't take a swing at God himself, he took out his hate on someone God loved. Cain killed Abel, but he hated God.

What happened to Cain could happen to the best of us. Sin crouches just outside our own doors and licks its chops the same way it did at Cain's house. What makes this a real horror story is the thought that, without God's grace, Cain's story could be our own.

9

GOD'S MYSTERIES

Prayer:

Lord, we don't always understand what is happening in our lives, but help us trust in you. Help us really believe that you know best.

Amen.

Read Genesis 7:1–10

A man named William Hazlitt once wrote, "No young man thinks that he shall ever die." Hazlitt was right. In fact, he was more right than he knew, for his statement is just as true of young women. It is nearly impossible for us to think about our own deaths.

But sometimes we're forced to think about death—whether we want to or not. Just recently I heard two young men, one in college, one in high school, profess their faith before our consistory. They came in separately, but both of them said they felt they were ready to say that God had saved them through Christ's death. What's more, they both said they were ready to say it out loud for all the world to hear. Both said they knew it, deep inside.

We asked them how they became convinced that God had actually chosen them. They gave the same answer. They both had been in bad accidents, one in a car and the other on a cycle. Both had looked death square in the eye. Both had been laid up helplessly in the hospital. Both knew they could easily have been dead. As a result, both saw their Savior's work more clearly, more powerfully than ever before.

Odd thing, isn't it, that occasionally it takes something as awful as an accident to help us see that our lives are not our own? But sometimes God sends things that seem sad or even horrible—things like the flood, for instance.

Imagine the story of the flood as a story for adults only, one of those programs that kids aren't supposed to watch. Think of the terror in the screams of people washed away by muddy creeks swollen far out of their banks. Think of families on rooftops, watching the crest rise by inches until there could be no escape. Think of swimming all night and never finding a bank or a beach or the side of a pool.

God sent a horrible flood to punish a wicked world. But the flood was first of all an act of grace. God saved Noah, his family, and a remnant of all that he had made during that first great week.

The flood was an act of God's judgment, but it was also a breathtaking act of mercy. He chose to save us.

Sometimes God acts in ways that seem incredibly strange to us. But he takes care of us. He always knows what's best, even when we think he's wrong. Take it from two guys with broken bones—or from a world cleaned up by the flood.

10

UNDER-STANDING GOD

Prayer:

Thank you for stooping to our level and helping us understand what seems so difficult. Help us to love you, to bend for you—because we know that's what you expect. Amen.

Read Genesis 9:8–17

Contrary to popular opinion, football takes some smarts. If a team wants to run a successful play, all eleven players have to know their assignments.

I once knew a great big tackle—let's call him Bozo—who was so forgetful he had to tape all the team's plays to the inside of his helmet. Nobody else was permitted to take off his helmet between plays, but this guy would flick off the helmet, listen to the quarterback's call, run his finger down the list, then snap the helmet back on. The guy was so big that no one—not even the coach—gave him any guff about it.

It's not hard for you to picture Bozo out there in the middle of the field without his helmet, but try this—try to think of God as forgetful. Not so easy, right? Most people are good at forgetting things, but certainly God doesn't forget. Or does he?

Listen to what he tells Noah: when I send the rainbow, I will remember my promise. The rainbow, it seems, is God's way of tying a string around his finger. That heavenly ribbon is meant to remind him, not us.

Of course, God really doesn't forget. Not the way people do. But sometimes the Bible has to speak to us in human ways, even when it speaks of God. Just a couple of chapters back, the Bible told us that God regretted having made people (chapter 6). Are we to believe that he got sour on us, turned cranky, and sulked like some kid who just struck out in the last inning? Not at all. When the Bible says God regretted something, it is using human characteristics to help us understand our Creator.

Because God is so much more than we can grasp, we need that kind of help, and he knows it. That's at least one reason why he gave us his covenant.

In today's passage the word *covenant* occurs eight times. A covenant is an agreement between two parties. In this covenant God promises never again to destroy the earth with a flood. In return, he expects us to obey him.

He gives us this covenant for two reasons: first, his promise helps us begin to understand his mystery; and second (and more important), the covenant gives us life itself. God bends over backwards for us. And the only condition for his bending is that his people do the same.

If you have to tape that to your helmet, do it.

11

JESSE'S ESCAPE (1)

Read Genesis 11:1–9

Jesse's black cycle stood alone in the school parking lot when he came out of the principal's office. Two or three dirt bikes were parked near it—little things with knobby tires and high fenders, like kids next to his own Big Daddy 500. But the other cycles, like the guys who owned them, were long gone. It was 4:30, and Jesse had just gotten himself kicked out of school.

It wasn't his fault either. He had just been giving some wimpy kid a little grief when Mr. Bronson came up out of nowhere and grabbed him around the arms—right in front of all his friends, right in the middle of lunch hall. Jesse had twisted his arms away in one quick snap and shoved Bronson so hard the man staggered, tripped on the next table, and fell back into a group of students.

Bronson had sat there snorting, really angry. And Jesse's buddies had laughed, making the humiliated teacher hopping mad.

The cycle cut a fine shadow over the gravel. Jesse pulled out his handkerchief and rubbed the fingerprints from the gas tank, then swung a leg over the bike and sat there for a minute. Jesse loved this cycle, loved it more than anything. He had spent years stacking boxes, carting out gro- ceries for little old ladies, mopping up aisles, doing a hundred inven- tories—all for the cycle. Even before he was old enough to work at the market, he had pedaled newspapers, getting up before the sun—all for the cycle.

His old man had warned him this time. "Jesse," he said, "you get in trouble once more and I'm locking that thing up for a year." His father wasn't playing around either. Whenever he got that mad, he talked slowly and stared hard. "I'm not kidding," he said. "Once more and that 500 gets dry-docked in the back of the garage."

When Jesse hit the starter, the cycle coughed lightly just once, then turned over and hummed, purring perfectly. No way was he going to let his old man park his bike that way. The cycle was his life. When he rode it, the other kids just stood back in awe. One flick of the wrist and the whole school stopped what they were doing— just because Jesse was taking off. He couldn't live the way he wanted to without the cycle.

That's why he went left at the light. Nobody, not even his father, was going to ruin what he had made for himself, what had taken him years to earn. The cycle was everything he lived for. That's why he took off, left everything back in that scummy town he grew up in.

Besides, it was a perfect day for a ride. Spring pulled in warmth that sweetened the air as it brushed back his hair and flowed across his cheeks. He didn't need anything else—not his mother, not his father, not the school. All he needed was the cycle. He'd show them. He'd take off and leave the whole mess.

Jesse watched an hour's worth of ditches pass—beer cans, waste- paper, snakes of black rubber from retread tires—before it struck him that he had no idea where he was going. No idea at all.

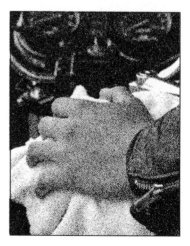

12

ABRAM TAKING LEAVE

Prayer:

Help us to

follow you,

even though we

may have to go

places we'd

rather not go.

Help us to obey

when we hear

your Word.

Amen.

Read Genesis 12:1–9

"We're leaving," your father says one day when you get back from school. Your mother's face is shadowed with streaks from tears she won't let you see.

"What do you mean?" you ask.

"We'll have a better life if we leave this place, so we're going across the ocean. We're going to start a new life."

Fear tightens into a fist beneath your ribs. You know he means it. You also know that you're not interested in starting over. After all, you've got your friends and your school—you're really not sure if life is worth living somewhere else.

But a few months later you leave anyway. The furniture sells in a huge garage sale; your bike goes too, and more than half your clothes. Everything goes.

You spend two weeks, maybe more, in one thin berth of a huge ship. All around you people get sick as dogs. Your father tries to help you through it, but you're sure he doesn't really understand. Your mother tells you not to call the old place "home" anymore. "We're going to have a new home now," she says. But her voice cracks. She's trying hard to convince herself.

Finally you arrive in the new country. Your first horror is that every word you know is worthless. You're like a baby without language, and it frustrates you. You cry a lot—too much. But the people look so different—they wear bright clothes and talk really loud and terribly fast. You hate them when they laugh. You're sure—you're always sure—that they're laughing at you.

You've immigrated. You've begun a process that millions of people have endured: you've left a home for some new place you won't quickly understand, and you're now a stranger in a strange new world.

Abram immigrated. No one said it would be easy, but God told him to leave the greatest culture of his time and live in the homeland of nomads, who knew little and cared less about him or his family. But Abram obeyed God.

And God made Abram a promise, a promise like the one he made to Noah with the rainbow. God told Abram that the entire world would be blessed because of what he did.

God armed Abram with a promise and sent him to a piece of real estate where the greatest story ever told would slowly, years later, unfold.

13

FAITH AND DOUBT

Read Genesis 15:1–6

Amy watched her father, deep in thought, bending over weeded rows of carrots. This was the fourth day he had spent in the garden, sweating in the hot afternoon sun. This was the fourth day since the funeral.

The night before, long after midnight had darkened the house, Amy had listened to the sound of his tears. She had heard her mother crying, too, but somehow Dad's sobs had bothered her more. She had also heard their words.

"If there really is a God, where was he a week ago?" her father had wondered. "How could he allow our little boy to drown?"

"I know how you feel," her mother had murmured brokenly. "I have doubts too. My faith isn't nearly as strong as it used to be. But we have to keep on praying. We just have to."

Doubt. Amy knew just what that word meant. Ever since the nightmare of Brian's death, Amy had been wondering too. Amy had a lot of questions. Somehow the death of her little brother seemed to have shattered her picture of a loving God . . .

Amy and her parents are not alone. Doubt is a natural part of every believer's life. Our passage today tells of Abram doubting God's promise of blessing: "What good is your blessing when I don't have a son?" he asks. God has promised Abram a son, but Abram, now already seventy-five years old, doubts God's promise.

If faith is a sure knowledge of God and his promises, then doubt is the nervous feeling that all this "Jesus saves" is a bit too much to accept. Amy and her parents couldn't understand how a great and loving God could allow something so horrible to happen to one of his children. It shook their faith and filled them with doubt. It made them, for the moment, question all of God's promises.

Amy and her parents could learn something by reading closely about Abram. "Come on, God," Abram says, "how are you going to do everything you promise, if you can't even get me a son anymore, huh?" That's doubt. So is, "God, how can we believe in any of your promises when you've allowed our little boy to die?"

But read on. God takes Abram outside in the night. From the earth's deep darkness, the night sky rolls through a haze of stars, hundreds of thousands of jewels on God's beautiful necklace. "Look at this, Abram," God says. "Your children will be as easy to count as these stars." And right then Abram believed God, and God called Abram righteous—because of his faith.

Abram and Amy and all of us have this in common: we live with doubts sometimes, and we will until that one day when our faith will be made whole—like Amy's brother is today.

14

WHO'S THE JOKE ON?

Prayer:

Turn our doubt

into trust, Lord;

give us joy in

the honor of

your grace

freely given.

Amen.

Read Genesis 17:15–22

Four guys sit in a circle around a five-dollar bill. A preacher comes along and asks what's going on.

Kid with the Yankees cap looks up. "Tellin' lies," he says. "Best lie gets the bill we found." He points at the money.

Preacher says, "When I was a boy, I never told lies."

Kid with the cap looks at his buddies and shrugs his shoulders. "Give him the money," he says.

Maybe if I were a preacher, I wouldn't think that joke was so cute. But I'm not—so I laugh. Laughter may well be the best medicine, but quite a bit of our laughing is usually at the expense of other people—in this case, preachers.

Here's a true story. Three brothers are building a house for a man. One Saturday morning the owner comes around, dressed in his jeans, ready to pitch in. Already the brothers are a little tired of the way the owner supervises, pointing fingers at them as if they don't know what they're doing, making sure they don't waste a penny's worth of lumber.

The owner picks up the scrap boards from around the block foundation, bangs out the extra nails, and drops them into a Folgers coffee can.

The three brothers watch him for a minute as he wrestles a tough nail from a two-by-four. The man whacks away until he gets frustrated, leans back and bangs the nail point. But the crooked nail still doesn't come out. The brothers smile.

Angry now, the man looks at the hammer as if it's not good enough. He picks the thing up, swings it down hard, and wham!—he blasts the end of his thumb. The brothers catch the whole show. The man dances and wiggles and hoots and jumps,

holding his thumb, whirling his arms through the air, his mouth stretched wide open. But he doesn't yell—not even once.

The brothers try to hold it back, but after the man gets in his car and leaves, still holding his thumb, all three fall on their backs and roar, squirming in the sawdust.

Abraham and Sarah laughed too. They laughed when God told them again that they would have a child.

Whom were they laughing at?

Themselves, probably. After all, Abraham was nearly one hundred now, and his wife, almost ninety.

But they were laughing at God as well. Abraham was seventy-five when God first promised him a son. He believed God then. But ten years later he doubted God's promise and took Hagar. This time, when God repeats the promise after another fifteen years have passed, Abraham and Sarah laugh. They can't help themselves.

And what does God do? He says the boy's name will be Isaac—meaning "he laughs." Abraham, this man of promise, the man God called righteous, laughs at God's promise. And God says, you just watch—this time next year, you will have a son. And his name will be "he laughs."

God could have laid out both of them, flat and cold, but his plans were too big. And Abraham knew it. Years later Jesus told the Jewish leaders that their father Abraham was overjoyed to see the day of the Savior: "he saw it and was glad" (John 8:56).

Abraham's mocking laughter, by faith, turned to joyful praise.

15

ROUGH
TESTS

Prayer:

Every day of our

lives you test us,

Lord, just like

you tested

Abraham. Give

us strength like

Abraham's to

pass your tests,

to be as faithful

as he was.

Amen.

Read Genesis 22:1–14

We've all had tests, but few human beings have faced as rough a test as Abraham faced. After waiting years for a child, Abraham and Sarah were finally given Isaac. He was the answer to prayers—a promise come true. So you can imagine how Abraham felt when God told him to kill their only child. That was the test.

All tests are meant to measure something. A page full of math problems measures the ability to figure. A playoff in band for first chair measures musical skill. God's test for Abraham measured something too. And it was a much harder test than anyone has ever taken in school. It reminds me of another story about a test, a story from one of Shakespeare's plays, *The Merchant of Venice* . . .

Once upon a time in an ancient land there lived a king with a beautiful daughter. The king wanted nothing but the best for his daughter, including the finest husband he could find. Because men from all over the world wanted to marry the princess, the king designed a test to determine who deserved his daughter's hand.

In the middle of his court the king lined up three chests—one made of gold, one of silver, and one of lead—and demanded that every man who wanted to marry his daughter choose among the three. First came the Prince of Morocco. He chose the gold chest, impressed by its inscription: "Who chooseth me shall gain what many men desire." Morocco wanted whatever it was that all men wanted—but when he opened the chest, he found nothing but a skull. He wanted the king's daughter, but he got nothing.

Next came the Prince of Aragon. He read the inscription on the silver chest: "Who chooseth me shall get as much as he deserves," it said. So Aragon,

thinking he deserved the princess's hand, chose the silver chest, opened it, and looked into the painted face of a blinking fool. Tough luck for the Prince of Aragon.

Finally, a man named Bassanio came along. He read the words on the lead chest: "Who chooseth me must give and hazard all he hath." Unlike the others, Bassanio was humble. He chose the lead chest because he knew that the greatest gifts come to those who give of themselves. Bassanio opened the chest and found a beautiful portrait of the princess.

The king's test was designed to measure a person's goodness. In that sense it was more like Abraham's test than some school test might be. When God told Abraham to sacrifice his son, he was testing Abraham's faith. God wondered whether Abraham still believed the promise God had given him years ago—a promise that Abraham would be the father of all believers.

Abraham did exactly what God told him to do. It couldn't have been easy for that old man to put his own boy on the altar, but he did. And when he did, he passed the toughest test with flying colors. The man God called the father of all believers kept the title because he continued to believe in the Lord.

16

NOT UN-EQUALLY YOKED

Prayer:

We like to think that we really know what's good for us and what isn't, Lord. We too often are sure that no one, not even you, knows better than we do what we need. Forgive us. Amen.

Read Genesis 24:1–21

Mindy had never had many dates—not in high school, not in the year since she graduated. That's why she was really excited when Carl, a guy at work, started asking her out. Mindy and Carl had good times together. They started seeing each other often. And before long they were talking about getting married. It was important to Mindy to be married in church—and, even more specifically, in her church—so she and Carl went to talk to Rev. Tyndale.

The conference with her pastor wasn't what Mindy had expected. As they left the church, Mindy was crying and Carl looked grim. Rev. Tyndale had told them in no uncertain terms that he wouldn't marry them—"at least not yet," he had said, "not as long as Carl doesn't care much about the God you worship, Mindy."

Carl *didn't* care. He wasn't raised in any church, and although he didn't like to talk about it much, he thought church people were a little silly. He loved Mindy all right, and it was fine with him if she went to church—but he didn't want to have anything to do with it himself. And that's just what he had told Rev. Tyndale.

After a while, Mindy went in to tell her folks what had happened. They were already asleep, but she woke them up and sat at the foot of their bed.

"He won't do it," she said. "Rev. Tyndale won't do it because he says Carl doesn't have faith . . . He said something about being 'unequally yoked'—"

Mindy's mother looked thoughtful. Her father leaned up on one elbow. "Maybe you ought to give some thought to what he says, Mindy," he told her.

Mindy, like most young people in love, wasn't ready to accept Rev. Tyndale's decision. She could see no reason for it.

Her story reminds me of my grandfather, the preacher. In at least one case that I know of, he refused, like Rev. Tyndale, to perform a marriage that he felt was destined for no good, a marriage where man and woman would have been "unequally yoked." His decison was not popular—after all, the kids were in love.

In that particular case, the couple got themselves married somewhere else. Twenty years later their marriage ended in disaster.

Did my grandfather know for certain that that marriage would be no good? Certainly he didn't. Does Rev. Tyndale know for certain that Mindy and Carl's marriage will fail? Of course not.

Did Abraham know for certain that any one of the local girls would make a lousy wife for his long-promised son, Isaac? No. But he did know, as did Rev. Tyndale and my grandfather, that those who walk with God should marry partners who walk with God. Does that mean all marriages between believers and unbelievers are bound to fail? Of course not. God has the miraculous ability to sponge up after a disaster, then ring out honey from the mess.

Marriage customs have changed since Abraham's time. No longer do parents hunt up proper partners for their children. What hasn't changed is Abraham's basic commitment to finding a God-fearing wife for his Isaac. Most God-fearing parents today want no less for their children.

Perhaps no single decision will be more significant in your life than your choice of a marriage partner. It's an investment that calls for large sums of thought and prayer.

17

PLAYING FAVORITES

Read Genesis 25:19–34

It was wrong for Isaac to love one of his sons more than the other, but it's not hard to see why Esau was his favorite. Esau was big and tough—a hunter forever tramping through the fields for game. Today, Esau would probably be the co-captain of the hockey team and king of the homecoming court. "Look, there's Esau," people would say, admiringly. Esau was the kid with muscles.

Jacob was another matter. While Esau was out hunting, Jacob hung around the tent cooking soup with his mother. Jacob never cared much about hunting with Esau; he had better things to do.

But before we start thinking that Jacob was some kind of sissy, we've got to read on a little. Maybe he didn't care to flex his muscles, maybe he didn't care what kinds of trick shots he could make with his bow, maybe he thought chasing rabbits was stupid—but he was no mama's boy either.

How do we know? Take a look at what he did.

One day Esau came in famished from a full day of hunting—hungry enough to chomp raw onions. As he entered the tent, he smelled the fine soup that his brother had been brewing all afternoon. The aroma floating through the place drove him crazy. "I've got to have food, Jacob," he said, leaning over the table as if he were about to die of starvation.

Jacob was no dummy. For all his years he'd felt his father's love for Esau. For all his years he'd been playing second fiddle because he was the younger of the two—even though it was only by a few seconds. For all his years he'd known that his brother had the birthright.

What's a birthright? Because Esau was the older son, it was his birthright to receive a double portion of his father's goods when his father died. That meant he would get twice as much as Jacob. The oldest boy in an Israelite family had an immense advantage over the younger sons, and Jacob knew it. Jacob wanted the birthright for himself. So when he saw his chance, he boldly took it.

Esau was roaring about his hunger. "Give me some of that soup," he said. Jacob calmly told him he could have as much as he wanted in exchange for his birthright. Esau's fists came down on the table. "Big deal," he said. "What good is the inheritance if I die right now?"

Jacob was no pushover, no sissy—but he *was* a bit of a schemer and a deceiver. He probably chuckled to himself as Esau foolishly gave up his inheritance for a bellyful of soup.

But God loved Jacob in spite of his scheming. Isaac may have loved Esau best, but for some reason God preferred the deceiver, Jacob. God doesn't judge us the same way people do. God does things his way.

18

BLESSINGS

Prayer:

Lord, help us to be as anxious for your blessing upon us as Jacob was for his father's blessing. Without your favor we can do little. Forgive us for trusting ourselves, when you deserve the praise and the glory.

Amen.

Read Genesis 27:1–41

I don't like meat loaf and scalloped potatoes, and I really despise pea soup. When I was a boy, I hoped my father's dinner blessing, prayed over a steaming pot of pea soup, would bring down some miracle to turn the whole ugly pot into a plateful of cheeseburgers. But it never happened.

I know now that at that point in my life I had the wrong idea of what a blessing is. When we ask a blessing, we're not asking the Lord to change spinach into pizza. Long prayers don't make liver and onions any tastier or pot roast any more chewable. We bless food every night at our house, but we don't expect God to change the food somehow. The blessing simply means that we are eating this food—no matter how tasty or how tasteless—in the presence of God himself. The blessing ac-knowledges that God is with us in whatever we do—eating or play-ing or sleeping or studying.

Jacob and his mother—and Esau and his father—had a slightly different idea about what *blessing* meant. To them, Isaac's blessing meant both favor and wealth. After all, God had told Jacob's grand-father, Abraham, that he, as the father of believers, would have all kinds of money. And Isaac himself was one of the richest men in his time. So when Rebekah heard Isaac say *blessing,* she was thinking about riches and power as well as spiritual blessing. And so were her sons. So it was the blessing that led to all that wretched scrambling and lying.

There's nothing beautiful about this story. In fact, if this story were written and published and set out for sale in a Christian bookstore, nobody would buy it. It's not sweet at all.

What's more, this story really has no heroes. Rebekah pushed her favorite son, Jacob, to deceive his own father, her husband. She plotted out the whole lie herself. Jacob, of course, went along with it. He stood there in front of his blind father and lied through his teeth. If he felt guilty about lying like that, we certainly don't read it in the Bible's account.

Isaac doesn't seem half so sinful as Jacob and his mother in this story. And Esau, Isaac's favorite, seems even less to blame—at least until he decides to murder his brother.

Actually, the whole family was a bunch of scoundrels. None of them seem to have been wonder-fully strong believers. Just think of Jacob standing there with sheep-skin glued to his arms and neck, all the while trying to lower his voice to sound as tough as his brother Esau. All of this wild scrambling was triggered by the potential of Isaac's blessing.

Somehow, God still sided with the schemer, Jacob. Even though Jacob was deceitful and wily as a snake, God knew he could make this man into someone strong and powerful. In God's own time, he would bring this schemer around, straighten out all his crookedness and make him a servant instead of a liar.

19

JESSE'S ESCAPE (2)

Prayer:

Lord, give us the ability to understand what you want for us. Give us the desire to obey.

Amen.

Read Genesis 28:10–22

The glow in the western sky slowly flattened into an orange belt at the horizon, and a thousand stars poked out from the canopy of night. Jesse felt fear in his fingers. Ahead of him was a cool late-spring night, and he had no sleeping bag, nothing at all to keep out the chill.

Jesse pulled off the freeway. He knew he would have to build a fire to keep warm, and if he built it too near the highway, someone would spot him. He stopped at a bridge where the road crossed a river snaking through the prairie. Carefully he climbed down through the ditch grass until he stood between the cement pilings, nothing above him but the loneliness of a country road. Beneath the bridge he could keep a fire going all night. Here no one would find him.

He had nothing to eat, so he fell asleep hungry, his jacket pulled over his shoulders like a sheet. At his feet the snapping sound of flames were a reminder of his vow to keep the fire going till dawn, no matter how often he had to wake up.

One odd dream recurred, flashed back and forth in his mind at will. Some strange power with a face like his father's and a voice much larger stayed in steady pursuit of his cycle, ran behind him while the cycle sang steadily in fifth gear, the prairie grass bending in its wake.

The grip of hunger woke Jesse at dawn, nearly doubling him up in pain. He sat up, rubbed the dirt from the side of his face, then slapped it off his palms. And then he felt something like a huge shadow behind him—a man was standing there.

"What on earth's a kid like you doing lying in this here mud?" a voice said.

Jesse turned slowly and looked up at a man dressed in baggy coveralls.

"You must be running from something, ain't ya'?" the man said. "You ain't set to be out here in the country all night. Ha'n't even got a blanket."

"I just needed to get some sleep," Jesse said. He pushed himself up and faced the man, who stood with both hands up on the edge of the bridge as if he were holding it there himself.

"You just come with me now, y'hear? What you need is the kind of breakfast only my wife can stir up." The gray-haired man twisted away from the bridge and stood there as if he were waiting politely for Jesse to leave first.

The cycle started easily. As Jesse rode behind the stranger's green pickup, he was nervous inside. But the man's finding him there, the man's offer of breakfast, reassured him that running had been the right thing. The man was like a guardian angel.

Dawn came up cool and bright. And right there on the cycle Jesse kind of prayed thanks, in his own way, for his guardian angel. He figured for sure that the man's offer of breakfast was a miracle sent by a God he really didn't know, a sign that running away was the only right thing for him to do.

20

THE TABLES TURN

Prayer:

So many times
we think we
know what's
good and right
and best for us,
God, but you
come along and
teach us clearly
about our own
pride. Give us
the strength to
trust you, in
faith.
Amen.

Read Genesis 29:15–35

It's not hard to dislike this Jacob character. Even his name means "deceiver." He lied to his brother, and he lied to his father. He was everybody's choice for the season's most wretched schemer. He had all the cockiness of a mosquito, and he was just as bothersome.

So when we read about Uncle Laban's trickery, it's hard to feel much sympathy for Jacob, to feel sorry about his seven long years of farm work for a wife he didn't want. Tough luck, Jacob, we can say. You got what was coming to you for being such a liar in the first place. There's even some kind of justice in what happened. Now the tables are turned, aren't they? Remember the time you glued that animal hair on your arms and pulled that mean trick on your own blind father? This time you're getting a good taste of your own medicine.

In order to appreciate what Laban did to Jacob, you've got to read verse 20 again. Jacob worked seven years for Rachel. Because he loved Rachel so much, those years just flew by. But when Jacob woke up the morning after the first night of his honeymoon, lo and behold the woman next to him wasn't Rachel. No sir, it was the tender-eyed, but not-so-beautiful Leah. Imagine what Jacob thought when he looked over and saw that he had married the wrong girl.

It was easy for Laban to pull that dirty trick, because custom dictated that the bride had to wear a veil until the morning after the wedding. It was also easy because Leah was more than willing to cooperate. She was no fool. Obviously, she wanted Jacob for herself.

People talk quite a bit about justice. So does the Bible. And to our minds at least, there's something almost wickedly just about a two-faced character like Jacob taking a good smack across the face from somebody else.

But what we think is just is often something different from what God thinks is just. Even in this story of deceit and treachery, God's will scored a knockout over what we think is right or wrong.

Judah, Leah's fourth son by Jacob, was the boy from whose family line Jesus would descend. So even though Jacob wanted Rachel, God had other plans in mind—plans that included Uncle Laban's dirty wedding trick of switching daughters.

Maybe it was God's idea that Jacob get his just reward for all the tricks he had pulled before. God's plan for his people moves in his own, sometimes mysterious, ways.

21

JACOB BECOMES ISRAEL

Read Genesis 32:22–32 and Genesis 33:1–4

I know this guy who once cheated on a history test. Hold it—I may as well admit it. I know this guy because I *am* the guy. Long ago I cheated on a history test, and I got caught. It wasn't fun at all.

Years later I worked with the teacher who caught me. Whenever I talked to him, I felt sort of weird inside because of what had happened so many years before. I was sure he was always saying to himself, "You stinker—I know about you."

Jacob had a similar problem. He was going to face his brother, Esau, and he was worried about what had happened so many years before when he had cheated Esau out of his birthright and Isaac's blessing. He remembered that Esau had threatened to kill him. Jacob was scared.

On the night before the meeting, a late-night, surprise visitor came to wrestle with Jacob. Those of you who have wrestled know how terribly tiring it can be. When you wrestle someone hard, you use every little muscle in your body—and all the big ones too. A few minutes' worth of wrestling is enough to knock anybody out.

This stranger came to Jacob and picked a fight that lasted for hours—in fact, all night long. What a match! Boxing matches last ten or fifteen rounds, but the rounds are only three minutes each. Jacob wrestled with this stranger all night long.

Finally the stranger told Jacob that the fight was over. "Let me go," he said. "It's getting light."

But Jacob wouldn't let go. "Not until you bless me," he said. Jacob knew that the stranger wasn't just some burglar or an old enemy. Jacob held on because he believed in this stranger. Jacob had faith.

Then something strange happened. The visitor gave Jacob a new name. If you were to change your name tomorrow, all your school records would have to be changed. All your friends would have to call you something else. Changing your name would be a big step. To Jacob, it was even bigger: he became a new man with his new name.

The night-long wrestling match was over, and Jacob, covered with sweat, got something he desired. Because the stranger who wrestled him was really God, Jacob became a new person. All his life Jacob had been wrestling with God, and on this night, the night before he would meet again with his brother, God himself came down to wrestle him. And Jacob held him tight.

"You will be called 'Israel,' " the stranger said, "for you have wrestled with God." And Jacob became, at that moment, a new man.

By the way, one day I asked my old history teacher if he remembered having caught me cheating. His jaw dropped. "You?" he said. "You're kidding—" And he just shook his head.

The next morning Jacob met his older brother and enemy, Esau. Jacob must have been a little scared, but it didn't last long. Right away Esau ran to him and kissed him.

Jacob, the new man, had become Israel.

22

LEST WE FORGET

Prayer:

Lord, sometimes

we start to

think that only

perfect people

can be called

your children,

but the story of

Jacob shows us

that you love us

even when we

aren't perfect.

Thank you for

your great

promises to us.

Amen.

Read Genesis 35:1–7

Just east of the little town of Cedar Grove, Wisconsin, one small highway marker stands in a half circle off an old highway called Sauk Trail Road. The marker tells the story of Dutch settlements there on the western shore of Lake Michigan. Carved into the wood of the marker is a summary of the sinking of the *Phoenix,* a passenger ship that went down in flames just a few miles offshore from that point in November of 1847.

When I was a boy, that sign seemed almost sacred to me. When that ship sank on a Sabbath evening, over two hundred Dutch immigrants died in the heat of the fire and the cold of November lake waters. Within sight of their new home in a new land, helpless Dutch passengers cried their last tears and prayed their last prayers before going to a cold lake grave.

Historical markers, like the one in Cedar Grove, spot the highways of this continent and others, reminding passersby of people, places, and events that shouldn't be forgotten. Near Custer, South Dakota, a highway marker describes the encampment of the yellow-haired general whose cavalry company was soundly defeated by the Sioux Indians at the battle of Little Big Horn. Around Niagara Falls, Ontario, highway markers commemorate the British and American cannonade battles of years ago. Smack in the middle of Nebraska's cornfields, a series of markers traces the path of the Pony Express, for a time the only overland mail route from eastern to western United States.

Old conniving Jacob erected historical markers so often you might think he was in the construction business—or the tourist trade. He set one up the night he saw the ladder going up to heaven (chapter 28). He named the place "Bethel," then told God, in typical Jacob fashion, that he would worship him—*if* God would bring him safely back to Isaac someday.

But God told Jacob that this time he was looking for more than a historical marker. Bethel, the place where Jacob made his solemn but cocky promise to God, would become a place of worship, not just a place to remember a dream. And the place would be marked with an altar, not just a marker.

This was a turning point in the life of the deceiver. Instead of simply building another memorial and then going on with his plotting and scheming, Jacob now collected all the idols he had allowed his people to keep and commanded the whole company to take baths. Clean yourselves up for God, he told them, and bury all your sins.

Then the new Jacob built an altar—for worship. Bethel wasn't simply a place to buy postcards and souvenirs. It was a place of action. It was the place where this new Jacob began to accept the responsibilities of the covenant he had made with the God of his parents.

IN MEMORY OF THE
SOLDIERS AND SAILORS
WHO FOUGHT IN THE WAR
OF THE REBELLION, 1861—
1865.

23

THE DEADLIEST SIN

Read Genesis 37:1–11

Everyone likes lists—some people even make money off them. Most of us are eager to read about the ten best-dressed movie stars, the twenty richest industrialists, the five ugliest animals, the four worst-fast-food restaurants, the ten most disgusting poems of all time, or world history's five silliest wars.

In the Middle Ages, people took religion about as seriously as we take sports. You could get in a fairly dangerous argument by claiming to know how many angels could dance on the point of a pin. But back then, people liked lists just as we do. They kept lists of things that were important to them—religious things: vices and virtues and the seven deadly sins.

It's still worth knowing the seven deadlies, though people today seldom talk about them. For the record, the seven deadly sins are gluttony, avarice (or greed), lust, sloth (laziness), wrath, envy, and pride. The king of these seven deadlies is pride. And it's pride that triggers all the action in the story of Joseph.

It's one thing to dream that you're so much greater than your brothers and sisters; it's quite another thing to proudly broad-cast it, especially when the rest of the kids are already angry about the fact that your father loves you more than he does them. But Joseph tells his brothers every detail of dreams they don't want to hear about. And he does it not once, but twice.

Jacob, the man who committed himself to God at Bethel, ob-viously favors Joseph. His pride in Joseph leads him to neglect his many other sons. That pride is rooted in the fact that he loves Rachel more than Leah.

Joseph's brothers' anger is rooted in their sense of injured pride—the idea that Joseph could, in fact, ever rule over them. Jealousy, anger, and resentment pour out from their injured pride.

And yet—it seems as if we've seen this before—God's mercy still extends to each of these victims of the sin of pride, even though every single one of them should know so much better. God loves them and he forgives them.

What's even more wonderful and incredible is that God loves and forgives us too—even though we also are victims of pride.

24

TWISTING PLOTS

Prayer:

Lord, even our own best laid plans don't always go the way we think they will, or should. But give us the faith to know that you are guiding our lives and that you love us. Make our faith strong.

Amen.

Read Genesis 37:12–28

Every story has a plot, a sequence of actions. Half the fun of watching TV or reading a book is trying to guess how the plot of the story will turn out. Generally, we enjoy plots that twist around like pretzels, surprising us at every bend.

In one of the finest plots in the Old Testament, Jacob's boys sold their brother Joseph into slavery. They had resented Joseph for a while, of course—ever since father Jacob had given him that flashy coat. But when they saw him strolling across the field while they slaved away with the sheep, they'd had enough.

"Let's kill that dreamer," one of the boys said. "We'll dump him in a well and tell Father that a wild animal got him."

"There's no need to kill him," said Reuben, the oldest. "Let's just toss him into an empty well and leave him to die." (Reuben planned to return in secret later and pull Joseph out of the well.)

While Reuben was away, along came a caravan of traders bound for Egypt. Judah had an idea. "Let's sell Joseph to them! That way we won't be responsible for his death. After all, he is our brother." So the brothers sold Joseph for twenty pieces of silver.

Sometime later Reuben returned and hurried to the well to rescue Joseph. When Reuben saw that his younger brother was gone, he went wild with grief. "Now what am I going to do?" he wept to his brothers.

Finally the brothers came up with a plan. They grabbed Joseph's flashy coat—which they had stripped from him before they threw him into the well—doused it with blood, and brought it to their father, pleading their innocence.

"Look at this, Dad," they said."
We think it's Joseph's coat."

Jacob fell to the ground in anguish, certain that his favorite son was dead.

The brothers must have thought that this was the end of the story for Joseph. They were unprepared for the "O. Henry" twist.

O. Henry was an American writer who became famous for a plot twist at the end of his short stories. He had knack for surprising his readers, for pulling the rug out from under them.

The story of Joseph has a perfect O. Henry twist. Jacob's boys were sure they were done with Joseph, as sure as a person could be with a bloody coat of many colors and a pocketful of silver.

But God himself was writing this story, and God is a master-plotter. O. Henry's stories seem cute, at best, when matched with God's stories. God had his own plot for Joseph, and he used Joseph's jealous brothers to spin it out.

Before long the whole bunch of them would be standing before some strange government official in Egypt, begging their hearts out for his favor. And that government official, as all of us know, would be none other than the dreamer, Joseph.

25

RAGS TO RICHES, ETC.

Read Genesis 39:1–6

"I was in my working dress. I was dirty from my journey; my pockets were stuffed out with shirts and stockings, and I knew no soul nor where to look for lodging. I was fatigued with traveling, rowing, and want of rest, I was very hungry; and my whole stock of cash consisted of a Dutch dollar.

"I went immediately to the baker's. I bade him give me three-penny worth of any sort. He gave me, accordingly, three great puffy rolls. I was surprised at the quantity, but took it, and, having no room in my pockets, walked off with a roll under each arm, and eating the other. Thus I went up Market Street as far as Fourth Street, passing by the door of Mr. Read, my future wife's father; when she, standing at the door, saw me, and thought I made, as I certainly did, a most awkward, ridiculous appearance."

So begins part of the auto-biography of Benjamin Franklin, one of the most famous of the patriots of the American Revolution. Franklin included this description of his arrival in the city of Philadelphia for a purpose: he wanted to sing the praises of the new country, a country in which people as poor as he was could become rich and influential. Franklin helped build a basic doctrine of American life: that anyone who had some smarts, a little nerve, and a healthy supply of elbow grease could attain success in this new country.

The rags-to-riches story has been part of American philosophy for more than two hundred years now. It's stayed there because it has, in many notable cases, worked. Wealthy and influential people from Benjamin Franklin to Abraham Lincoln to Jay Van Andel and Richard DeVos illustrate that such a climb to success is pos-sible.

Joseph's story, however, is more than rags to riches. Joseph started life as the son of a wealthy landowner. Later he was sold as a slave, worked as a slave, and slowly, through his own hard work, made it to the office of steward, where he controlled just about everything the rich Potiphar owned. Joseph's story is riches to rags, then back to riches.

It couldn't have been easy for him, being a slave for this rich Egyptian. But the Bible says he did his job well, worked hard, and was a good man. With those credentials, he gained an important position in a society in which he was a stranger. It wasn't easy. Joseph made himself a suc-cess. Just like Franklin did.

Right?

Wrong.

God was creating the plot. God was in control. He gave Joseph the strength, the intelligence, the business sense to accomplish the work Potiphar asked of him. Furthermore, God gave him the moral sense to refuse Potiphar's wife when she asked him to sleep with her (vv. 7–12). And, when Potiphar believed his wife's lies about Joseph's behavior with her, God gave Joseph his favor: the Lord was with him, and whatever he did, the Lord made it prosper (v. 23).

Joseph didn't forget who was guiding him, both in his rags and in his riches.

God had his hands on Joseph's life.

26

DREAMS

Read Genesis 40

Reading the Bible can get a little tough at times. Most of chapters 40 and 41 tell us about Joseph's amazing talent for interpreting dreams. As long as we read the story as if it is some Disney-like fairytale, it's easy to accept everything that happens. But as soon as we try to match the story up against real life, things get a little bit hard to believe. After all, how many licensed dream interpreters have offices on your block? Can you really believe Joseph?

It's not that we don't dream, of course. Almost all of us have some nightmares, some sweet dreams, and more than a few dreams we wouldn't dare tell anybody about. Some dreams come back time and time again, as if to haunt us.

When I was a high school teacher, I used to dream quite regularly of walking into a full classroom. I'd ask the kids to be quiet, but nothing would happen. I'd raise my voice. Still, nothing would happen. I'd yell. No one paid me a dime's worth of attention. I'd scream—"Be quiet!" But it was as if I wasn't even there. For me, that dream was a nightmare.

I suppose some psychiatrist (perhaps the closest thing we have to a dream interpreter) would tell me that my subconscious was merely showing me my greatest fear as a teacher—that I could lose complete control of the class. She'd tell me we sit on some thoughts—we don't really allow ourselves to think some ideas that actually float around in us. I really didn't allow myself to think I couldn't keep kids quiet—even though that fear was in me. So the fear came out in a dream. I sat on it, so it had to find another way out.

But the dreams in chapters 40 and 41 of Genesis are more than mere reflections of someone's secret fears. They are dreams especially designed to prophesy what's going to happen to the dreamer. Joseph comes back to power—big power—by using Pharaoh's dreams to explain the future of the nation. God uses these dreams to bring his plan to fulfillment.

That's where the Bible reading gets tough. Does God speak to *us* in our dreams too?

There's two easy answers: yes and no. Yes, he does—so from now on keep close track of every dream you have (and then go crazy trying to interpret what on earth is being said). Or no, he used to use dreams, but he doesn't anymore. Both are easy answers.

Robert Mason, author of a book named *Chicken Hawk*, begins the story of his life by explaining that when he was a kid, he frequently had dreams of simply rising off the ground, dreams of levitation. During his two years of combat service in Vietnam, he flew more than one thousand combat missions in— guess what?—a helicopter.

Joseph probably could have told him as much. But Joseph would have added some important advice (40:8): interpreting dreams is *God's* business.

27

SWEET REVENGE

Prayer:

Lord, help us to forgive others. Help us to remember that hatred can eat us alive if we don't control it. Thank you for telling us to love our enemies. Amen.

Read Genesis 42:1–17

What we need here are a few instant replays.

Flashback 1: Joseph is sitting in a deep hole in the ground, nothing but darkness around him, nothing above him but a round circle of light. His coat is gone now. He is cold, maybe crying.

Flashback 2: His brothers sell him for twenty pieces of silver to some strange men on camels. Joseph has never been to Egypt; he has never been a slave. The men look dangerous. They lead him away from the fields he knows so well. They bind his hands with ropes that dig into his skin, making his wrists raw with blood.

Flashback 3: In Egypt he devotes himself entirely to doing the best work he can, organizing Potiphar's business concerns. He has no choice. He is a slave to whatever Potiphar desires.

Flashback 4: He is thrown into prison because Potiphar's wife tells her husband Joseph raped her. It isn't true, but who listens to a slave?

Now the camera rolls to the present. Even though Joseph is not an Egyptian, he has become incredibly powerful. God has blessed him; he now controls the farm policy of the whole country. One day, in the middle of a work week, his brothers stand before him, twenty years older now, but still recognizable to their younger brother. How *could* he forget them after what they put him through?

Ah!—sweet revenge. He remembers the dismal hole in the ground, all his hours of sweat, the smelly prison. They were responsible for all his agony.

Ah!—sweet revenge. One scratchy little voice in Joseph's mind tells him to send his brothers back to their father without food. "Give them what they deserve," the voice growls.

"They aren't your brothers anymore; men who act like they did don't deserve the title 'brothers.' Starve them out. Make them pay for what they've put you through."

Ah!—sweet revenge!

But there's another voice too, a much louder voice. This voice rises from Joseph's twenty years of experience away from his family—years in which he felt God's hand in his life. Joseph knows that the bad chapters are only part of the story. After all, today he is second in command in the entire country of Egypt. Joseph knows now how God has used him and blessed him.

That second voice comes up with a plan. Check these brothers out, the voice tells him. Put them to the test. See if these men are still full of the anger they once had. See if they have changed. "After all, Joseph," that voice reminds him, "you have—haven't you?"

Joseph knows something— something each of us should learn. He knows that although revenge may be sweet, that doesn't make it right.

28

JUDAH, THE TYPE

Prayer:

Lord, thank you

for your gift of

life. Thank you

for showing us

the power and

the grace of

sacrifice in these

biblical

characters.

Amen.

Read Genesis 44:18–34

Quite often we use people we know to describe new ones we don't. If your friend claims her teacher is a regular Indiana Jones, you probably get a pretty clear picture of what her teacher is like. Character types are handy that way.

Judah stood up for his little brother. He told Joseph that he would stay in Egypt as a slave, rather than leave Benjamin behind. In doing so, he was—even though he didn't know it at the time—becoming a character type, a type of Jesus Christ. Just as Christ stood in the place of all of us—just as he died in our place—Judah gave himself for his brother.

Judah's sacrifice sets a pattern that will recur in our readings. In fact, it will recur so often as we read through the Old Testament stories, that by the time we get to Christ's own sacrifice, the pattern itself will be very familiar and understandable. Judah's sacrifice points ahead to Christ's.

A whole lot farther along in the Bible, in the first letter to the Corinthians, the apostle Paul explains Christ's gift this way: "God made him, who had no sin, to be sin for us, that in him we might become the righteousness of God." It's the same pattern of sacrifice, only this time God's gift isn't only for one little brother loved by his father, but for all of God's children.

Isn't it something that it was *Judah* who stood up the way he did? After all, it was Judah's idea to sell Joseph into slavery to begin with (chapter 37). Not only that—and this is even more special—it was Judah whose children's children's children (and then some) would include none other than Mary and her most favored son, Jesus Christ.

Who can believe all of that is coincidence?

29

TEARS

Prayer:

Thank you for

the story of

Joseph, for the

story of your

own abiding

love for your

people. To your

name be all

power and glory

given, yesterday

and today and

tomorrow.

Amen.

Read Genesis 45:1–15

Some people cry at weddings. Most people cry at funerals. I have a confession to make: I cry at track meets. Well, not cry exactly, but my bottom lip starts to jiggle and I start rubbing the inside corners of my eyes, as if with the last gust of wind I picked up some dust that needs to be poked out.

You can imagine what the Olympics do to me. It's embarrassing. When I see some sprinter standing up on the victory stand while the national anthem is playing, I turn to pudding. And if I even get a hint that his or her own lips are quivering, I turn into a slobbering fool.

Joseph cried too—for a different reason. Look at that first verse: he simply couldn't hold it back anymore, and he cried. Think of how long it'd been since he'd seen his brothers. Then think of how long he waited before he told them who he was. He held it back for two long visits, swallowed his excitement, until finally he simply couldn't anymore—out it came, like the whoosh of air from a balloon. He couldn't hold it back: he cried.

Then, while his hands were still up to his eyes, he yelled, "Everybody out!" He cleared the place with one long swoop of his robed arm. Egyptians flew like scattering chickens from this strange bearded man who had become their leader. And he was left with nothing but his destitute brothers, dressed in rags probably, poor as abandoned children, skinny, dirty travelers there from miles away simply to beg, on their knees, for food.

"And he wept aloud." He cried so loud the flustered Egyptians, standing around outside the room, heard his whooping through the closed doors. Finally, he raised his eyes, held his hands to the arms of his chair for strength, and tried to speak. "I am Joseph," he said. "Is my father alive?"

The poor brothers bumbled about, hemmed, and hawed. They hadn't the slightest idea what was going on. Just seconds ago they had been scared to death that someone from their family would have to stay in Egypt if they were to take any food back to their father. Now this madman ruler—the man who had set them up so clearly with the silver cup in their bags, the man who had made such wild demands on them—now this guy broke into tears and started talking about Joseph! Things had gone mad.

So Joseph told them again, "I am your brother Joseph, the one you sold into Egypt!"

That scene can't help but tug at your lower lip. And it gets even better. Read verses 5 through 8 again. "It wasn't you who sold me into Egypt; God sent me," Joseph told them.

Now let's go back a minute. This was the son of Jacob the deceiver. This was the cocky kid who went around telling his less-favored brothers about dreams he had, dreams that put them down badly. This man, Joseph, had come a long way—a long, long way.

At this point in his life Joseph saw everything clearly—because he saw God's will. He had been made whole. He understood God's power in his life.

And Joseph didn't even know it all. God had used his life to preserve his people so that someday a Savior would be born to save the world—that includes you and me.

Now that's really beautiful. (Pardon me, I must have something in my eye.)

30

JESSE'S ESCAPE (3)

Read Genesis 47:1–12

"What do ya' know about farm work, boy?" the man said, swinging his big leg over the seat of the tractor. His name was Arlen, and Jesse's full belly reminded him that Arlen had been right: what Jesse had needed was the kind of breakfast only his wife could stir up— eggs, bacon, toast, and rolls.

"Never been on a farm before—not to work at least," he said.

Arlen had told him over breakfast how it was he needed some help. The neighbor kids were back in school and there was still some late haying to be done. Jesse never questioned the idea of working for a while. He had nowhere to go, and Arlen said he'd pay him well. Things were looking good.

By mid-morning both of them were up in the barn together. Arlen had two bales of hay laid flat on the edges of two others packed edgewise. "Think I can get the two of them into this one space?" he said.

Jesse looked at the width of the gap. Arlen had told him that the rows of bales had to be stacked tight. The space left in the row looked too big for one bale, but not wide enough for two. "I don't know," he said. "I don't think so."

"You watch now," Arlen said. He leaned his weight on the inside edge of the two flat bales so that both of them seemed to wedge into the gap. Then he pulled at the outside edges, forcing them both down with his arms first, then with his knees, until they fell together into the space—fell tight, the entire row of stacked bales as flat and packed as a floor.

"Ain't nothin' to learn that trick," he said. "But it's something that's got to be done. If you're going to walk on a row of bales later on, it's got to be tight or you can crack an ankle sure as anything." He jumped on the row and walked back and forth to demonstrate.

"It's your old man you're running from, I bet, isn't it?" Arlen said, sitting back on the edge. "I was sixteen myself once." He poked a piece of hay into his teeth. "I took off too. What you're doing ain't nothing new to me."

Jesse sat at the edge of the row, his knees pointed away from the man. "I don't have to live with his rules anymore," he said.

"Course you don't. You're free as a bird all right. But I think you got to learn somehow to respect him. The both of you got to fit together like these bales of hay."

"I don't need him anymore—"

Arlen flicked off his cap and ran a hand over his red hair. "I made it all the way to California thinking I didn't need my old man anymore. I know what you're doing better than most—"

"You don't even know my father," Jesse said.

"Got me there, sure enough." He put both hands at his sides and brought his legs up beneath him. "But I know you already, and what I see tells me all I need to know about him."

The chains on the elevator jingled through the silence.

46

31

LEAVING AND ARRIVING

Prayer:

Thank you for delivering the Israelites from slavery. Thank you for delivering us from sin. And thank you for your promise that all of us will enter the promised land. Amen.

Read Exodus 1:1–14

There are lots of things I don't understand about computers—even though I'm using one right now. For instance, I type out a sentence and it appears across the TV screen in front of me. Then I type another one. If I look back and figure I don't need the first one, I get rid of it—but very mysteriously.

The computer uses a little flashing blip called a "cursor" to tell me where I am on the screen in front of me. As I type, the letters jump out of this little flashing blip. If I want to erase a sentence, I put the little blip on the first word of the sentence and hit a couple different keys. In just a matter of seconds that little cursor eats the words—just devours them—as if the whole sentence were one long Hershey bar.

What I don't know is where those words go. If I erase a sentence I've written on paper, I figure that if I were to pick up all the little specks of rubber from the eraser and unroll them or something, my words would still be there. Right? At least the lead from the pencil would be there. But that little cursor just eats words, and I have no idea where they go. It's as if they go out the door and disappear into space, never to be seen again.

That's not the way things went for the Israelites. Sure, one day they marched right off of Pharaoh's screen, just like my letters. They made their exit from the land of Egypt, from Pharaoh's cruel slavery. That's why we call the second book of the Bible *Exodus*—it tells the story of the Israelites making their *exit* from Egypt.

But that's only half of it. The door out of Egypt opened to the promised land. Their exit was a kind of deliverance—from the bondage of slavery under the Pharaohs to the blessings of freedom in the promised land. The Israelites didn't leave simply to get away, but to get somewhere. Unlike the sentence my cursor eats, the Israelites didn't simply disappear. They went somewhere when they walked off Pharaoh's screen.

So the theme of the whole book of Exodus is not simply an exit, but a deliverance: God reached into the affairs of his people and delivered them *from* the misery they suffered at the hands of Pharaoh, and *into* his own promise.

What happened to the Israelites is what happens to us as God's people in the twentieth century. God's gift of his Son delivers us from sin and death in the same way he delivered his people, the Israelites, from the slavery Pharaoh locked them into—and all of us are bound for the promised land outside the door he opens for us.

Let's remember that as we read Exodus. The Israelites didn't simply take the door marked "exit." They'll walked into new opportunities to serve the God who had delivered them.

So should we.

32

LUCK

Read Exodus 2:1–10

You're sitting at home with your parents. It's 1943, and you live in a city in the Netherlands. Nazi soldiers with rifles stand around on street corners all day. You've seen them beat up people. Your own father has hidden from them for months; at nights sometimes he disappears. You know very well the Nazis might kill him for what he does during those hours he's gone.

Suddenly, without warning, a black car stops out front and Nazis run into your house. Your father has just enough time to hide in the only way he can—by winding himself into the curtain. You see his shoes sticking out where the folds at the curtain's bottom barely reach the floor.

The Nazis search the house; a young German checks the room in which you've been sitting. You watch his eyes burrow into every corner. You see him spot your father's shoes beneath the curtain. You're sure he's seen your father. Your stomach turns.

"Find him?" the officer yells. The young German watches the curtain. You wait for the horrible words.

"Not here," the young man says. When the Nazis leave, you cry . . .

That's a true story. I heard it from the man who remembered the fear he felt for his father wrapped in the curtain.

It would be easy to call that family *lucky*. But *luck* is a Las Vegas word. It's not in the Bible anywhere. Neither is *fortunate*: we might say the man in the story was *fortunate* not to have lost his father. We might say it that way, but it wouldn't be true.

We might say that the baby Moses was lucky not to have died like so many of the other Israelite children. In fact, we might say it was fortunate for the whole Israelite nation that Moses stayed alive, that he was groomed in the Pharaoh's court, that he was given the kind of power he needed to lead God's people out of bondage. "Whheew," we might say, "all of that was so lucky."

More than three hundred fifty years ago, the church adopted a confession that most of us still claim is true, even if we don't know it as well as we should. This "Belgic Confession" says that God rules his world, that he doesn't forsake his creation to fortune or chance.

For years, God's hand in our lives has been called *providence,* not *luck* or *fortune.*

My father used to tell me there was no such thing as luck. Even today, whenever I catch myself, wishing someone "good luck," I can't help but think that it's a stupid thing to say. I don't believe in luck, really—neither should you, even if the rest of the world does.

You think that's silly? Look at how Moses was saved from death to lead his people. Look at Joseph's story in Egypt. Look at the man whose father is alive today because of a young German who for some reason chose not to tell his commanding officer. And remember that if God watches the common sparrow, he watches out for us too.

Prayer:

Lord, it's hard to believe that you watch all the sparrows in the world. It's even harder to imagine that you also watch all of your children. Help us to believe that you are with us every moment.

Amen.

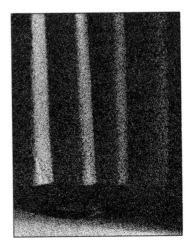

33

MOSES' APPRENTICESHIP

Prayer:

It's impossible for us to understand who you are, Father. But help us to realize that you are the God of all generations. Give us faith in your power and your love.

Amen.

Read Exodus 2:11–15 and 3:7–15

The way Moses was raised, you'd think he had no reason to be a tough kid. After all, most Israelite boys his age were dead. He was brought up in luxury, in the courts of Pharaoh himself.

But then, think of this: he must have always known that he was really not an Egyptian at all, but an Israelite. He must have felt terrible seeing his own people whipped while he rode around in chariots and ate big dinners in the palace.

One day he took the law into his own hands and killed an Egyptian who was hammering on an Israelite. Pharaoh was furious. So Moses fled for his life and hid in the desert.

We might think of those years in the desert as Moses' apprenticeship. An apprentice is someone who learns a skill or trade from a master worker. Masons still learn by apprenticeships—so do carpenters, plumbers, and many other persons in a wide range of jobs.

But Moses didn't really learn his future profession in the land of Midian. In Midian he was only a shepherd. Instead God used Moses' apprenticeship to teach him to wait, because in waiting one learns patience, and in patience, one learns trust. Moses went off half-cocked and killed an Egyptian, his anger triggered by his own hate. God wanted Moses to learn to trust, so he put him through years of an apprenticeship, miles away from the fight he would wage later on with Pharaoh.

Then, finally, God called Moses from a burning bush. Still, Moses didn't trust enough. "Me?" he said. "You've got to be kidding. I'm no giant. I can't bring off Israel's deliverance."

"Who said you'd be doing it alone?" God said. "I'll be there, I promise. Furthermore, once all of you get out of Egypt, the whole nation will worship me right here,

at the very spot you're standing on right now."

Moses wasn't brought up as an Israelite. "Who are you?" he said, hunching his shoulders. "I don't even know your name."

"I AM," God said.

Strange name, you might say— I AM.

Not really. Generations had passed since Joseph. Moses didn't know the covenant God of his fathers. "I AM," God said— "Jahweh," or, as we know the word better, "Jehovah."

God told Moses to tell the people he was the I AM, the eternal. Not the I WAS, God only to Moses' grandparents, but the I AM, the holder of Abraham's promise. I AM is both I WAS and I SHALL BE. "I AM," he said.

Moses, the apprentice, facing the burning bush, was becoming Moses, the master of trust, the man of faith.

34

PHARAOH'S ISRAELITE PROBLEM

Prayer:

There are times, Lord, when troubles just keep building up. Give us faith to believe that you are in charge of our lives. Help us feel your love. Amen.

Read Exodus 5:1–14

Let's try to look at this Israelite problem from Pharaoh's point of view.

He probably excuses himself; he figures it isn't his problem. After all, when he took the throne there were hundreds of thousands of Israelites around the country already. He didn't ask them into Egypt. They were already there—and multiplying like flies. It isn't his fault that one of his grandfathers let them into the country. It's a problem he's inherited—that's what he tells himself. Besides, he thinks, these people are terrific workers. Israelites seem to be born to make bricks. They take to hard work like ducks to water. They don't know anything else. They'd be lost without a full day's work—without some boss with a whip leaning over them. It's the only thing they understand. No Egyptian really considers them fully human—not the slave Israelites.

What's even more important, Pharaoh knows very well that his whole country will shut down tight if he gives Moses his wish and lets the Israelites take three days off to worship their silly God. I've got a country to run, he tells himself. I can't just sit around in the palace and let some slaves fan me with palm leaves. If *I* can't get three days off, how can *they* expect to just walk away on a vacation?

Pharaoh's big problem is that his people have grown fat on slave labor. Because there are Israelites to do the really hard work—making bricks and building new dwellings in the hot sun—the Egyptians themselves can sit around and sip cool drinks. Pharaoh knows very well that one million Israelites on a three-day vacation will shut down his whole economy, bring the whole country to a standstill.

And what's worse, he has this fear that the Israelites will get too big for their own britches. If he lets them go this time, he's afraid they'll make demands like this more often. What if Egypt should lose one million free workers? After all, somebody's got to make bricks. Somebody's got to build cities. How would he ever get the Egyptians to get their hands dirty when they're so used to making the Israelites do the work? How could he possibly get them out of the pool and into the hot desert sun?

So he tells his secretary of labor that from this time forward the Israelites will collect their own straw. And even though finding straw will make it tougher on them, he won't tolerate any letup in the number of bricks they've been producing per week.

What he has to do, he knows, is punish them for their ideas. We can't let those people think, he tells himself. We can't give them a moment to use their heads. The straw thing, he says, is a perfect solution. Shove their noses in the dirt.

Poor Pharaoh. All of that makes so much sense to him.

Poor Pharaoh. His god is not the I AM.

Poor Pharaoh. He's going to catch it—but good . . .

35

THE LORD GOD

Read Exodus 11:1–10

One of the first movies I ever saw was an epic called *The Ten Commandments*. The director of the film created an unearthly fog to represent the coming of the tenth and most horrid plague. The city was in darkness—I remember it clearly. Slowly, like a deep mist, this silent fog wound its way through the empty streets, around the corners of houses, and, like some huge, poisonous snake, into the homes of the Egyptians.

Where the fog crept in, sharp, piercing screams ripped through the stillness, echoed through the silent streets, then slowly deepened into anguished moaning. All over Egypt men and boys were dying in just a few nightmarish hours—firstborn grandfathers, firstborn fathers, and even firstborn children and babies. And all one could see was the thick fog creeping in stillness into the hearts of the Egyptians.

The scene was really scary, I remember.

And the Scripture is kind of scary too. We are now at one of those places in the Bible when the I AM shows power so great that even believers have to sit back in silence and in awe.

Why did it have to happen? A flood of frogs should have been proof enough of God's power. Boils on every man, woman, and child should have shown Pharaoh that he wasn't just messing with some two-bit magicians. Three days of darkness should have burned God's signature into everything Moses and Aaron had ever told the man, everything they had done to Pharaoh's people.

But Pharaoh wouldn't give in. God "hardened his heart."

Is God to blame for dying children who had nothing to do with Pharaoh's refusal? Couldn't God simply have allowed Pharaoh to change his mind. Couldn't he have told him to let Moses and Aaron have their way? Why did God harden Pharaoh's heart? Is God to blame for all of this death?

God told Moses ahead of time that Pharaoh wouldn't be bested by any of the plagues, even mass death (v. 9). But listen to what he says: "This will give me the opportunity to do mighty miracles to demonstrate my power." God flexes his power to show that he is the I AM.

God's punishment rained down on the Egyptians for their treatment of his people. But it also rained down to demonstrate his power to his own chosen people—even us, years later.

As long as we believe in the I AM, we will have questions about who he is and how he operates. We will never understand everything about his way or his will, even though he wants us to try, always.

This much we know from the story of the plagues. The Lord God has promised his grace to his people. Nothing—not stubborn Pharaohs, not great rivers like the Nile, not slick governments—will stand before his promise of love to those who love and fear him. He is the I AM.

Prayer:

Almighty God, even our best ideas don't help us understand you completely. You are so great. Help us give you praise through the chorus of our lives as your people. Amen.

36

SYMBOLS

Prayer:

Lord, thank you

for our

deliverance.

Thank you for

being the Lamb

who died that

we might live.

Amen.

Read Exodus 12:1–13

Most people have a drawer full of junk they never look at but wouldn't toss in the garbage.

One of the things in my drawer is a miniature white flag with a green, embroidered eagle perched on a symbol that looks like this ⊬. This odd, broken-looking cross is called a "swastika." Even if you didn't know its name, you probably know that the swastika was a symbol of Nazi Germany and its madman leader, Adolf Hitler. It's been almost forty years since the fall of Nazi Germany, but that symbol still has a piercing sting to people who remember it better than I do.

Symbols are strange things. I don't know one shepherd, and I've never been close to a lamb. Yet look how often we talk about Christ as "the lamb of God," or "the sheep who was slain." We talk about lambs as if we knew something about them. Not many of us do. What we've done is use Christ's own words to his disciples, even if we don't know the difference between a ram and a ewe. The disciples knew shepherds, and they knew sheep. So when Jesus called himself a lamb, he was making himself very understandable to the people around him.

Of course, the lamb was a Jewish symbol long before Christ started comparing himself to one. Lambs were important to the Jews since the days of slavery in Egypt. When the angel of death swept silently through Egyptian streets and took the lives of firstborn males, he skipped those homes where the families had splashed lamb's blood on their doorposts. Lamb's blood meant deliverance. It meant the angel would "pass over" that home and move on somewhere else to do his awful job.

Not only did that lamb's blood give deliverance to the Israelites, but the lamb's meat nourished them. Christ is our nourishment as well. That's another reason he referred to himself as the lamb.

Sure, the disciples understood sheep, but they also understood the celebration of the Passover. They'd celebrated it for years. When Christ told the disciples he was the lamb, he wasn't talking about the sheep eating grass on the hills outside of town.

Jesus Christ *is* the Passover lamb. He died so that we might be passed over by death itself, so that we might nourish our lives with joy.

The swastika is a powerful symbol all right, but the lamb is even stronger. Even those who marched under the big, black, crooked cross can find forgiveness and life in the blood of the simple and innocent lamb of God.

37

GOD DESTROYS AND SAVES

Prayer:

Prayer:

Dear Lord, you delivered the Israelites from slavery, and you've delivered us from sin and death. Thank you for your promises that last forever. Amen.

Read Exodus 12:31–42

If you've ever seen an area a hurricane has hit, you'll never forget it. Years ago, I rode along Louisiana's gulf coast highway just a week or two after waves high as stadium walls had battered homes and businesses. Locomotive winds had snapped every tree for hundreds of yards into the shoreline. What buildings still stood were gutted by the storm, and huge ships lay belly-up in the sand, as if they had been tossed there like dead fish. It looked like a war zone.

Maybe you've seen pictures of Berlin, the capital of Germany, at the very end of World War II. Allied forces opened a floodgate of bombs and beat the whole city to a pulp. Dust and debris from buildings and factories clogged otherwise busy streets.

It's not hard to understand why people give up when everything is destroyed by hurricanes or wars.

It's strange, but it wasn't that way in Egypt. Pharaoh called for Moses and Aaron. It was the middle of the night—that night when the angel of death was making his rounds. This time Pharaoh was singing a different tune. He didn't *command* them to leave—he *asked* them. "Please," he said, "please go away. Take everything with you—I don't care—but leave, *now!*"

What did Egypt look like on that horrible night? Were its streets filled with destruction? No. Were the people's homes flattened or gutted? No. Were its downtowns ruined? No. Most of its cattle were dead, but otherwise Egypt bore no scars from the plagues—at least nothing you could see. In Egypt, things still *looked* pretty good.

Yet Pharaoh begged Moses to take off. And then he said something odd. "Oh yes," he said, almost crying, "one more thing. Please," he begged, "give me a blessing."

When he asked for a blessing, Pharaoh revealed what had really happened to him and to his country. The Egyptians' hearts had been ripped in two, their belief in their own gods ruined by the power of the I AM. Jehovah, Moses' God, hadn't gone for the juggler; he'd gone directly for the heart. He'd not destroyed cities; he'd destroyed the proud soul of the tyrant and his people. "Wait!" Pharaoh begged, "Give me a blessing."

It wasn't only Pharaoh either. All the Egyptians begged the Israelites to take whatever they wanted. "Take our gold and silver. Take our fanciest chariots and our best living room furniture. Take whatever you want, but leave—please leave!"

So Moses moved the sons and daughters of Jacob out of Egypt four hundred and thirty years after God had brought them to that land. The one thing left intact in all that time was God's own promise to love and protect his chosen people.

The proud Egyptians, so rich and healthy, were left crying in the streets.

38

BREAD OF LIFE

Prayer:

We're sorry for getting a kick out of seeing other people punished. We deserve punishment for how we act, but you give us love. Thank you, Lord. Amen.

Read Exodus 16:1–17

Here's a bad story. Unfortunately, it's also true. It really happened . . .

There's a kid in school that nobody likes. He complains a lot. He's always in trouble.

One day the teacher catches him doing something bad—maybe cheating on a spelling test, maybe throwing spit wads. The teacher is angry. He makes the kid stand up in front. While everyone watches, the teacher takes a ruler out of his desk drawer and tells the kid to hold out his hand. "Smack," the ruler comes down on his palm. The kid cringes. Because we dislike him, we have to laugh at the way he crumples up. He's really a tough kid, and we think he's acting. He's always acting.

The teacher looks at the class. "Should I hit him again?" he asks. "Yeah," we say—all of the rest of us together. What do we care? We don't like the kid anyway. The teacher swats him again. And again.

You don't think that could really happen, do you? But it did. I know, because I was there telling the teacher to whack him again.

Often it's fun to see other people punished. Something beastly in us (something called sin) makes us get a kick out of seeing others "get theirs," especially if we think they deserve it.

So it's easy to read this story and shake our heads at the Israelites. After all, here it is only two months since the plagues, only two months since God opened the Jordan River to let the whole mess of Israelites walk through, then closed the opening up tight, swallowing Pharaoh and all his villains. It's been only two months.

And yet just two months later, here they are in the desert complaining that they'd rather be full-bellied slaves than hungry, but free, men and women.

"How dumb can those people be!" we wonder. "God must be furious with them! Are they ever going to get it from him! And we sit back and kind of wait for God to smack them a hard one.

But what does God say? He tells Moses that he has heard their complaining. "Tell them," he says to Moses, "that by tonight they'll have so much food they won't know what to do with it. And then tell them that I AM is their God. You tell them, Moses."

Do any of us deserve God's love? No. And yet listen to Christ himself: "I am the bread of life. Your forefathers ate manna in the desert, yet they died. But here is the bread which came down from heaven which a man may eat and not die."

So God feeds us too—with the bread of life. Jesus is our manna—even though we don't deserve a single crumb.

39

SUNDAY CLOTHES

Prayer:

Lord, forgive us for judging other people by the way they walk or the way they dress. Help us respect your holiness. Help us feel the power of your hand in our lives and to know you're always there. Amen.

Read Exodus 19:9–25

Bessie poked Frank the minute she saw the kid in shorts and grubby shoes sitting in the back pew of the church. She pointed with her thumb and lifted just one eyebrow. Frank knew what she meant. Bessie and Frank both figured it was a sin for someone to come into the house of God dressed up for the barn. When the usher took them down the aisle, they made sure they didn't give the kid even a glance—no sir.

"I can't believe it," Frank said once they were seated.

"Who'd of ever thought it could happen right here in our church?" Bessie pulled her hanky up to her nose . . .

Not long ago, every kid had a special hanger in his or her closet. If you were a boy, your hanger held a suit coat, a pants, a shirt, and a tie—a dark one probably. Girls had dresses, fancy ones with lace, that hung directly above a pair of shiny black shoes. Only on Sunday could they wear those special clothes, so they called them "Sunday clothes." The rest of the closet was filled with "everyday clothes." Maybe some of you still have special clothes for Sunday.

In today's Bible passage God told Moses to make the Israelites clean themselves up before they came before him. He demanded it. He did say that clean clothes would be kind of nice; he told Moses the people *had* to be clean or he'd "break out against them." That sounds dangerous.

Bessie and Frank know passages like the one we just read, and they think of church as the place where God's people come together to meet God. Bessie says going to worship calls for their very best Sunday clothes; after all, nothing could be more important than talking to God. Would you dress up if you were going to meet the Queen of the Nether-lands? Of course you would. Isn't meeting God even more important? Of course. You can't fight with that logic.

So Bessie and Frank aren't wrong in dressing up. But they are *dead wrong* in judging someone else on account of his shorts and dirty shoes.

Does being cleanly dressed in Sunday clothes mean you can enter God's presence? No. Look what happens in the passage. The people pleaded with Moses to talk *for* them. They needed someone to come between them and God. Moses went up the mountain alone.

Some things don't change. We need someone to come between us and our holy God too, even though we may have the best clothes in the greatest fashions from the latest catalogues. Clean bodies and clean clothes aren't enough. The Israelites needed Moses. We need someone even cleaner. We need Christ, our go-between, our mediator.

40

SIGNATURES

Read Exodus 20:1–17

Some people make a big deal out of handwriting. They claim that if you take a pen and fill up a sheet of paper, they'll discover all kinds of silly secrets about you, things that will help you find "the real you"—whatever that is. Oh yeah—it will cost you a couple of bucks too.

You don't have to be Einstein to figure some of it out yourself, of course. Kids who draw little bubbles over their *i*'s like to be fancy. If you like to be fancy, you probably don't mind a little attention now and then. Really shy kids don't dot their *i*'s with bubbles. And so on.

How you write probably does say something about who you are, but so does *what* you write. For instance, here are two opening sentences from that world-famous essay topic, "What I Did on My Summer Vacation":

Student A: "Last summer we went to the lake for a few days—it was OK."

Student B: "The glorious rays of sunshine poured like honey from the beautiful azure sky."

Chances are, reading those sentences will give you a pretty clear picture of the two kids, even though you don't know them.

Some authors say that whatever they write is really a self-portrait. When a young woman writes a story about an old man, parts of that story (maybe what he chooses to see while sitting on a bench in a crowded shopping center) probably describe the author as well as the old man she's writing about. Everything we write—in fact, everything we say—describes us.

We can learn a lot about God by reading the Ten Commandments, the Law he wrote for our lives. God wants us to think of him whenever we read his Law; that's why he begins by reminding the Israelites—and us—what he has done for them. "*I* brought you out of slavery," God says. "So make sure that you worship only *me*."

The Ten Commandments aren't simply some extra laws we should add to the laws that govern our country. We don't really know who wrote most of those laws. Who said, for instance, that we should cross the street only with the green light or that we should walk along the road facing the traffic? Sure, somebody wrote those laws, and we must obey them, but we don't really know the person behind the laws.

The Ten Commandments are different. They point us directly at the I AM. When we read them and obey them, we point our hearts and our souls and our minds directly to God and give him the love, obedience, and respect that he demands.

Think of the Ten Commandments as God's own signature on stone. When we see that signature, we can't help but see the Lawgiver himself behind it. And so we do our best to obey that Law, because we know and we love the God who wrote it.

41

DOUBLE-CROSSERS

Prayer:

Dear God, we know that we forget just as easily as the Israelites did. Give us strength to follow our promises. Thank you for giving us salvation through Christ. Amen.

Read Exodus 32:1–14

Aaron may have been Moses' brother, but he wasn't much like him. While Moses was up on the mountain with God himself, Aaron was listening to the Israelites complain about not having a leader. While God was talking to Moses, Aaron was telling the Israelites to grab all their gold and bring it to him.

First he made an idol for them—a golden calf. Then he declared the next day a holiday—a special day to worship the calf.

How quickly Aaron and the others had forgotten. Just a short time before the Israelites had heard the thunder and seen the mountain smoke. They had been terrified. But already they had forgotten their fear.

How could that be? How could these Israelites—who had just been led out of Egypt, who had seen the most amazing miracles, who had been so close to God himself—how could they forget him so quickly?

Easy. It happens all the time.

Mary wanted her basketball team to win the championship. That was all she wanted—nothing else, just to win. She sat on the bench, waiting for the man with the mike to announce her name to the crowd.

The gym was packed. Everybody was there; after all, it was the championship game. The Vikings had made it through a whole season with only one loss—to the team they were playing tonight.

So Mary prayed. She sat right there on the bench, closed her eyes, and prayed. The crowd went wild, yelling for her teammates as they left the bench, one at a time, for the middle of the floor. But Mary sat there and prayed.

"Dear God," she said, "I want us to win this game so bad. Please let us win. I promise I'll do whatever you want me to do if you just let us win."

When the announcer read her name, she ran off the bench and slapped her teammates' hands in front of hundreds of fans.

The Vikings won in double overtime. Mary scored thirty points, and when it was over, she left the gym on the shoulders of her coach and teammates.

But Mary forgot. Ten years later she barely remembered the game, much less her frantic prayer to God. She forgot her promise, even though she stayed a Christian.

How quickly we all forget! The golden calf shows us that. It's easy to blame Aaron, to think of him as some kind of doublecrosser, leading the people away from their God. But we all do it. And what's worse, we do it all the time.

That's why we need a savior—someone like Moses to come between our God and ourselves, the double-crossers. Many of us go to church every week and sing praises to our God. Yet on Monday we forget. It's just that easy. We need Christ.

To say we'll obey is not enough. God has to teach us to obey him. Sometimes that means he has to punish us—as he did the Israelites—for the times when we so easily forget.

42

JESSE'S ESCAPE (4)

Read Exodus 40:1–16

Being alone in a church at night was a strange feeling. Every time Jesse had been in church before, hundreds of people filled the pews. An organ played, and somebody stood up front and talked. But now it was perfectly quiet. The only sound in the sanctuary came from crickets outside and the dim whirr of power lines out front.

Jesse didn't know why he had left Arlen's farm. Maybe it was because he had been left alone that Sunday while Arlen and his family went visiting. He had sat alone, nothing to do at all, and it was the loneliness that scared him. It seemed as though the whole world had been suddenly emptied and only he was left in the quietness.

That's when it dawned on him to take off again. Arlen had paid him; money was no problem now. So he didn't think long. He didn't want to allow himself to think about it, because he was afraid he would decide against it.

So he headed south, threading through towns and countryside bright with spring greens. Back on the cycle, he felt sure running was the right thing to do. As long as he felt the cycle beneath him, he felt at home. And he loved the way teenagers in little towns watched him from the sidewalk, envying his freedom, his long hair flying back in the breeze, both hands on the bars.

By nightfall some silly little fear came back inside him. He had to sleep—he couldn't run from having to rest. But there were no easy answers.

Finally, when he came across a country church along a country road, Jesse stopped. The church made him think of Arlen. Jesse had never been very interested in church, but when Arlen had carted him off to church with them that morning, he hadn't complained. "You live here with us, you live like we do," Arlen had said. And although Jesse wouldn't have admitted it, something about the church service made him feel a little less lonely. Maybe that's why he decided the church would be a good place to rest for the night. No one would find him there, alone in a church at night.

Darkness sealed much of the sanctuary, except for the corners where exit signs blazed in red. Jesse found a comfortable spot on the carpet in the aisle and waited to fall asleep.

But the quietness kept him awake. He sat up and looked around him. His imagination created horror stories—long-veiled figures marching over him down the center aisle . . .

He raised himself with his arms, staring into the darkness. On the front wall he saw twin signs, only their shapes visible in the dim red glow from the corner doors. Jesse stood, then walked up to the front pew. On one side the tablet read, "Lo, I am with you always," and on the other, "even unto the end of the world."

He lay back down slowly, quietly, as if he might awaken someone else there sleeping beside him. His cycle was out next to the oil barrel in back of the church.

Silence pounded through Jesse, and he shook, alone with his fear, until finally he slept.

Prayer:

Lord, we meet you daily in our lives, not just on Sunday. Help us recognize you when we see you; help us listen to your voice when you speak to us. Help us know that we are your temples, and you are within us.

Amen.

43

YOM KIPPUR

Prayer:

Lord, thank you for washing away our sins in your blood. The only way we can show our thanks is by giving you our lives for your service. In whatever we do, may we work to glorify your name in your world. Amen.

Read Leviticus 16:1–10, 20–22

It's hard to believe what the high priest had to go through just to worship God, isn't it? If you read this passage closely and try to imagine what things looked like, you can't help but be amazed at how much blood must have been spilled over everything. Here's how things went, once a year, on the Day of Atonement:

The first animal to die was a ram, a big male sheep. At the front entrance to the tabernacle the high priest (Aaron) had to slaughter a ram as a sacrifice for his own sins. The ram's blood made Aaron clean so that he could serve as a priest for the other Israelites.

Next two goats were sacrificed. The first was killed for the sins of the people. Some of its blood was taken in a bowl and sprinkled on the cover of the ark. God himself lived above the cover of the ark, and beneath the cover lay the Law, the Ten Commandments. The first goat's blood assured the people that their sins against God's Law were forgiven.

Then the high priest took the second goat in his hands and held it, making the people believe that all of their sins were absorbed by the animal. As they watched, he sent this goat into the desert to die, a real scapegoat for the sins of the Israelites.

This was only the beginning, of course. If you read any further in this passage, you'll see that God's long list of instructions for worship just keeps on going. This "Yom Kippur"— Day of Atonement—of the Israelites was full of ceremonies and rules that seem strange and bloody and foreign to us today.

And yet it all makes some sense. Christ's blood on the cross *was* real blood, far more significant than the blood of any animal. And when he died, he took with him all of our sins.

The dead ram only *represented* Aaron's sins, and the two goats were nothing more than scapegoats. But Christ's sacrifice was more than a ceremony. When he took on our sins, he carried us into life—real life—with him forever.

God told the Israelites to celebrate the bloody Day of Atonement every year. He wouldn't let them forget. The Israelites' Day of Atonement points at the real day of atonement we still celebrate.

And yet think how easy it is to forget all of it, every second of Christ's suffering just for us.

Then remember, like the Israelites, never to forget.

44

THE OUTSIDER

Prayer:

We so often think that we know best about things, Lord. Help us to know that what you want comes first.

Amen.

Read Numbers 12:1–16

Have you ever noticed that people tend to marry someone of the same nationality or race? Dutch Protestants, for example, often marry Dutch Protestants and Irish Catholics often marry Irish Catholics. Sometimes parents get upset when one of their kids marries an "outsider," someone from a different nationality or ethnic background.

Don't misunderstand. We're not talking about Christians marrying non-Christians. The Bible tells us clearly that such marriages are wrong. No, we're talking about something different. We're talking about marrying someone whom people like us might be tempted to call an "outsider."

I have a Jewish friend who is a Christian. He told me that his father fell in love with an "outsider," someone from the group the Jews call "Gentiles." We'll call this someone "Katherine."

Katherine's future in-laws hated her so much for not being Jewish that they refused even to meet the woman their son loved. But one day Katherine accidentally met her Jewish mother-in-law-to-be. It happened this way: Katherine was riding at the front of an elevator. When the doors opened at the ground floor, Katherine's future mother-in-law was standing there in the lobby, waiting to get on. Even though the two women had never met formally, they recognized each other.

Imagine the scene. The doors opened quickly, and there they stood looking at each other, eyeball to eyeball. The Jewish mother took one look at Katherine, and suddenly, without even thinking about it, she spit directly in Katherine's face. That was it for their first meeting.

Moses, a Jew, married an "outsider," a Cushite woman who may well have been darker-skinned than most Israelites. Miriam didn't like it at all. She told Aaron, her younger brother, that Moses wasn't the only person God talked to. (If you read chapter 11:25, you'll see that she was right.) Miriam was trying to undermine Moses' authority because she was angry about his Cushite wife.

But the Lord heard Miriam and Aaron talking together, bad-mouthing his own chosen servant. And the Lord was angry. "Maybe I do talk through other people, other prophets," he told them, "but if I do, it's through dreams and visions. That's not the way it is with Moses. When I talk to Moses, it's face to face."

Why did God get angry? Was it because he approved of Moses' Cushite wife? That's probably part of it. If he didn't like Moses marrying some girl who wasn't a Hebrew, you can be sure he would have said so.

But what really angered God was Miriam's rebellion against her younger brother's leadership. He was furious that she bad-mouthed Moses. That's why he gave her leprosy for seven days. That's why he threw her out of the camp of the Hebrews she claimed to love.

By rebelling against Moses' authority, Miriam was also rebelling against God. That's why, for seven days, God made her an "outsider."

45

FAILURE FOR LACK OF FAITH

Read Numbers 13:25–33; 14:20–25

A doctor who is not a Christian once told me that he had seen miracles with his own eyes. The bones of an old woman he treated were rotting with cancer, he said. Yet she walked to his office for appointments. She shouldn't have been able to move, he said. Her pain should have been that bad. But what should have been, wasn't. Why? "Her faith," he told me. As she came closer to her death, she looked forward to life with her Lord. Her faith gave her the ability to take pain that no one "should have been" able to take.

Of course, that doesn't mean that those who feel pain have no faith. What the doctor remembered, he remembered as a miracle. But faith *can* do things we think are impossible.

Here's an old story you may have heard before. It's a little naughty, but the point is worth making.

A man falls from a cliff. Somehow, in his fall, he reaches for a sapling growing from the rocks, and he catches it with both hands. But he finds himself hundreds of feet above ground, and he's scared.

"Help!" he yells.

A voice comes out of nowhere. "I'll help you," the voice says. "This is the Lord. Listen to me. Let go of that branch with your right hand. Have faith."

The man looks beneath him, then lets go with one hand.

"Now let the other one go too," the voice says. "Have faith."

The man looks way down again. He looks back up and sees no one anywhere. The fall, he's sure, will kill him.

"Hey," he says, "anybody else up there?"

You can't really blame the man for not listening. In fact, it's easy *not* to have faith.

You really can't blame the ten spies for chickening out of going into Canaan either. They've seen the forts of the Canaanites. Sure, there's milk and honey, and everything's really rosy in this new land. But there are also giants running around. The place is crawling with fighters. No way, they say. No way can we take all those Hittites and Jebusites and Amorites.

Caleb and Joshua pooh-pooh the other ten (14:16). "The Lord loves us," they claim. "He'll bring us in safely."

But ten-to-two odds don't win elections. The Israelites believe the ten and run scared. And it's easy to understand why. Because it's easier *not* to have faith.

Just like that the Israelites forget everything the Lord God has done for them. They forget the exodus, the manna, the quail, and the Ten Commandments. They forget all about God's power and sit there shaking with fear.

God doesn't like it—not at all. "If you're so scared," he says, "then why don't you just back up and start over?" Then he tells Moses the bad news. Not *one* of those who complained, not one of those who are over twenty years old, will ever make it to the promised land.

That's their punishment for faithlessness. A whole new generation of Israelites will have to be born into the kind of strong faith their parents lack. Then, God's chosen people will make it.

What the Israelites forgot—and what we so easily forget—is that faith can move mountains.

Prayer:

Lord, please give us the gift of faith. Help us to be strong in our belief that you love us and that you are in control.

Amen.

46

MOSES AT THE END

Read Deuteronomy 32:48–53; 34:1–12

Some Bible stories tear your insides right out. Picture Moses climbing that huge mountain. He's one-hundred-twenty years old, but still strong enough to make the climb. Higher and higher he goes, leaving his people far behind.

For years he has listened to his people complaining. For years he has scolded them for their lack of faith. For years he's known that God is angry with the way the Israelites so quickly forget what he has done for them.

Moses will never forget the time God gave him the Ten Commandments. Up on the mountain, alone, nothing around him but lightning and thunder, Moses listened as God told him the rules for living. And then, his insides still shivering with fear and excitement, he went down to his people—and found them worshiping some dumb golden calf, acting as if they had already forgotten Pharaoh and the Angel of Death, the Red Sea opening up, and food from the sky.

Always, every step of the wilderness trek, God has talked to Moses. God has been angry sometimes and pleased some-times. He has praised Moses and scolded him. No one before Moses was ever so close to the I AM. From the burning bush to this day of climbing Mount Pisgah, Moses has walked with God.

That's why it doesn't seem fair. Just because of one tiny thing, one moment when he didn't listen, God tells him that it's over. Years of guiding a sometimes ornery people through the wilderness aren't enough. God tells Moses that because of just a few seconds of unbelief he'll never get to that promised land.

Toward the top of the mountain, the air keeps getting thinner. It becomes more and more difficult to breathe. The muscles in Moses' back grow tight as cables across his shoulders. His arms hang like lead as he tries to keep moving— upward, upward, following God's command.

"Look, Moses," God says. "Look out at the promised land."

Moses reaches for a boulder to steady his legs. His eyes clear slowly, his breath settling in even heaves. He raises his hand up to his eyes and looks.

There it is. There it is.

"That's Naphtali and Ephraim and Manasseh," God says. "And there's all the rest. I told Abraham and Isaac and Jacob that someday it would belong to their children. Now, soon, it will."

Moses looks at the glory of the promise, spread out before him in soft greens and yellows. But it won't be for him—not this promised land. Not for the old warrior, the old leader. He can do nothing but look.

Horrible story, isn't it?

Not really.

Read on. Verse 10 says there has never been another prophet like Moses, for the Lord talked to him face to face. *Never* another like Moses. Never!

And what is Canaan if you compare it to the promised land with the I AM? What are green fields if you compare them with eternity?

Only one will ever be greater than Moses. And Moses, leading God's people, has helped speed his coming into the world.

47

LEAP-FROGGING

Prayer:

Lord, we don't like to think about people we love dying, but we know it will happen eventually. Help all of us— whenever it happens—to know that we have to go on believing, being strong in faith. Amen.

Read Joshua 1:1–9

My kids are still young enough to be a little silly. Last May I took them out to the cemetery where their great-grandparents are buried. The grass was nicely cut, and the sun was warm, even though the afternoon was turning into evening. Like most seven- and five-year-olds, my kids haven't been to too many graveyards. So I suppose they thought the place was just some kind of new playground lined with nice big stones you could jump over or ride like ponies.

There's something wrong in playing games in a cemetery— that's what I thought, at least. So when they started playing leapfrog over the tombstones, I stopped them and told them it just wasn't right to tear around a cemetery like a couple of coyotes. They didn't understand. Maybe next year they will.

Today I'm thinking that maybe it was wrong of me to stop them from playing leapfrog. Let me try to tell you why.

Last week my friend John died. He was a fine Christian man, a member of the little Bible study group my wife and I belong to. In some ways it wasn't a sad funeral—everybody knew that John had gone to be with God.

What scares me is that he won't be at Bible study anymore. John knew answers to hard questions. There's something nice in being able to let the older people answer the hard questions. As long as John was around, I could count on him for the answers. But now John is dead. And now I'm the oldest one in the Bible study group. That makes me the one who has to come up with the answers first. And today, out here in the cemetery where we're burying John, I'm not so sure I like having to be the one with the answers.

Joshua probably didn't like

taking over for the great Moses either, but he had to. God said so.

I guess that's the way it goes. Like it or not, death gets everybody sometime. It'll get me, it'll get your parents, it'll get you—it gets all of us. And what's there left to do when someone we know, someone we trust, someone who has the answers gets called by God himself? The only thing we can do is go on.

When Moses died, Joshua had to lead the Israelites. When my friend John died, someone had to take his place in Bible study. Somebody has to stand at the graveside and jump over it.

So maybe my kids weren't wrong. There will come a time when each of us has to leapfrog the graves of those people we love and respect the most. And when we do, we'll have to ask for God's grace to do it. It won't be easy. But it wasn't easy for Joshua either.

48

HOMELAND

Prayer:

It is easy to

think that we

earn things, to

think that our

best works gain

for us what we

want. Yet we

know that all

the blessings

and things that

we have are

gifts from your

hand.

Amen.

Read Joshua 2:1–24

When I was a kid, my favorite possession was my baseball glove. Usually a brand-new glove is as stiff as a bushel basket. It takes a summer's worth of games to soften it up until it fits your hand perfectly. Just borrow someone else's glove and you'll know it's not yours. A borrowed glove never feels quite the same as the floppy one you've beat into shape to fit your own hand.

Baseball gloves are to kids what homes are to some grown-ups. Take the Israelites, for example. For years they wandered in the desert, looking for their own home. More than anything else, perhaps, they wanted a homeland, a land they could work into shape like a favorite baseball glove.

Rahab's story shows us very clearly that the land the Israelites wanted so badly would come to them—but only as a gift from their God. No matter how brilliantly they schemed or how hard they fought to get a homeland, they'd get it only when God himself gave it to them.

Rahab is a story in herself, of course. She was a prostitute—not the sort of person the people of Jericho would give a good neighbor award. Yet God worked through Rahab to give the Israelites the land they desired. Rahab, the prostitute—Rahab, the believer.

No matter what kind of past she had, Rahab had faith in the future. Even though she didn't know the great I AM as well as the Israelites did, she *knew* that he was a great and powerful God. Without so much as a question, she told the spies that she wanted safety because she *believed* in the Lord's power. Everybody's talking about it, she said.

Her faith wasn't weak-kneed. She acted. She made a deal with the spies, telling them that she would save them from the Canaanites if they would save her and her family. She didn't question them or their God one bit. She didn't say, "Who is this God and what should I believe about him?" She simply acted. She had a unique faith, an unquestioning belief that this God of the spies was someone to be respected and obeyed. That's why she's listed with the heroes of faith.

The point is that the spies couldn't have handpicked Rahab to save their lives. God picked her. And later, when God's people got their land, they got it because God chose to give it to them. The homeland they had been searching for, the homeland they would shape like a trusted old baseball glove, would be theirs as a gift from the God who loved them.

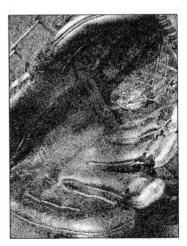

49

DÉJÀ VU

Read Joshua 3:7–13

Have you ever been riding on the bus or sitting in school or visiting at your friend's house when all of a sudden you get this really odd feeling that you've done exactly the same thing before—that you've lived these same moments at an earlier time? It's really a weird feeling, but lots of people get it—so many, in fact, that there's a name for it—*déjà vu.* It means something like "seen already."

Psychologists say that déjà vu is caused by your mind dreaming up the situations you're in. Sometimes—when you're sleeping maybe—your mind creates some familiar scenes, complete with events that you may be looking forward to a lot. Then, when that moment actually arrives, it's just as if you've been there before. It happens all the time.

The Israelites may have thought they were all suffering from a bad case of déjà vu when Joshua directed the men holding the ark to step in the waters of the Jordan River. Certainly they'd heard about how Moses had raised his staff over the Red Sea to let the Israelites escape the Egyptians. Now it was happening again, right in front of their eyes, on the banks of the Jordan River. The moment the ark touched the river, the water turned right around and piled up. The Israelites must have thought they were seeing an instant replay of one of the greatest stories of their escape from Egypt.

Maybe God did this miracle to remind them of where they'd been before. God didn't want his people to forget where they'd been. "Now watch this," he said, when the waters turned right around and went backwards. "Watch this, remember Moses, and don't forget that I'm your God."

The God of the ark of the covenant wasn't just stuck in that box the Israelites carried around. He even ruled the waters of the Jordan River. And he wanted the Israelites to know that.

But God also had another reason for such a show of power. The Israelites were stuck. They had to get their armies, not to mention their cattle and their families and all their household supplies, over to the other side. On top of that, their enemies were over there waiting to ambush them.

So God pushed back the water, just as he had before. And the Caananites, hungry for Jewish blood stood on the side of the Jordan and watched. Can you imagine what they must have thought when they saw the water rolled back, when they saw the old Jordan turn on a dime and flow the other way? It must have scared them silly!

To the Israelites, the Jordan turning its course was like an old memory all of a sudden coming alive. For the Caananites, it was their scary introduction to the Israelite God, the God of his promises, the God who would lead his chosen people to the land he had picked out specially for them.

Prayer:

You are the only God and the greatest God. Help us to rely on you for our needs. Help us to feel that without you we can do nothing. Amen.

50

THE FALL OF JERICHO

Prayer:

Dear Lord, the story of Jericho shows us your power and your loyalty. Keep us in your grace. Help us to bring praise to your name for the rest of our lives. Amen.

Read Joshua 6:1–21

Two of Jericho's finest lieutenants stand together on top of the wall. Outside, the Israelites march quietly round and round.

"It's always in silence," Gola says. He pulls nervously on the side of his helmet. "Every day it's in silence."

Farez stands there, both arms over the wall. "It's some kind of silliness. That's all it is. Six days of marching—"

"But it's always in silence," Gola says.

"What is it with you, Gola? You afraid of these stupid people?" Farez pulls out his sword and smashes it hard against the stone wall. "You think they can get through this? Is that it?"

Gola stares off into the empty plains.

"Twenty years already we've fought together, you and I, Gola. Twenty years and not one moment of fear. We've taken armies much greater than ours and *now* you are scared?" Farez takes Gola's shoulders and faces him, trying to look into his eyes.

Gola turns away and looks toward the center of the city where people walk in and out of their houses as if there is nothing wrong. "Something is strange about these people. Look now how they march again in silence— every day, as if they expect something to happen just from the marching. Look, Farez—look at them!" He pushes Farez back to the wall.

"Let them come up these walls, I say. Let them come." Farez pounds the top of the wall with his fists. "Let them feel our sharp swords, these strange people."

Dust rises from the feet of thousands of marchers. Together, their steps sound like a fierce whisper across the stones outside the city walls. Suddenly, the swish of their footsteps ceases.

"Farez, they've stopped!"

Farez turns back to the wall, his eyes narrowed.

The Israelites assemble themselves slowly, their horned ark out front.

"What now?" Terror whines through Gola's voice.

The two men stare out at the marchers, who wait, their tense faces all turned in one direction as if watching for some signal.

"I am afraid, Farez." Gola can't help thinking of his wife and children. "These people are different."

Suddenly a wail like a low-toned siren arises from the marchers; higher and higher it climbs until it hits a howling pitch.

"What are they doing?" Gola asks.

The walls begin to shake fiercely, but Farez clings to the stone, his eyes aflame.

"I am afraid," Gola says. "Not in all our years have we fought people like these. Their God is real."

Beneath them the stones buckle, and the two men fall awkwardly, still clutching their swords, until their bodies pitch off the block. They are buried with all of Jericho under tons of stone.

51

REVIEW DAY

Prayer:

Help us to want to remember what you have done in our lives and in the lives of our ancestors. Give us the desire to be faithful to the God from whom our blessings flow. Amen.

Read Joshua 24:1–16

On the day before a big test, some teachers go over all the things you'll have to know. They call that review day.

The day before he retired as the Israelite leader, Joshua had a review day. He talked to the Israelites about history as if he were preparing them for a really big test. History is important to God. That's why Joshua went over the same old story again.

I'm wondering what Joshua would say to me if he were sitting in my study. What facts would he have me remember on my review day?

"Schaap," he'd probably say, "you know how God was with your great-grandparents when they came to this country from across the ocean. They didn't have peanuts really, did they? In fact, your great-grandfather wasn't even a farmer, he was a sailor. Yet he got to South Dakota and picked up a hoe. He had faith, didn't he?"

I'd probably nod at the old man as he sat there in my easy chair.

"But they had five bad years in South Dakota in the early 1890s—no crops at all. Your great-grandfather couldn't make it out there, even though he was sure that America would be the land flowing with milk and honey. Did he give up?"

I'd probably shake my head.

"No way. He believed in God, even when his dream failed in the dust. He picked up his family and went back east to a farm. And it wasn't easy. But God blessed him for his faith, didn't he?"

That would make me feel good—to hear about his faith.

"And what about that other great-grandfather, the drunk. He wasn't too good to his wife and kids, was he?"

I'm not so proud of that story, so I'd probably blush.

"But did your great-

grandmother give up on God when her own husband didn't treat her well? Of course not. She kept on loving God and never stopped telling her children about how blessed they were—even if their dad wasn't the greatest dad in the world."

I know that's true, even though I never knew my great-grand-mother.

"And what about the time your grandfather the preacher lost his sweet little daughter to that strange disease? You've heard about how much that hurt him, to have to bury his own little girl. But did he give up? No, not for a minute. He kept believing and kept asking God for strength.

"And what about your parents? For those long times during the war, when your dad was thousands of miles away—did they stop believing in God? No way."

Most of the time I'd just sit there nodding, I suppose. And then he'd tell me what he told the Israelites.

"Who is it going to be, Schaap? The God your ancestors loved and believed in or some other—money maybe, or fame, or power? Who are you going to serve?"

Joshua would say it to me in the same way he said it to the Israelites, because Joshua knows that tomorrow there will be tests—and the next day, and the next. Every day, tests. That's the way it is in life.

Joshua wanted the Israelites to be ready, because God himself is the teacher. Joshua knew that when God sees his children getting *F*'s, he weeps. Yesterday and today.

52

WINNING BATTLES/ LOSING WARS

Prayer:

Lord, if the story

of the Israelites

teaches us

anything, it

teaches us how

quickly we can

forget about

you. Give us

better memories

than the

Israelites, and

help us stay true

to you.

Amen.

Read Judges 2:6–16

When I was in the ninth grade, I played forward on the freshman basketball team. We used to practice in a little grade school gym— except on those days when the high school varsity team had games. Then we'd get to practice in the big gym. Just practicing in the high school gym was a thrill.

We really looked up to the seniors, guys who could run faster and jump higher and shoot straighter than any of us. We dreamed about the day we could play ball as well as those big seniors played. We dreamed about the day we could play in the high school gym in front of hundreds of people and long lines of cheerleaders.

Then something happened that I'll never forget. That varsity team was really good; they won a lot of games. Everybody thought we had one of the best teams in the history of the high school. But one day seven of those big seniors were kicked off the team for drinking. Our heroes had let us down.

Their behavior brought about a lot of changes. Junior varsity players were called up to take over the seven places on the varsity team. And seven of us freshmen were called up to the junior varsity team. Suddenly, we found ourselves playing in that big high school gym. We looked around and saw bleachers full of people, and we were scared.

Playing against older guys from other schools, we got whomped every game—in front of all those people who cheered for us. It was embarrassing. We had looked forward to the glory of winning, but all we got was the misery of defeat. And it all happened because those heroes of ours— those great players, our idols, who had won lots of games—had lost the whole season when they broke their promise not to drink.

They had won battles all right, but they lost the war.

The Israelites broke their promises to God. Instead of staying faithful to him, instead of trusting in him and worshiping him, they chased the stupid gods of the Caananites. Joshua's review day wasn't enough. They failed their tests.

How did God react? Did he destroy them for breaking their promises? Did he just let them go and find some other people who might be more interested in staying faithful to him?

Our passage tells us that whenever the Israelites went out to fight a battle, God made them lose. But he didn't desert them. After a while he provided leaders to save them from their enemies. Why would he do that? Because his people loved him? No, simply because *he* loved *them* so much.

That's called "grace," and it's grace that's absolutely undeserved. It's typical of our God, Jehovah, who loves us in spite of how easily we forget him.

Because of his grace, we can lose all the battles and still win the war.

53

JESSE'S ESCAPE (5)

Read Judges 4:1–10

On any morning other than Monday, Fred and Deborah Ellengson were pretty much retired, but on Mondays they worked at getting the church clean. Every Monday morning they picked up coffee cups from the tables in the fellowship hall and wandered up and down the rows in the sanctuary, pulling bulletins and paper from the hymnal racks.

On this particular Monday morning they had finished the fellowship hall and were working their way through the sanctuary when Fred had his surprise. For a moment he stood frozen at the edge of a pew, staring down the aisle as if he'd seen a ghost.

"What's the matter, dear?" Deborah said.

Fred stood there pointing; then, he raised his finger to his lips, begging her for quiet.

She edged out of her pew, leaned out into the aisle, and saw the boy lying on the floor.

She looked at Fred, motioned him up slowly toward the front with a nod of her head.

"Who?" her husband asked with his eyes and with his lips.

She shrugged her shoulders. The both of them stood there above him, checking every inch of his body for a spot of blood, for some sign of how he died.

"He's alive," she whispered, making exaggerated motions of breathing with her chest.

"Cops," Fred said, leaning toward the back door.

"Wait," she said.

Fred grabbed her arm and jerked her toward the back door. "He's got to be a criminal," he said. "The cops better be here when he wakes up—"

"He's just a boy," Deborah said. "Pete's sake, Fred—he's about the same age as our grandson. Why would a kid like that come in a church and sleep?"

"We got to get the cops—"

"Settle your nerves now," she said. "You call the cops, but I'm going to talk to the boy."

"Deborah, don't you dare. He's maybe dangerous—"

"He's maybe dangerous all right, but he certainly is no more than a boy. He needs help—"

Fred moved toward the door, then swung around back again. "Don't do it, Deborah. Let the police take care of this—"

Deborah pulled the candy wrappers out of her apron and jammed them in the basket by the visitors' book. "I'm going to talk to him. I think he needs us—"

Fred took her arm as they walked up the aisle toward the front of the church, the spot where Jesse lay, fast asleep, on the carpet. He brought the broom handle out in front of him and poked it toward Jesse, but Deborah whacked it away before the end reached his chest.

"That ain't a way to wake up a dog," she said. She knelt down next to the boy and laid a hand on his shoulder.

When Jesse opened his eyes, he looked up into a mist and saw only the backlit outline of a face.

"We're here to help you, boy," he heard her say. "You come to the right place when you come to the church."

54

MURDER IN THE TENT

Prayer:

Lord, you
control us with
your power.
You even
control those
who don't
confess that you
are their God.
Help us to give
you honor and
praise through-
out our lives.
Amen.

Read Judges 4:17–22

Today lots of people consider themselves genealogists. Genealogy, as you may know, is the science of hunting up information about your long-gone ancestors. It can be a whole lot of fun—until one day you find a bum in your family. Then it can be embarrassing.

I'll tell you a family secret. (I can do it because all the people who wouldn't want me to tell you about it are dead anyway.) I had two very well-known great-grandfathers: one was a distinguished seminary professor—the other, a town drunk.

Most families have at least some secrets like that about their ancestors. The families in the Bible are no exception. Again and again the Bible tells some rather embarrassing stories about our biblical ancestors.

Jael was one of God's less honorable people, and the murder detailed in today's passage is one of the most treacherous murders in the Bible. The story may be exciting, but it certainly isn't uplifting. You don't come away singing when you've just read the story of Sisera's murder.

Why is such treachery in the Bible? Good question.

We do know some things about the murder that aren't obvious from a first reading of the passage. We know that Sisera was a hated enemy of the Israelites. He was a feared army commander, fierce and powerful, and he scared the stuffings out of almost everyone he came into contact with.

Jael was nothing more than the lowly wife of a Kenite, a nomad friendly to the Canaanites but living on their land by special permission. Sisera, the mighty, entered her tent, where he was fed and given a place to sleep. But as soon as the mighty one fell asleep, Jael proceeded, very calmly, to drive a tent spike through his skull. End of story.

So why is the story in the Holy Scripture? Well, for one thing, it reminded the Israelites how the proud and mighty warrior was nailed to the tent floor by a lowly nomad. Sisera, one of their great enemies, was killed in his sleep by a woman who had befriended him. It's a simple story of treachery, but it's also a story of how God saved his people from their enemies. Sisera's horrible death is a gift from God to his people.

The danger facing Israel in their new land was that they would start to act and look like their neighbors. God used his judges to keep that from happening. He used their ugly violence, their treachery, their deceit, to keep his people trusting in him.

Likely as not, the Israelites laughed when they told the story of Sisera and Jael. We may not like to think of them sitting around a fire and chuckling about such a horrible murder, but they may well have done just that.

The story may have made them laugh with joy—because it re-minded them that they were in God's hands. And that's what they needed to remember.

55

GIDEON'S DOUBT

Prayer:

Dear Lord,

forgive us when

we doubt—like

Gideon—that

you are mighty

enough to do

exactly what

you want to do

in our lives and

in our world.

Help us to know

for sure that

you are the

almighty God

who can do

anything.

Amen.

Read Judges 6:11–24

When Henry David Thoreau decided to live for a time at Walden Pond, the railroad had just been built. Alone in the woods, Thoreau saw the peace and tranquility ruined by the roaring, steam-belching locomotive, and he wondered, in his book *Walden*, whether the huge black machine wouldn't make slaves of the people it was meant to serve.

Anne should have read Thoreau's thoughts before she insisted on the car. She had just turned sixteen, and she'd always wanted a car. She figured a car meant freedom. She could take it to school and cruise Main just like the others kids. What she didn't know was that it would cost her an arm and a leg to pay for the insurance. She found out that gas wasn't cheap, and when the transmission went out, she watched her savings disappear in the repairs. She took an extra parttime job to handle all the expenses, and the job kept her so busy that she didn't have time to drive around in the car. Anne never read Thoreau, but she should have. That car became her master as she became its slave.

The Israelites wanted a homeland, some place to call their own, but they never considered the demands a homeland would make on them. As long as they were wanderers, they were dependent on God. Once they became rooted, they started to depend more and more on the land itself. The land created new problems, problems they had never guessed would come to them.

No longer were the Israelites the attackers. Now the nomads from the east—the Midianites, Amalekites, and Arabians—swarmed down on the landowners, stealing food during harvesttime. The land the Israelites had wanted so badly created new headaches.

The land also affected the Israelites spiritually. Perhaps we can see that best if we contrast a character we've seen before, the prostitute Rahab, with Gideon. You remember Rahab. She was the woman who hid Joshua and the other spies when they sneaked into Jericho.

Rahab had an unquestioning faith. When she discovered the spies were Israelites, she took their side immediately—because she believed in their God. "I've heard about all the marvelous things this God of yours has done for you," she told Joshua. "I know he's the one and only true God." So she hid the spies, lied to her countrymen, and saved her own life. Rahab really knew very little about the I AM, but she knew enough, more than enough, to convince her that the Israelites' God was someone to be feared. She had no doubt.

Now look at Gideon, out threshing wheat in a winepress to hide it from the Midianites. An angel of the Lord told him that he was specially blessed as a fierce warrior. And what did Gideon do? He did what any of us would do— he doubted. Sure, he said, give me a sign or else I can't be sure that you're not just blowing hot air. Besides , he said, don't you think it's a little silly to believe that my little tribe can do anything against the Midianites?

Look at the doubt and the fear. Think of Rahab, who didn't hesitate for a minute. Look at the difference. All-too-human doubt had dug its way into the soul of God's people.

56

THE LONG SHOT

Prayer:

Lord, make our

belief strong.

Give us the will

to put

everything we

have in your

care, and help

us rely on your

love and power

in everything

we do.

Amen.

Read Judges 7:2–22

If we think God's aim in trimming down Gideon's army was to create some lean and mean fighting unit, some special-forces brigade who fought like panthers, then we're missing the point. God wanted to make very clear that victory would come only through his power, not through the bravery of a bunch of crack troops.

Gideon's soldiers weren't even a long shot in the battle with the Midianites. After 22,000 left because they were scared, and another 9,000 lappers were sent home, Gideon had only 300 left—300 Israelites against 135,000 Midianites. Gideon's army had no chance whatsoever. For every one of his men, there were 1,350 Midianites. Such odds were more than steep—they were impossible. Swinging one of those heavy swords 1,350 times, even if the targets were fresh-baked loaves of bread, would leave even the toughest of Gideon's men wheezing for air. Let's not misunderstand: there was *no way* the Israelites could win—unless they relied on God's power.

God was working for Gideon by working against the Midianites. Look at the interpretation of the dream (v. 14) and you can tell how scared the Midianites had become. Fear drenched their bodies in sweat as they anticipated the fight.

Why were they afraid? Because the unbelieving Midianites had heard of Israel's mighty God and they believed he was for real.

The Irish author James Joyce returned to his mother's home when he heard she was dying. Although Joyce had given up on the church years before, his mother remained a strong Catholic. So when her son stood by her bed, this mother asked for one final favor. She wanted Joyce to take communion once more—for her sake. She said seeing him take the sacrament would make it easier for her to die.

Joyce thought about it for a long time. He figured if he really didn't believe in God, he couldn't hurt anybody by taking communion—and of course his mother would be pleased. At first, it seemed very simple to him.

Yet, the more he thought about it, the more convinced he became that he shouldn't take the sacrament. Communion was such an important thing, he reasoned, that he would be wrong to take it for any motive other than a sincere desire to be part of God's people. He let his mother die without allowing her the comfort of her last wish for him.

Joyce, the unbeliever, still believed in God enough to fear him and to respect the sacraments of the church.

God made the unbelieving Midianites into firm "believers" too. They were terrified of only 300 men because they "believed" in the awesome power of Israel's God.

What's really odd is that the Midianites believed in God's power more firmly than did those thousands of Israelite troops who went home afraid.

57

SAMSON THE GREAT

Read Judges 15:9–17

The Samson in my mind looks like some Saturday-morning cartoon hero. His powerful arms are wound with huge muscles. He wears a little triangular swimming suit, like a weight-lifter, and the bulging muscles in his back ripple when he rolls his shoulders. He's bearded, of course, and his perfectly brushed hair falls neatly to his shoulders. He's an Israelite Tarzan.

Of course it's possible—though not likely—that Samson was actually an eighty-pound weakling. After all, his massive strength was not his own. The whole point of the Samson story is God's *gift* of strength to him. He didn't spend his waking hours pumping iron or taking steroids to make himself Mr. Israel. His strength was phenomenal because it was greater than any other human had. It was a miracle—it came from God.

God made Samson strong so that he could fight the Philistines, Israel's enemy from the west. The Philistines had a different way of attacking God's people—they did it from the inside out. Instead of coming on with hordes of troops, ready to die for the cause, the Philistines weaseled their way into the lives of the Israelites. The Philistines beat them with smiles instead of swords.

The Philistines were like cancer, eating away at the values of God's people. Even Samson, our hero, was infected. He had married a Philistine girl, and most of his friends were probably Philistines too. He fought without a sword because the Philistines had a law against the use of iron weapons. At first he fought alone because God's people were too threatened by the Philistines to help him. And finally he gave in to the pleadings of a Philistine temptress named Delilah. Yes, Samson and God's people were infected with the cancer of Philistinism.

But God used this infected hero in a mighty way. The Great Jawbone Slaughter described in today's passage began to unite the Israelites and to help them realize how they had fallen into the deceptive hands of the Philistines. The people of God began to look to Samson as a leader. Why? Because God had given their hero strength—not because he had it all along.

We all need our heroes, and Samson can certainly be one of them. But let's not forget who gave the big man his muscles.

58

BEFORE
THE FALL

Read Judges 16:4–21

A Greek philosopher named Aristotle would have loved the story of Samson and Delilah. He would have loved it because the story seems to fit his definition of the word *tragedy.* Aristotle claimed that tragedy is the account of some strong human being who is destroyed by a single character flaw.

In today's Scripture we read of Samson's downfall. Delilah was in cahoots with her Philistine friends, who offered her big money to try to chain down the man who had become the symbol of strength to the Israelites. "Get him to tell you how he keeps all that strength," they pleaded, "and we'll line your bathtub with silver." (They didn't say exactly that, of course.)

Samson may have had big muscles, but he certainly didn't have Solomon's brains. Four times Delilah tried to subdue him before she finally won. You'd think he would have gotten the hint. The Bible says she nagged him so long he was "tired to death." But he kept joshing along. Why didn't he just throw the woman out on her ear? Why?— because of his pride.

Aristotle had something to say about that too. He claimed that the one character flaw that most often leads the tragic hero to his downfall is nothing other than pride.

Samson's pride blinded him to the truth. Like so many heroes, Samson began to believe in his own myth. People had told him how they worshiped his power. He'd listened so long to the cheers of the Israelites that he started to believe he was as invincible as they told him he was.

Look what happened. On Delilah's fourth attempt he gave up and told her the truth about his vow. But when he woke up to find his hair gone, he really didn't believe that his strength could have left him: "I'll go out as before and shake myself free," he said (v. 20). Samson the Great had come to believe everything people said about him. His pride had swelled far out of proportion.

Samson's tragic fall led to the end of his freedom. He was a prisoner of the Philistines, a sorry figure they used for entertainment. So goes the great hero.

One more thing about this philosopher, Aristotle. He claimed that tragedy should deeply affect those who see it. He said tragedy should lead to a *catharsis* in those who truly understand what has gone on. *Catharsis* is a big word, but its meaning is not so difficult. It means "a cleansing." Having seen a great person fall, people should be cleansed of their own pride, Aristotle wrote. They should see themselves in the great fall of the tragic hero.

That's something for all of us to think about when we're patting ourselves on the back and taking the credit for ourselves instead of giving it to God.

As the old saying puts it, "Pride goeth before a fall."

Prayer:

Mighty Father, help us to avoid trusting in ourselves and forgetting that you are the source for everything we have and are. Keep us close to your hand. In Christ's name we ask this. Amen.

59

A SERVANT'S MEMORY

Read Judges 16:23–31

"I am an old man among children," he says, and he stares at his hands as if the thin flesh were proof of his age. "But I too was once a child."

He sits beneath a shade tree, and his legs run straight out before him, their thinness clearly outlined beneath the folds of his robe.

"I was the servant who was sent for Samson," he says.

A young boy sits there in the grass, his legs folded beneath him. He hears the raspy depth in the old man's voice.

"I went to the prison and told him he was to come with me. It was dark, but for Samson it was always dark in his dungeon. In the light of my torch, I saw him rise. He came to me. He followed the sound of my voice."

The old man stops for a moment, his jaw still trembling, his eyes closed as if it is hard to remember.

"Samson asked me where we were going. How was I to answer? I could have said to him that they wanted to jeer him. 'Samson,' I could have said, 'they will humiliate you. They are drunk and they are wild—and you will be their sport.' I could have told Samson the truth."

The old man's face drops. "I answered him only with silence."

The young boy waits for the old man to start again. He knows the story, knows how the blind man looked that night, years ago, his face streaked by the dirt from the dungeon.

"I know what Samson's death means," the old man says. "I know how Jehovah works in the lives of his people." He looks up into the leaves, and the child sees the milkiness in his eyes.

"The Philistines were crazy with drink. 'Bring on this Samson,' they yelled. 'Bring him on so we may laugh at him—this man of wondrous strength, this man of Israel's God!'

"It was a long way to the temple, and as we walked together we could hear the Philistines laughing and yelling. 'Where do you take me, my son?' Samson asked me. And always I answered in silence."

The young boy sits up closely and waits for the end that already he knows well.

"In the temple they screamed at him, and he sat there, a blind man with such long hair. In the middle of all of their screaming and spitting, he stood. And he said to me, 'My son, you put me where I can stand between two pillars.' "

The old man holds out both hands as if those pillars are standing in the long grass there beneath the tree.

"And I knew what he would do. His prayer to God was there on his lips. I could see his lips move, but the noise of their screaming was too strong."

His hands push out slowly from his chest. "Many of them died and Samson too," he says.

The old man looks straight at the boy and points. "Jehovah will have his way, my son," he says, and he nods, several times, in a way the boy will never forget. "Jehovah will have his way."

60

THE ROOKIE AND THE VETERAN

Prayer:

Whenever we get bored by the same old stories, whenever we start to think about other things in the middle of our prayers, whenever we yawn through Bible reading, remind us of Ruth, Lord. Amen.

Read Ruth 1:15–21

The story of Ruth is probably one of the greatest stories in the Old Testament. It's the story of an outsider, a Moabite named Ruth, who married one of God's chosen people, an Israelite named Chilion. Chilion, his brother, and his parents, Elimelech and Naomi, had moved to Moab because there was no food in Israel.

When Chilion and his brother died, Naomi planned to return to her homeland. Ruth wanted to join her. "No," Naomi said— "What's there for you in my homeland?"

Then comes one of the most memorable lines in the Bible. Ruth told her mother-in-law, "Wherever you go, I will go, and where you stay I will stay, Your people will be my people, and your God my God."

Now remember, Ruth was a Moabite. She wasn't born and reared with Israel's I AM. What she knew about Jehovah, she knew through her husband and her mother-in-law. Ruth was a convert, a rookie. But she had incredible faith. "Your God is my God," she said.

This is also the story of Naomi. Naomi, with her husband and her two sons, had lived in Moab for many years. Sadly, both her boys and her husband died, and she was left alone with her two Moabite daughters-in-law. She was getting older and knew that this land of Moab was really not her home. So she returned to her home in Israel, and Ruth went with her. That much we already know.

The moment Naomi got back to Israel, she told all her old friends how bad she had it. Right there in front of the woman who had forsaken everything merely to be with her mother-in-law, Naomi told the Israelite women not to call her Naomi anymore, but to call her Mara, which means bitter.

In spite of the loving beauty of her daughter-in-law's pledge of life-long loyalty, Naomi was bitter and angry.

Naomi should have been the great believer. She was the veteran. She was the one who was reared in the way of Jehovah. She was the one whose heritage included all the wondrous stories of the deliverance. She was the one who should have known God, who should have known that God wouldn't want her to be bitter.

Ruth was the rookie. She shouldn't have loved God as much as Naomi did. After all, Jahweh wasn't the God of her parents. The whole story of the deliverance was new to Ruth. Ruth had heard about the I AM only because she happened to marry an Israelite.

The contrast between Ruth and Naomi should tell us something. Just because we were born in Christian homes and have Christian parents and grandparents doesn't insure us of anything. Naomi was the bitter one. Naomi, the daughter of God's covenant people, thought only of herself and of her problems. Ruth, the outsider, really believed and really loved. Ruth, the outsider, was a mother in the family Jesus Christ himself was born from eleven hundred years later.

Sometimes all of God's promises get so old and worn to those of us who've heard them so often that we stop caring. We just take them for granted. We're like the Israelites that way—like Naomi.

Sometimes we need to be much more like Ruth, the rookie.

61

BOAZ AND RUTH

Read Ruth 4:1–6, 13–17

Some people claim that it's tough being a woman today, but it was probably a whole lot tougher in the days of Ruth. Just think about what Ruth faced when she came to live with the Israelites.

The law of Moses said it was okay for a widow like Ruth, a woman who had no children, to marry another man. But whom could she marry? She didn't have many choices. She "belonged" to the nearest male relative of her dead husband. If that man wanted to have her, he could. A wife was really not much different from a piece of property.

But the law had one catch to it. If any children were born to the new couple, the kids would take the name of the first husband, not the second—even though the second husband was the father. In addition, the first husband's property would stay with his family—but the second husband had to work that land.

You can understand why that law made men a little reluctant to marry a widow. They didn't look forward to giving their children another man's name or to spending a good part of their time working land that would never belong to their own family.

But this man Boaz was willing. He was willing to marry Ruth even though there were many good reasons why he shouldn't. For one thing he wasn't Chilion's closest relative. Also, he was much older than Ruth. And, let's not forget, Ruth was still a Moabite, not a Jew. On top of that, if Boaz married Ruth, he would have to spend a lot of time working land that would never belong to his own family line.

So why *did* Boaz marry Ruth? Read verses 10 and 11 in chapter 3. Boaz said Ruth was a beautiful person—not because she looked like she should be on a magazine cover, but because she loved her mother-in-law so much. Boaz knew that Ruth wanted an heir for the family of Elimelech—for her mother-in-law. Because she loved Naomi so much, she was willing to do anything for her. That's love!

Also, Boaz knew what others thought of Ruth. The whole town recognized her as a kind and loving person. Boaz was willing to marry Ruth because he knew this Moabite woman was a just-plain-wonderful, believing human being.

There's more: Boaz was a redeemer. He and Ruth had a baby, thus preserving the line of Elimelech. By taking Ruth as a wife, Boaz redeemed, made alive, the family line of Elimelech.

That's important. David, the greatest king of Israel, would come from the line of Elimelech. And after David, generations later, would come Jesus Christ. Somewhere, way, way back, Christ would have great-great-great-great grandparents by the names of Boaz and Ruth.

Through God's incredible plan for his people, Boaz married an outsider, Ruth the Moabite, and kept the line going. Boaz redeemed the family line for the great Redeemer himself.

And Ruth, who was not even a Jew, became a bloodline parent of the Savior of the world.

62

DEDICA-TION

Read 1 Samuel 1:11–28

"I'm going to tell you something that I've never told anyone else before." Lillian Bode sat on the edge of her chair, holding a cup of tea she was drinking in the Chinese fashion, very slowly. She was more than eighty years old.

"I came into this world at the beginning of this century," she said. "My mother's parents were from Illinois. They had a lot of miscarriages, but somehow she lived—she was precious, you see. Then I came into the world—and I got sick with pneumonia. It was fatal back then.

"Mother wondered, 'How can I ever live without this child?'

"And then she came up with an idea. 'She could be a missionary,' she said to herself. At that moment she gave me to the Lord. I was just a baby, but I got better right away. She never told me about her promise until years later when I came home on my first vacation from school."

Miss Bode's eyes sparkled when she told the story she had never told anyone before. They sparkled because for close to sixty years she actually *had* been a missionary. She had learned how to drink tea like the Chinese during her years in Taiwan and China.

Then she told me more. "All through my life my mother held up mission work to me. But she never told me to go into missions. When I was a teenager, we had Mission Fest—one whole day of preaching. Mother made sure that I went to hear the missionary's speech by having me tell her all about it when I got home. She encouraged me in that way."

More than anything, Miss Bode's mother wanted her daughter to be a missionary. Since the day she asked God to spare Lillian's life, this mother continued to pray that her daughter would choose mission work as her vocation.

Mrs. Bode sounds a little like Hannah, doesn't she? There was nothing Hannah wanted more than a son. When, at last, she was able to have a child, she named him "Samuel," meaning "asked of the Lord."

But Hannah did something that Mrs. Bode never did; she literally gave her boy to God. She left him at the temple for the Lord to use.

It took supreme dedication for Hannah to give her child up to God. She had to forget her own desire to have her little boy around the house and to watch him grow into a man. She had to remember that God had given her the boy, and that God wanted Samuel back to serve him.

Samuel became one of the great prophets of God's people.

Mrs. Bode didn't deliver her little girl to the church, but she did pump her full of the desire to tell everyone about Jesus. Mrs. Bode found every way she could to teach Lillian how important it is for each of us to preach the gospel to those who haven't heard the good news.

Lillian Bode, the little girl who almost died, started churches single-handedly in Taiwan. Lillian Bode, God's own missionary helper, became one of the greatest missionaries in the history of the Christian Reformed Church.

One God, and two dedicated mothers, were very happy.

Prayer:

Lord, give us the kind of dedication that Hannah and Mrs. Bode must have had. Help us to see that giving our lives up to you is the most important thing we will ever do.

Amen.

63

IMAGES AND KINGS

Read 1 Samuel 8:1–9

Some people claim it's easier to worship a God you can see than one you can't see. Maybe they're right.

I remember the first time I saw a picture of Jesus. It was hanging on the wall in a Sunday school room. Most of you have probably seen a picture like it: Christ sitting with both hands folded on a big stone, his eyes up toward heaven, his long hair flowing over his perfectly white robe. I've never forgotten that picture.

Years later, during the Vietnam War years, I bought a picture of Christ myself. It was a strange pencil drawing that made Jesus look just like a hippy. His hair was long and scraggly, his beard untrimmed. He had an angry expression on his face. He looked like he could have carried a big sign on a stick and marched in a protest.

I used to have that picture up on my wall.

The Israelites felt the need for pictures too. That's why they asked for a king. Many of them weren't sure who was running their government. No one seemed to be in charge. The other countries in Canaan had kings, and it seemed to work out well for them. So the Israelites wanted a king too.

Now of course they *did* have a king. Their king was God. But nobody could see God, could they? Not even God's chosen people, the Israelites. So the people told Samuel, "We want a king! We want to see who's in charge."

If we look at the entire history of the Israelites from this time forward, it's pretty clear that having kings led to big, bad problems. But the people were sure they knew what they wanted. They screamed at Samuel, "Give us a king like all the other nations around here. We want to see the person who's leading us."

God's people then, and God's people now, often want some *thing* or some *body* to worship. If we can *see* a king, we'll know we have a leader, they told Samuel. If we can see Christ on our walls, we'll know he's there in our hearts.

Maybe I'm a little old-fashioned. But I know this from personal experience: when we draw pictures of Christ, or when we buy them, it's very easy for us to give him the shape or form *we* want him to have. If we're angry, we can make him look angry. If we're sweet, we can make him look like sugar candy.

It's easy to make God in our own image—just as easy as it was for the Israelites to reject the great King for a king they could see. Like them, we don't know what God, our King, looks like. And we don't need to. The important thing is that we know that he is within us and within our world.

64

ISRAEL'S BIG MAN

Read 1 Samuel 11:1–15

The people of Israel didn't have a democracy, so they didn't get together and vote for their first king. God chose Saul, and it's not hard to see why the people thought he was a good choice.

The Bible tells us twice (9:2 and 10:23) that Saul was a head taller than the rest of the Israelites. Whether or not we like to admit it, height means something. It's no joke to say that we look up to tall people. Saul stood out in a crowd.

Another good thing about Saul is that he wasn't proud. In fact, like Moses, Saul didn't seem to be too anxious to take a crack at such a big job. Back in chapter 10, Samuel told all the tribes that their king was coming. "Where is he?" they asked. Samuel told them he was hiding. Modesty, folks say, is a virtue.

In addition to being tall and modest, Saul was young, handsome, and popular—the kind of guy people like to be around. If the Israelites themselves had chosen their first king, they might well have decided on a man like Saul.

Today's passage shows us the new king in action for the first time, and you can't help but be impressed by the way this tall and handsome king handled things. Israel was in bad shape. The people were so desperate for help that they were willing to submit to their enemies. But the price was far too steep. Nahash told God's people that he would accept their surrender only if the whole bunch would stand there and have their right eyes gouged out. Nahash figured he'd show these gutless people who was boss.

When the new king heard the horrid terms of the surrender, he acted. He wasn't about to let the enemy humiliate them.

The Bible says Saul "mustered" the people. *Mustered* is a strange word—sounds like something a person does to a hot dog. But Saul's "mustering" showed that he was a terrific leader, popular and persuasive. When Saul "mustered" the people, the Bible means he stirred them up—but good. In a very short time, he got thousands of Israelites geared up to battle the Ammonites. Don't forget—just a few days before, these same people had been scared to death of Nahash and his barbarians.

Some coaches have the ability to psych up their teams so high that they come out of the locker room steaming. Saul seems to have been that good. With only a few hours of inspiration, he got 330,000 Israelites just humming, huffing and puffing for a shot at the hated Ammonites.

And the Bible says they whaled the daylights out of Nahash and his villains. By the middle of the day, no two of Nahash's soldiers were left together. God had given Saul a great victory.

The new king was a hero—the tall man was really a big man. The people loved Saul because he had kept them free and happy. Everything looked just fine.

But looks can be deceiving.

65

DAVID, SON OF JESSE

Prayer:

Lord, be with us

as you were

with David.

Give us strength

and power

through your

gift of the Spirit.

Amen.

Read 1 Samuel 16:1–13

Way back in 1501 a young Italian artist named Michelangelo sculpted a statue of young King David. It's a huge statue, almost seventeen feet tall, of a nearly perfect human form. David's arms are thick and rounded, bursting with power. His chest is almost triangular from the broad shoulders down. His hips bulge with muscle, and his thighs and calves are packed with strength. Michelangelo's *David* is just a young man, maybe sixteen, but he stands tall and proud.

Jesse's David may not have been like Michelangelo's. We *do* know that he was "a man after God's own heart." And we know that he brought Israel to a power and stature that the young nation would never reach again.

But we also know that Jesse's David was the youngest of eight sons and that his father was certain David would not be the one God would choose to be king. When Samuel came around to anoint one of Jesse's boys, this father told his youngest son to stay out in the fields with the sheep.

Samuel took one look at Jesse's oldest boy, Eliab, and figured he was the kingly kid. Maybe Eliab looked something like Michelangelo's *David.* "This has got to be the one," Samuel said.

"Don't be silly, Samuel," God said. "Men and women judge themselves by appearance, but I don't."

So Jesse brought up the other six sons. But Samuel, almost as astonished as Jesse, had to say no to each one of them. "You have any other boys?" Samuel asked.

"Come to think of it, there's David," Jesse said.

The Bible says David had a fine appearance with handsome features and a ruddy complexion. It doesn't say anything about bulging muscles or a fierce personality. David was just a shepherd boy—no all-American linebacker.

Likely as not, he wasn't anything like Michelangelo's *David.* But as beautiful as Michelangelo's *David* is, that sculpture has nothing on Jesse's David.

David was the greatest king of Israel, the writer of many of the psalms, and the ancestor of Jesus Christ, the Savior.

Jesse's David may not have had the perfect human body, but he was really awesome: the Spirit of God came upon him and gave him great power (v. 13).

Beats lifting weights any day.

66

THE FAITH OF THE UNDERDOG

Prayer:

Lord, help us to get as angry as David when we see your name being dragged in the mud. Give us David's faith.

Amen.

Read 1 Samuel 17:17–27 and 41–51

Once a week at school a kid named Jay gets picked on by a big mean guy called Morf. Morf's so tough he's got muscles in his fingernails, and he loves to show off. Sometimes Morf just yells; sometimes he grabs Jay's books and dumps them in the mud. Jay gets sick of it.

One day when Morf is calling him names, Jay flies into him and knocks him off his feet. Both of them flop in the mud. Morf is so shocked that he stomps off, leaving a trail behind him. Jay hasn't won the war, but he's notched himself one big battle.

Jay and Morf are something like David and Goliath. People who like the story of David and Goliath like the story of Jay and Morf too. Both stories have little guys who work up a head of steam and pop off at big bruising bullies. Stories like that make everybody feel good.

Maybe that's why David and Goliath is such a well-known story. It's one of those stories like Noah's ark or Jonah and the whale or the first Christmas—everybody has heard it before. The trouble is, not everybody listens closely.

David and Goliath is more than a story about an underdog who smashes a giant. Yes, Goliath was nine feet tall and carried some awesome weapons. Yes, David was only a kid who'd never been more than a mile from his father's sheep. But there was another character in the championship match, and David knew who that character was: his God.

Let's look at three verses, starting with verse 26. David saw this huge soldier shooting off his mouth at God's people. All around him, the teeth of the Israelites chattered. "Who's this guy who thinks he can take on God's own chosen people?" David asked.

Now look at verse 37. Saul heard about David's bragging and called him into his tent. The big king reminded David that he was only a boy. David got a little angry. He was convinced that he could take the loudmouthed bully. He listed all the wild animals he'd killed while out with his father's sheep. He told Saul that the Lord who saved him from all those animals would save him from this character Goliath.

Finally, verse 45. Goliath got angry when he saw the wimp the Israelites had sent, and he told David it was all over for him. Little David wasn't scared at all. "This day the Lord will hand you over to me," he said. "The whole world will know that there is a God in Israel. All those gathered here will know that it is not by sword or spear that the Lord saves; for the battle is the Lord's, and he will give all of you into our hands."

If we see David and Goliath as *only* the story of a boy beating back a huge bellowing bully, then we're missing the real reason for David's courage at the Valley of Elah. David knew Goliath was taunting Israel's God, and David was absolutely sure that his God wouldn't stand for it.

David's God killed Goliath; David's sling just whipped the stone.

67

"THE GREEN-EYED MONSTER"

Prayer:

Dear God, bless us today and every day. Keep us from feeling those bad emotions like jealousy and rage. Help us put all our trust in you. Through Christ, your Son, Amen.

Read 1 Samuel 18:1–16

Almost twenty-five years ago a high school kid named Marvin drove off in his Chevy with my girlfriend. I was in the eighth grade, and so was my girl—you'd better make that Marvin's girl, I guess.

I'm embarrassed now to think of how jealous I was—pedaling my bicycle while the two of them sat all cozy-like in big-time Marvin's car—but I burned inside, just burned. That was twenty-five years ago, but when I remember it today, I still feel as if I've just swallowed a shoebox full of hot peppers.

My girlfriend didn't marry Marvin. She didn't marry me either, for that matter. All three of us have our own families. But when I remember them in the car, I can still growl.

Jealousy does that. "It is the green-eyed monster which doth mock the meat it feeds on," Shakespeare says in *Othello*. The green-eyed monster turns you inside out with anger. It eats you up and, when it shows itself, always makes you look stupid. For instance, throwing a rotten egg against Marvin's pretty car would have done nothing at all but make me look dumb. Jealousy mocks the person it feeds on.

In a matter of a verse or two, Saul, Israel's handsome king, became insanely jealous of David, the man he had once loved as a son. Why the change? The sound of the women's song tied him up in knots: Saul's killed thousands, they chanted, but David's killed tens of thousands.

And deep inside, Saul knew what else had happened. Verse 12 says Saul knew the Lord had left him and gone instead to David. So Saul sent David away. But when David proved to be a great general, the king was overcome with jealousy. He couldn't think about anything but the upstart David. The green-eyed monster was like a cancer, eating him up inside.

I can imagine how Saul must have felt—even worse than I did about Marvin. I really don't hate Marvin anymore. I don't even know him. He's probably got a son who drives a car and looks for girls. But I can't forget what happened twenty-five years ago. Why not? Because it hurt my pride.

Saul's pride was shattered too. Israel's big-man king had become an also-ran to a new folk hero. And nobody likes playing second fiddle.

Jealousy grows like a weed in places where great chunks of human pride have crumbled into dust.

68

READING GOD'S WILL

Prayer:

*Dear Lord, we
know that you
rule our lives.
When we face
tough decisions,
help us
understand
what you want
us to do. Help
us know your
will. Help us
obey.

Amen.*

Read 1 Samuel 24:1–22

"O Lord my God, I take refuge
in you;
save and deliver me from all
who pursue me,
or they will tear me like a
lion
and rip me to pieces with no
one to rescue me."

Psalm 7:1–2

Some people who study the Bible
think that David may have written
Psalm 7 during the time he and
Saul were enemies. If those
people are right, then these verses
show us how scared David was of
Israel's king. What's more, they
illustrate David's real danger.

Imagine, then, what it must
have been like for David to stand
there in front of sleeping Saul.
Full of fear for his own life, David
could easily have killed the man
who was always trying to kill him.
What should he do?

David's friends made the
decision more difficult. "Kill him
now," they told David. "After all,
the Lord has promised that he will
deliver Saul into your hands."
David's friends gave murder
divine approval. "God wants you
to slay him! Do it!"

But David didn't kill Saul; he
snipped off a corner of Saul's
robe—and even felt guilty about
doing that (v. 5).

David didn't kill the man who
was constantly threatening his life
because that man was still God's
anointed king. And despite his
own desire to free himself from
Saul's constant hunting, David
knew that killing Saul would be
wrong—against the will of God.

But this passage shows us a
tough problem: David's own men
told him it was God's will that he
kill Saul. David argued that it was
God's will that he spare the king's
life. What we have here is two
versions of God's will. Both David
and his advisors think they know
it.

There's an old story that's told

about most every war. Two
soldiers fight each other hand to
hand, until one kills the other. The
one left alive looks closely at the
man he's killed. He sees a cross
hanging around the enemy's neck,
a cross just like the one he wears
himself. Both men believed they
were fighting for a cause God
himself supported. Both felt God
was on their side.

It's not always easy to read the
Lord's will for our lives. Some
people struggle their whole life
trying to understand whether the
Lord wants them to be preachers
or plumbers.

What David's decision seems to
show, however, is that principle is
better than coincidence. David's
friends wanted David to kill Saul
because Saul's death would rid
them of danger. "Do it now," they
said, dreaming of peace. "God
wants you to do it or he wouldn't
have brought you here." David's
friends used God like makeup to
give their *own* motives—no
matter
how understandable—a better face.

David wasn't worried about
himself. He was worried about
disobeying God by taking God's
will into his own hands.

David was right. His friends
were wrong. David put his own
feelings for staying alive—no
matter how strong—in second
place to his regard for God's law.

90

69

JERUSALEM THE GOLDEN

Prayer:

"O sweet and blessed country, the home of God's elect! O sweet and blessed country that eager hearts expect! Jesus, in mercy bring us to that dear land of rest; who art, with God the Father, and Spirit, ever blest."

Amen.

Read 2 Samuel 5:1–12

David may have been only thirty years old when he took over as king of Israel, but he was already striped with scars from his years as an army commander. In dozens of previous battles, he had found out that there were a number of ways to skin a cat—even if that cat were a bunch of rowdy Jebusites holding the city of Jerusalem, the city David wanted for himself and for his God.

The Jebusites weren't exactly a sophisticated bunch. They probably did a whole lot of spittin' and screamin', all the while poking their noses up in the air as if they were really big time.

"You can't take this city, you zero," they might have said. "We're so tough we could blindfold our third string, and they could still take your army. Come on up—we dare you"

David had been a scrapper since the day he met Goliath. So when the Jebusites taunted him, he didn't take it sitting down. Besides, more than anything he wanted Jerusalem to be the home of the Lord God. The Jebusites were merely in his way.

David had a plan. He told his men that the whole city would fall if they would merely sneak up through the ducts in the walls—those shafts where water was drawn up into the city. The Jebusites were expecting them to attack the walls. David knew better. He told his men to wind their way through the water ducts and turn the whole place inside out, to win the battle for God and his people.

And the soldiers did. They took Jerusalem, and Jerusalem became "the city of David." David, in fact, gave the city its name; the word *Jerusalem* means "foundation of peace." The fort city on the hill became the center of David's kingdom, the place where God lived with his people.

Today, of course, Jerusalem is not a "foundation of peace." Today the Jewish nation of Israel owns part of the city; for them it is a holy city because it is the city of David, their own ancestor. But part of the city belongs to the Moslems too, Arabic people who feel that the city is as important to their religious tradition as it is to the Jews'.

Because of that rivalry, Jerusalem is no model of peace. Probably no area of the world has suffered so much, seen so much destruction and needless killing as the Middle East. Not since World War II has any region of the globe been so burned by the fires of warfare as that area surrounding the city which David called "foundation of peace."

Was Jerusalem given the wrong name? Not really. David's kingdom laid the foundation for the *new* Jerusalem of everlasting peace. Once Christ came, David's kingdom expanded to include believers throughout the world, not just those who pitched their tents around Jerusalem. The I AM sent his Son, through David's line, to bring peace and salvation to *all* people from Timbuktu to Talahassee.

This new Jerusalem is the place God has promised to those who are faithful to his Word. This new Jerusalem is heaven itself—that's the real "Jerusalem the golden." That's the real city of peace. Eternal peace.

David knew what was worth fighting for.

70

THE COM- FORTER

Prayer:

Thank you,

Lord, for the

comfort you

give us, for the

warmth and the

love that you

make us feel.

Thank you for

the gift of life

through your

Son, Jesus

Christ. In his

name,

Amen.

Read Psalm 23

If you live in the north, your toes know what a cold night is. On January nights, the backyard snow glows in the shiny brightness of the moon. The still air bites your nose and fingers, and snow chirps beneath your boots.

No matter how thick your storm windows, the cold inches unseen into the house and lies there on the floor like a frozen lake. You tuck your feet up beneath you on the couch like a cottontail, as if heat from your insides will warm your toes.

If the furnace heat doesn't reach upstairs, your bedroom floor feels like a cold sidewalk beneath your bare feet. The bed's not much better—the sheets cold and stiff as sheet rock.

On just such nights, my mother used to take out what she called a "comforter," a thick pink quilt, shiny smooth, pumped full of a million goose feathers. It didn't weigh much, but it was at least four inches thick, and it buried a kid's frozen body beneath the covers. Once my body heat swelled through the sheets, the comforter turned my icy bed into a warm little nest. In fact, that comforter was so warm that in a few minutes my big toes would wander over to the corner of the bed and poke out from beneath the covers for a breath of fresh air. On a winter night there was nothing quite as nice as that thick pink comforter.

There were times when God was like a great pink comforter to David—a source of warmth and comfort in an ice-cold, shivery world. Perhaps no chapter in the entire Bible is as well known as Psalm 23. Not all of us need the courage to fight Goliaths, but all of us—young and old, rich and poor, smart and not-so-smart— need the comfort of God's love, the warm trust that he's there, wrapping us in the greatest quilt

we can imagine. David knew it— that's what made him sing.

Not long ago I had to speak at the County Home, a place for people with mental impairments. The little room held six long rows of people the world thinks are most forgettable. Our kids sat there quiet as mice, a little afraid. I was scared when I was a kid too. Visits to the County Home were not my idea of a good time.

First we sang a couple songs, and lots of the residents sang them by heart. So I wondered if I could get them to say Psalm 23 together. "Do you remember this?" I said. "The Lord is my shepherd—" And immediately they started in.

I don't think we would have won a speech contest, but it was beautiful—absolutely beautiful. Even my kids joined in.

Psalm 23 is forever in those folks' minds. It gives them the same kind of comfort it gave David and you and my kids and me and everyone else who knows our Lord in their hearts.

Why don't you say it together right now? You don't have to wait for a January night.

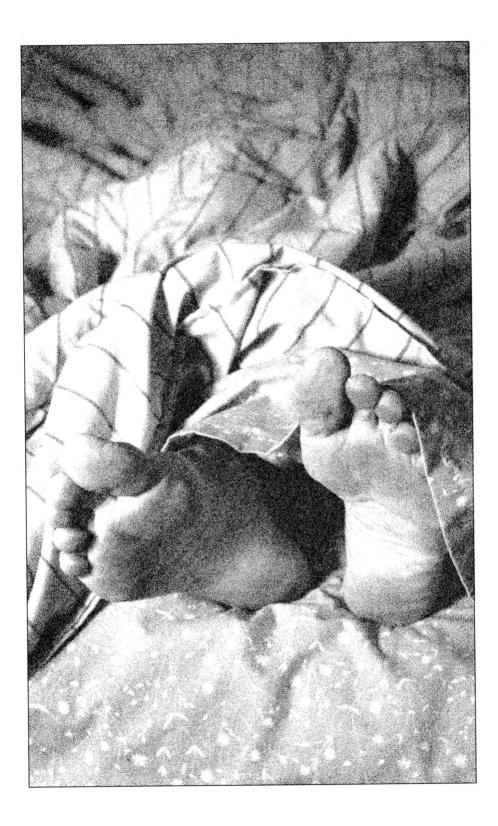

71

SIN

Read 2 Samuel 12:1–14

"The Lord is my shepherd, I shall lack nothing."

When you read Psalm 23, you can't help but wonder how David, such a strong believer in God, could have let himself fall into sin the way he did with Bathsheba. Things like that aren't supposed to happen to our greatest heroes.

One night David got out of bed and walked around on the flat roof of his palace. Down below he saw a beautiful woman bathing. Quicker than you can imagine, David ordered his soldiers to bring her to the palace. David wanted her for his own (and the king got what he wanted). Bathsheba, Uriah's wife, became pregnant. And David—God's shepherd boy, Israel's deliverer, the great soldier, the strong believer, the man of principle—David ordered Uriah killed to hide what he'd done with Bathsheba. Now he was guilty of both murder *and* adultery.

How could such a thing happen?

Sin. The answer seems too easy. But we all sin, even those people we admire most for their faith—even the preachers, even the teachers, even our moms and dads. Even ourselves.

Still, the story of David and Bathsheba saddens me. We expect sin from the skid row bums and Hollywood producers and pornography peddlers. We expect it from the people we call "filthy rich." But we don't expect it from Davids. We don't expect it from those whom God himself sets up in front of us as the good people.

We want our examples to be clean as glass, pure as Eden itself. But they aren't. They never are. Neither are we. The garden is gone.

What's even worse, we don't see sin in ourselves. Listen to Nathan, God's messenger. He spells out a story that parallels David's own story as closely as the two lanes of a freeway.

Just to hear it made David angry. "As the Lord himself lives," David roared, "that man deserves to die." Righteous David, the killer and adulterer, could not see himself in Nathan's story mirror.

Then come some of the toughest words in the whole Bible. "You are the man!" Nathan said. Notice how Nathan didn't give David a chance to speak. He just poured on the coals, listing the indictments that God himself had handed down to his chosen king.

When it was over, David shook. "I have sinned against the Lord," he said.

And immediately he was forgiven. God was confident of David's confession of this horrid sin, and God forgave him. "The Lord has taken away your sin," Nathan told him.

Try as we might, we can't ever fully imagine God. I'm not sure *I've* ever forgiven David for what he did, but God has. Just like that, David was forgiven. I don't think he deserved to be forgiven—not so quickly. But I'm not God. God forgives because God loves in ways that we can't begin to imagine. Even on our best days, in our best behavior, at our most loving, we come nowhere near to being like God.

Of course, forgiveness isn't easy. It doesn't come cheap. It's painful and costly. David and Bathsheba's son would die because God does punish sin. God forgives all of us—even David—but someone else takes the punishment in our place, earning our forgiveness. Someone innocent—like David's son or like God's own Son, Jesus Christ.

Prayer:

Lord, be with those people who are in positions of power. We know that you expect great things from them. Give them strength and faith. And help us to understand that they are no more or less human than we are.

Amen.

72

HITTING THE BOTTOM

Prayer:

Dear Lord,

thank you for

the confession

of David. Help

us confess our

sins as David

did. And forgive

us as surely as

you forgave

David.

Amen.

Read Psalm 51 (Today read the meditation first.)

My friend Bill used to run a treatment hospital for alcoholics. He got tons of calls and letters from people who wanted to know what they could do about the man or woman in their family who had a drinking problem.

Bill told me he couldn't say much to those people. In fact, all he could tell them was that nobody could do anything. "Your Johnny's just going to have to hit the bottom sometime," he'd say, "and until he does, there's nothing you or I can do." Bill said it seemed cruel to tell moms or dads or wives or husbands or children just to sit there and watch their loved ones drink themselves into idiots.

But Bill claimed that only alcoholics who know they need help can get any. "We can help them only when they admit that they can't do anything to stop drinking on their own," he said.

Psalm 51 is a record of David's feelings when he hit bottom after his sin with Bathsheba. Once Nathan helped David to see his sin, the mighty king was in misery. He knew that the only way to live again was to confess his sin and ask forgiveness. He knew he needed God's help.

"My sin is always before me," he said. The memory of killing Uriah was like a huge wall before his eyes. No matter how he tried to see past it, it stood there motionless.

"Surely I have been a sinner from birth." He wasn't making excuses here, but instead telling God that sin ran so deep in him that it came naturally.

"Let me hear joy and gladness; let the bones you have crushed rejoice." David knew that sin had robbed him of joy. God's knowledge of his sin had crushed him.

"Create in me a new heart, O God." David, one of God's strongest believers, asked God to start completely over on him. He confessed that he was so full of sin that God would have to begin again—as if there never had been a Goliath or a sleeping Saul.

"Then . . . sinners will turn back to you." David had faith in what God could do. He asked for forgiveness so that someone so broken as he could be a witness to all sinners.

"A broken and contrite heart, O God, you will not despise." David's pride had been shattered by seeing the ugliness of his own sin. He was humbled so low that his face was on the ground, and he knew God's arm was the only support that could get him back on his feet.

His sin had proven that when he relied on himself he was nothing. What's more, he knew that everything—his pardon for sin, his purity, and his joy—all depended on God's grace.

David confessed his need for help. He knew that what he needed only God could give.

73

BIG SHOES

Prayer:

Teach us to be

humble, Lord.

It's easy for us

to think that if

we just had a

little more

money or a

little more time

or a little more

brains, we

could do it all

ourselves.

Forgive us for

our pride, and

bless us.

Amen.

Read 1 Kings 3:4–15

I know a kid who was probably the best trombone player in her whole eighth grade class. She was good—she was very good. Today she's in her twenties, and she never plays the trombone anymore. She gave it up long ago. You know why? Because her older brother was always better than she was. Too many people tried to compare the two of them. She finally got tired of people expecting her to be just like her older brother.

It's really hard to fill somebody else's shoes, especially when those shoes are really too big to fill. For several years Vince Lombardi was the best football coach in the whole country. His team, the Green Bay Packers, won championship after championship.

Finally, Lombardi left. He took another job, and the Green Bay Packers had to find another coach. The team picked a man named Phil Bengston.

Phil Bengston had a tough time. He didn't last long as coach of the Packers.

Nobody likes to follow in the footsteps of someone whom everybody loved. It's not pleasant constantly to be compared to someone else. It's not easy to try to live up to someone else's achievements—especially when that someone was a "superman" or "superwoman."

That was Solomon's problem too. It was hard being king. It was even harder trying to fill King David's shoes. Not only did Solomon have to rule over lots of people and do it well, but he also had to be compared with his own father—everybody's favorite, King David, the musician-king.

So one night Solomon had a dream. He saw himself talking to God. The first thing he told God was that he knew God was always faithful to his father. But he confessed that he felt like a little

kid compared to his father. And then he asked God for help in ruling. It's just as if he told God that he couldn't do it all alone—the shoes were too big.

And in the dream God loved the humble way in which Solomon talked. "You didn't ask for money or long life for yourself, Solomon," God said. "I like that. Instead you asked for brains to run this nation of people—my people."

God told Solomon that he'd give him the wisdom he asked for. What's more, that wisdom would help him get rich. "And one more thing, Solomon," God said, "if you honor me, I'll bless you with long life." God repeated something similar to the covenant he had drawn up with Abraham many years earlier.

God gave Solomon the wisdom he wanted—and a whole lot more. Why? Because Solomon confessed that without God he couldn't fill anybody's shoes. Solomon put his faith in the right place.

Solomon, like his father, was blessed.

74

JESSE'S ESCAPE (6)

Prayer:

Sometimes things happen to us because we let our fear or our excitement or any kind of emotion we have get out of control, Lord. Teach us how to get along with others.

Amen.

Read 1 Kings 3:16–28

It took a while for Jesse to assemble all the pieces in his mind—that he had left the farm, that he had slept in the church, that these people must have come in and found him.

"I needed a place to sleep—," he said, sitting up.

"Can't have this, you know," the old man said. "We got laws to keep you vagrants out—"

Jesse wasn't sure what a vagrant was.

"You'll be all right," the woman said. "This here is my husband, Fred, and I'm Deb.

"Don't go cozying up to him, honey. No telling what he's done—"

Jesse didn't trust the old man. It seemed as if fear had made him slightly crazy.

Jesse tried to reassure him. "I'm not about to do—"

"Quiet down! We ain't going to believe anything you say anyway." The old man glowered at him, holding the broom up like a rifle.

"Fred—"

"This is a dangerous one all right. You can see it in the eyes, I always say—"

The sun streamed through the windows to the east, cutting long, bright rectangles over the benches. Tiny specks of dust floated in the sunlight's radiant gaze.

Again Jesse tried to quiet him. "Listen, believe me, I just needed to get some sleep. Now I'll be—"

"We're not letting you get away now, boy. You hear me? We already called the cops."

Jesse got to his feet. He was smaller than Fred, but he could see the fear in Fred's eyes, fear that made him almost wild.

"I'm sorry," Jesse said. "I'm leaving now." He had no choice, of course, not with the cops coming.

"I say you're staying," Fred said, and he raised the broom up to Jesse's chest. "We got breaking and entering on you for sure, and who knows what else you already done—"

When Jesse jerked the broom away from Fred, the old man's hands shrieked along the handle. Jesse threw it hard away from him. The broom spun out toward the wall and smashed through the stained glass, shattering the window. Jesse stood there, dumbfounded, staring at what he had done.

"I knew you couldn't trust him. I can see it in his eyes," Fred said.

Jesse saw Deb's tears and ran for the cycle, the explosion of glass echoing through his ears. He was in trouble now. Maybe it wasn't his fault completely, but he knew it wasn't smart of him to throw that broom.

The cycle started on the second kick, and the gravel spit up by the back tires cracked against the side of the church when he left.

98

75

GOD'S TEMPLE

Prayer:

Thank you for being the I AM. Thank you for being with us always and everywhere. May your name be praised forever. Amen.

Read 1 Kings 8:12–27

One night after Bible class some of my friends and I were left in our church alone. It was years ago, but I remember it well. There was something kind of scary about being in such a big, old building with no one else around. We snuck upstairs to the sanctuary, the place where Sunday worship was held. It was as dark and quiet as the rest of the building.

I don't know who thought of it or how we started, but one of us got down on the shiny, wooden floor. Rugs ran down the aisles of the church, but the floor beneath the pews was smooth and slippery. And the floor wasn't flat; as it ran toward the front of the church, it actually pitched downhill. Here's what we did: we got down on our backs beneath the pews, put our hands up on the edges of the benches, and pulled as hard as we could. Whoosh!—we zipped along the slippery floor up toward the front of the church. We turned the church into a playground.

What I remember best about that night is not daring to laugh. Even though we had a great time, nobody dared to laugh out loud. And since our sliding down the floor didn't make any noise, it was almost perfectly quiet in the dark church.

Why didn't we laugh out loud?

I can only explain it one way— you see if you know what I mean. I think we didn't dare to laugh because we thought that goofing around in the church sanctuary was wrong. The only thing the church sanctuary was used for was Sunday worship, that one time of the week when everybody talked together to God through prayer and songs. It was like God himself lived in that sanctuary. That's the way it seemed to us.

Some Israelites might have thought Solomon's temple was the place that God lived too. After all, nearly all of their neighbors had temples where their own gods lived. And Solomon's temple was one of the most beautiful buildings anyone anywhere had ever seen—it *looked* like a house for a god. So, for the Israelites the temple was a symbol of God's presence among his people. No kids would have slid up and down the floor of Solomon's temple.

Yet, take a look at what Solomon says in his prayer to God in verse 27: "The heavens, even the highest heavens, cannot contain you."

Did the great I AM actually live right there in the temple Solomon had built? Did he live in the old church I remember as a boy? Nope—not at all. The I AM is much too big to be contained in one or two—or even a million— buildings.

And don't forget this—Christ told the people that he would destroy the temple and build the whole business back up in three days. If you think about a temple the size of Solomon's, then Christ seems to be talking nonsense.

But, of course, he did exactly what he had told the people he would do. He died, and three days later he was raised to life again.

What about the temple? Jesus was talking about his body. And he talks the same way about ours, because our bodies are God's temples today. God lives in us— not in a building.

76

AFTER A FASHION

Prayer:

It's hard for us

to understand

how a smart

man like

Solomon could

forget about

you so easily.

Help us to

remain strong

followers of

your will and

your Word.

Amen.

Read 1 Kings 11:1–8

Years before Solomon was born, the people of Israel claimed they wanted a king to make their nation "like other nations." First came Saul, then David. Solomon was the third king, and by the end of his reign, lo and behold, the Israelites had become exactly what they wanted to be—"like other nations."

Solomon, you see, had a problem with women. Counting wives and girlfriends, Solomon had almost a thousand women. He collected women the way some kids collect baseball cards or little charms for silver bracelets. He picked them up wherever he could find them, and he never gave a hoot what God they worshiped.

Just "owning" that many human beings is bad enough, of course. Each one of a thousand women couldn't possibly be a human being to Solomon; he couldn't possibly know their names or their real feelings. To him they probably were something like slaves.

What's odd is that in some ways, the wise Solomon became a slave to them. Those women didn't own him, but in an odd way they began to control his life. They became his god.

Many teenagers like clothes. But clothes aren't cheap. To keep in fashion—to really keep up with all the latest fads—takes a lot of money. If a teenager has to pay for her own clothes, keeping up can be a problem. If she has to work like a slave to make enough money to wear the latest, you can't help but wonder if she owns the clothes or if the clothes own her.

That's how it was with Solomon. He pursued his women with such devotion that he started following their gods. It's not hard to guess how God felt when Solomon, the great temple builder, started using all his money to build temples for the stinking gods of the Ammonites and Moabites.

What an incredible turn of events! It hadn't been that long since Solomon had been given the blessed job of building the great temple that his father, David, always wanted to build. When he got older—just when you might expect this very smart man to get even smarter—he turned his back on the God of his fathers and mothers and ran like an animal after women, chased them so hard that he even worshiped their dumb gods.

Solomon the wisest Israelite turned into Solomon the fool. As a result, the whole nation followed the direction of their beloved king and worshiped at altars that were horrid in the eyes of God. Solomon made pagan worship respectable, and the whole nation of God's chosen people started looking exactly like any other pagan people.

Finally their wish had come true. Israel had become exactly what they wanted to become—just like other nations.

77

FANTASY

Read 1 Kings 11:26–40

Some of us have a fantasy that goes something like this: Suddenly, out of nowhere, a very wealthy and generous person appears and hands us a million dollars. "It's yours to do with as you wish," says our mysterious visitor. And we're off and dreaming about what a million dollars could buy: all the clothes we'd ever need; a room full of the latest video games and stereos and TVs; a dozen trips to Disney Land, and much more.

Well, in today's Bible story Jeroboam is promised a real-life fantasy. "You're going to be king over ten tribes," God tells him. "And you will rule over whatever your heart desires."

God was going to split the kingdom in two. Ten tribes would go to Jeroboam. One tribe—the one that would continue "David's line"—would go to Rehoboam. The ten tribes of Israel would always be tangling with the tribe of Judah—even though they were neighbors and even though they worshiped the same God.

I grew up in a little town that was always tangling with another little town just around the corner. Both towns were full of people who went to the same kinds of churches. Lots of people in one town had cousins or even brothers in the other. But somehow, in spite of all the things they had in common, people in the two towns just couldn't get along.

Gradually the rivalry between the two—especially at high school sports events—turned into a kind of hate. We used to call the other town "Skunk Town," and they called us the same thing. The two towns were a little like Israel and Judah—they could never really get along.

It could have been different, at least for Jeroboam and his ten tribes. As king, he had money and power beyond anything we can imagine. Servants waited on him hand and foot. Not bad! Kind of a fantasy come true for Jeroboam.

There was a catch, of course, a big *if* attached to God's promise. "*If* you do whatever I command you and walk in my ways and do what is right in my eyes by keeping my statutes and commands, as David my servant did, I will be with you."

Though the Bible says Jeroboam was a very capable young man, a man with lots of leadership ability and status in the community, he wasn't able to live up to his end of the bargain. And so his fantasy, like that of even the wise Solomon, crumbled into dust. What might have been a long and prosperous reign turned into disaster. The same prophet who promised Jeroboam so much would one day tell him that God was going to give Israel up because of Jeroboam's sins and the sins he caused Israel to commit.

Why do God's people always turn their backs on God when they'd be so much better off listening to him? It seems that no one can be true to God—not Jeroboam, not the Israelites, not Solomon, not even David.

We can't either. That's why we need a Savior. And we know that Jesus, our Savior, is no fantasy. He's for real.

Prayer:

Thank you, Lord for being our God, now and forever. Help us to be faithful to you, through Jesus Christ, our Savior and Lord. Amen.

78

THINGS GET WORSE

Read 1 Kings 14:21–28

Every night millions of people watch the TV comedian Johnny Carson. They have for years. All of that attention has made Carson filthy rich. Recently, Carson's third wife filed for a divorce and asked the court for a mere $2.6 million per year in support from her ex-husband.

Mrs. Carson claims she needs $37,000 a month—more than many families earn in a whole year— for jewelry and furs alone. She says she got used to spending that much money while she was married, and now that she's alone she couldn't think of spending a dollar less.

Solomon probably used the same excuse to justify spending loads of money for himself and all his women friends. He just *had* to have a summer palace on the seacoast, didn't he? After all, once you get used to living so high, you can't go back to peanuts.

Solomon's immoral use of money and slave labor led directly to a split in the nation of Israel. Jeroboam, a good worker and leader, was appointed to collect money and recruit slave labor in Ephraim, a tribal district of northern Israel. However, Jeroboam didn't particularly like Solomon's rough demands. He got angry about them—so angry that he led a rebellion against Solomon, his boss. The rebellion failed, and Jeroboam had to run for his life.

When Solomon died, his son Rehoboam was crowned king. In a flash, Jeroboam came back to Israel, rounded up many of his old friends, and told the new king the same thing he had told Solomon—take it easy on the taxes. This time he put some teeth into his demands: he told Rehoboam the whole nation would split up if Rehoboam didn't listen.

Rehoboam refused, so the northern territories broke away and left Israel split, creating two warring nations where once God had ruled a faithful people. Rehoboam was left with just one tribe—Judah. Jeroboam became king of the ten tribes, which were together called Israel.

Both Israel and Judah rejected the I AM. Both kings followed the religion of their pagan mothers, and the people they led turned into horrid sinners, ugly before the eyes of God. Both nations forgot completely about their loving God.

But God's mercy still reached out to his people. Israel was split into two sin-blackened countries, but still God held Judah in his hand. From Judah would come the Savior of the world.

Judah's people did things that made believers weep. Yet, Judah would be the source, eventually, of Jesus Christ.

Sometimes it seems so clear that we don't deserve the love of God. But then, God's love is something else, isn't it?

79

DROUGHT AND FAITH

Prayer:

Lord, thank you

for the faith of

the widow.

Teach us to

have her kind of

faith.

Amen.

Read 1 Kings 16:29–30; 17:1–16

"'For everything there is a season,' the Bible says. One Sunday as we were coming home from church, we noticed a cloud bank along the western horizon. It looked like the much-needed rain was finally on its way. By the time we got home, the sky was black. The sun had disappeared. But instead of the familiar gentle roll of thunder and the welcome patter of rain, we heard the sound of blowing sand and dust as it began to tear at the siding of our house.

"The boys quickly changed their clothes and went out to the barn to do the chores. While they were outside, I decided to go upstairs to hang up their Sunday clothes. When I picked up their clothes, I could see the outline of them on the bed.

"This was the first of many dust storms we were to experience. They would usually begin about the same way: a nice sunny day would look like it was going to give way to rain, but instead would give way to driving dust. These storms would last for days and sometimes even weeks.

"Finally, the wind would die down and things would brighten up. In the house we would begin the job of dusting out everything and washing the clothes. We would sometimes get a small pailful of dust out of the house.

"Outdoors the dust would lie in banks around every building, tree, or post. Fences would collect long snakelike banks of dust. Sometimes the farmers would jerk these fences out with a tractor to keep from getting dunes of dust in their fields. Whenever we would get a sprinkle of rain, the boys would get out the Fordson tractor and start disking, but the tractor would soon stop because of the dust getting into the carburetor . . ."

Those words belong to Mrs.

Hattie Los, a great-grandmother from Delavan, Wisconsin, who has written down her memories of life during a bad drought in South Dakota. Today, with our huge supermarkets full of food, it's helpful to feel the gritty dust between our teeth when we read her memories. We might otherwise think that drought is something only a movie-maker creates.

When you think of what life must be like during a drought, you have to be shocked at what the widow of Zarephath did for Elijah. She was out scrounging for firewood to prepare what she thought would be the last meal she would ever have with her little boy. Husbandless, and therefore penniless, she knew that she was facing death head-on.

Elijah looked over her meager provisions and made an unbeliev-able demand. "Look," he said, "you make me a cake with what you have left, and I'll guarantee you'll have food."

What kind of lunatic would believe this guy? Give me what you have, and "poof," you'll get all you want? But the widow believed. Like Rahab before her, the widow had a tenacious faith.

Maybe she believed because she saw this man Elijah for what he was: God's chosen prophet. Whatever it was, the widow of Zarephath never blinked. She believed Elijah. Her faith—the faith of a serving widow—kept both her and her son well fed.

80

CHEAP THRILLS

Prayer:

Dear Father,

help us to be

obedient to you.

Help us to love

you above all

and our

neighbors as

ourselves. We

know that isn't

easy.

Amen.

Read 1 Kings 18:17–46

Today's passage presents two incredible stories; one happened on stage, the other off.

In the first, thousands of people stood on a mountaintop while hundreds of priests tried to prove their god's power: would it be Baal or Jahweh? After Baal failed badly, Elijah asked that water be poured over his offering. We know what happened. The Lord came through with a spear of fire so intense that "it lapped up the water."

But there are *two* incredible stories here. One is about God's victory over Baal, the other about the people's reaction. In the very next passage, Elijah, who should have been made a national hero after the way he walloped the priests of Baal, had to run for his life. The second incredible story is about the way the people didn't care. For a minute or two they fell down on their faces and screamed that the Lord was God, but a day later, their worlds went on, spinning away from the God of their deliverance.

When I was a kid, I used to go to Bible camp. It was fun—at least most of the time. But all week long the adults talked about the bonfire on Friday night. We were expected to give "testimonies" at the bonfire.

"Testimonies" were a big deal. Every year you could count on one or two regulars to get up there and give a testimony. They seemed to like it; some of them even cried. But the camp counselors used to push everybody else to stand up too. Every night at devotions our counselor would remind us.

"Remember—Friday night I'd love it if you guys would give a testimony," he'd say after the lights went out.

The Friday night campfire made me terribly nervous. Talking in front of all those people scared the stuffings out of me. But my counselor was counting on me, after all, and a guy got the feeling that if he didn't give a testimony, he wasn't really square with God.

First we'd sing some soft songs. Then some preacher would talk real seriously. He'd say, "Now, does anyone want to say anything about their relationship to Jesus?" For awhile it would be very quiet. Then some of the regulars would start in.

I'm scared yet, just thinking about it. I know why all those counselors wanted us to testify, but the whole experience was so chilling. I mean, we felt weird while it was going on, and even after—so nervous and strange. Especially when people cried.

People forgot God after Mt. Carmel because the whole show, for them, was nothing more than a cheap thrill, an emotional experience, like testifying in the jumpy light of a campfire. Once their nerves settled, Israel forgot the whole show.

Following the I AM is a full life's dedication to obedience, not simply an emotional experience. If it were only an emotional experience, the blazing altar on Mt. Carmel would have brought God's people back to loving service.

But it didn't.

My camp counselor wasn't wrong in trying to get us to testify. Serving God *is* an emotional experience. But it's more—so much more. It's no cheap thrill.

81

GUILT

Prayer:

Lord, forgive

our silence

when we see

other people

hurt unjustly.

Give us the faith

to stand up for

you when we

see people doing

wrong to others.

Amen.

Read 1 Kings 21:1–16

Zoarash and Mandal walk slowly back toward town. Children run past, yelling and laughing, throwing stones at each other, mimicking what has just been done to Naboth, owner of the vineyard. Zoarash reaches for his wife's arm, but Mandal refuses him.

"I'll have no part of this," she says, eyes straight ahead.

"Mandal, please—people will hear you—" He stops quickly as if to seal his wife off from the stream of people returning with them.

"Naboth was innocent. You know it!" she says.

Zoarash looks around to see if anyone heard. He stands there momentarily, then walks ahead of his wife, unwilling to carry the conversation further.

Mandal watches him walk, his hands on his hips. "You have sold yourself, my husband," she yells. "God says—"

Zoarash turns suddenly and runs back. "How dare you?—I am your husband." He takes her arm and drags her along the road. Other men on the road smile when they see him take her this way.

Mandal reaches for her husband's shirt. "Please," she says, "let me say what I must."

Zoarash stops and looks around, then drags her off the road beneath a tree, away from the rush.

"Zoarash," she says, "please confess this sin to God. You know the lie. You know the lie, and the blood of Naboth is on your hands too. You were part of this treachery—"

Zoarash kicks at the dirt. He leans down towards her and speaks in a whisper. "The queen herself ordered this. Would you have me disobey the order of the queen? Would you have me die?"

Mandal wipes tears away with her sleeve. "You are already dead if you have sold your own soul to Satan—"

"It was the queen who ordered it. Who am I to disobey? 'Have him stoned'—you read the note. Is the life I've made for you so bad that you would lose it for my disobedience?"

"You have spit in God's face, Zoarash. Unless you confess your sin, this life you love so dearly will be worthless. All of it is worth nothing at all without obedience to God—"

"And what of God's king and queen? Am I not to obey them? Is that not also the commandment?"

Four men come back along the road, carrying Naboth's body.

"Look, my husband. Look at that and tell me that your soul doesn't weep for your own sin—"

Zoarash stares at the lifeless body, its arms dangling. The men who carry it laugh and joke. Dust cakes the blood against Naboth's temple. Zoarash drops on his knees in the ditch. He keeps his head up, because no one must see him grieve.

"What have we done, Mandal?" he says. With one hand he holds his head, as if to stop the constant pain.

"We have sinned, my husband," Mandal says. She rises and comes to him. "We have sinned against God."

82

THE TORCH IS PASSED

Prayer:

Sometimes we

wonder if

you've left our

lives, Lord.

Abortion,

murders, wars—

horrible things

happen

constantly. But

we know that

you have

promised to be

with us always.

Thank you for

that promise

which gives us

hope.

Amen.

Read 2 Kings 2:1–15

To the other prophets life without Elijah must have looked rather dreary. Elijah had been the conscience of God's people, the man God himself had made captain of the prophets. Time and time again, courageous Elijah, armed to the teeth with God's Word, had stood up to the most evil king of the Israelites, Ahab, and his wicked queen, Jezebel.

Elijah knew that he was going to be with God. So did Elisha, his obvious successor. But when Elijah tried to bring it up, Elisha said, "Don't talk about it." Elisha didn't want to think about life without the leader.

My daughter acts the same way about a dentist appointment. "Don't forget the dentist," I might say on the morning of her appointment. She just growls and looks away as if to say, "You don't have to remind me."

To the prophets remaining, losing Elijah was much, much worse than a dentist appointment.

But Elijah had to be replaced. God's work on earth had to go on, even if successors seemed few and far between. Elijah, like only Enoch before him, went up to be with God without really dying. Elijah's ascension in a fiery chariot was a testimony to his obedience to God's Word.

But what happened on that day also showed Elisha's preparation to replace a man nobody thought could be replaced. First, Elisha swore he would not leave Elijah's side, even though Elijah himself was not sure any mortal would be able to witness the fiery chariot's descent from heaven. Elisha's loyalty was itself a promise that he would be faithful to God, just as his friend Elijah was.

Then Elisha asked Elijah for a double portion of his blessing. The request was not like the hoggishness of asking for two helpings of ice cream; it was Elisha's way of asking for the faithfulness of Elijah. When Elisha asked to be Elijah's successor, he was showing his willingness to serve.

Finally the moment came. The fiery chariot's arrival on earth is one of those moments in biblical history which can only be drawn. I can't imagine it as a photograph. God allowed only Elisha to witness the flaming glory of that moment.

Once the chariot was gone, Elisha looked around him. Elijah was gone. The faithful were without their leader. The world must have looked slightly dingy without the great Elijah.

But Elisha remembered how Elijah had separated the waters earlier that day. So he picked up the coat and slapped it down on the Jordan. The waters divided, just as they had earlier. God was still with them. Assurance returned to all those who feared Elijah's leaving. When they saw the waters part, all who watched knew that the torch had passed. God had not deserted them or left them leaderless. Elisha would take up where the great Elijah had left off.

The Lord would not leave his people.

83

PAYING THE PRICE

Read 2 Kings 5

Mr. Pumpernickle keeps geraniums on his front steps once the weather gets warm enough. Mrs. Beadle, next door, has a cat named Sassafras, a Siamese that whines like a siren. One night Sassafras chewed up those pretty Pumpernickle geraniums for no good reason except that she was bored. Mr. Pumpernickle sued Mrs. Beadle for the despicable actions of her horrid cat. He claimed his sorrow for the chewed geraniums was worth $12,000.

Mr. Pumpernickle's actions are not all that unusual. People sue each other at the drop of a hat today, especially if the dropped hat makes somebody fall and sprain an ankle. So what's an ankle worth? A couple thousand—maybe more if you play Saturday afternoon tennis. What's a finger worth? What's a child's life worth? Everybody sues today, because it seems that everything—even life itself—has a price.

People have always been greedy, of course. Just look at this Gehazi, a servant of the great prophet Elisha. He's an odd character in this story of faith.

And this *is* a story of faith. The young girl in Naaman's court has faith that Elisha can heal Naaman of his leprosy. She tells her master to go see him. Naaman goes; he has faith—but only up to a point. When Elisha doesn't even come out of the house to greet such an important man, Naaman tells his servants that the strange prophet must be some kind of jerk.

But Naaman's servants have faith. "Don't turn your back on this prophet's advice," they tell him. So Naaman listens, goes to the Jordan, washes three times—and lo and behold, he's clean as a young boy.

Naaman's a man of the world. He figures any such miracle cure is worth a few bucks, so he goes

back to Elisha and tells him what happened. After confessing that he now believes Israel has only one God, Naaman asks Elisha to name his price—and he pats his saddlebags full of silver.

Enter Gehazi. While Elisha knows that God's healing hand has no price, Gehazi is looking to make a few quick bucks. When Elisha sends Naaman away, Gehazi sneaks out after him, finds him, and claims that, after some soul-searching, Elisha has reconsidered and will graciously accept a few pieces of silver.

But when Gehazi tries to sneak the silver back into Elisha's house, he discovers that he's in big trouble. Elisha knows what he's done.

Gehazi thinks he'll turn a quick profit on a deal that Elisha was silly enough to turn down. He figures it's free money. But Gehazi gets stung for his greed and his lying.

There is no price on God's healing hand. We can't buy grace in our lives. Christ's sacrifice is not up for sale. If anyone should have known that Naaman's miraculous cure didn't have a sales slip, it should have been Gehazi—a man who constantly attended the prophet Elisha.

But instead, poor Gehazi—not rich Gehazi—ended up with Naaman's leprosy. Gehazi paid the price for thinking too much of money.

84

ELISHA THE ECCENTRIC

Prayer:

Sometimes we doubt the power of prayer, Lord. Thank you for the witness of a man who was a true believer, a man of great obedience—this strange man, Elisha. Give us his faith.

Amen.

Read 2 Kings 6:8–23

From the sound of things, Elisha was one of those characters everyone talks about—maybe just a bit eccentric (unusual, strange), but never a bore.

You have to feel sorry for the king of Aram, though. Everytime he finds a secret place for an attack, God tells Elisha, and Elisha tells Israel's king. It's like cat and mouse almost. "It's as if Elisha is right there in your bedroom," the Aramite officers tell their king. That's how well Elisha knows the king's every move.

Determined to put an end to this pesky prophet, the Aramites surround Elisha one night. When Elisha's servant wakes up and sees a whole army hunting them, he's terrified. But Elisha just shrugs his shoulders. "We've got more than they do," he says, and he asks God to give his servant a vision. Poof!—just like that the hills are glowing with God's own chariots of fire, and Elisha's servant stops sweating.

Then the Aramites bolt down from the hills, bound and determined to kill this crazy character who has been confounding all their plans. But Elisha asks God to turn the whole bunch blind.

Poof! God turns the lights out for the whole charging army. Every last one of them loses his sight. Imagine the chariots suddenly out of control! Elisha could have asked for something else; he could have asked that they all die or that the mountains tumble down over them, but he doesn't. He asks God to strike them all blind. And just like that God does.

A thousand blind soldiers grope along, trying to find their way. "I'll show you," Elisha says. "Just follow me and I'll lead you to the man you're searching for." Now you can't tell me that Elisha isn't chuckling a little at this point,

out in front of a whole army, all of them trailing like a gaggle of baby geese.

Where does he lead them? Where else but directly to their enemies. Imagine the look on Israelite faces when the eccentric prophet comes through the city gates leading a whole garrison of enemy soldiers.

The Israelites are almost speechless. "What are we going to do with all these people?" they ask Elisha.

Elisha could have said, "Butcher them." He could have told them to lock these soldiers in jail; after all, let's not forget that the Aramites are out to get *him*.

What does God's prophet do? He asks God to restore their sight. Then he tells the king of Israel to treat them like special guests. "Put on the biggest feast you can come up with," Elisha tells the king, "and then send them all home."

The Israelites do just that. And then comes the surprise ending: the wars between Aram and Israel end!

All of Elisha's zany moves result from his obedience to and belief in Yahweh. God empowers him to be the character he is. And when you read this odd story, you can't help but think how true it is that God works in mysterious ways.

85

JESSE'S ESCAPE (7)

Prayer:

Lord, sometimes

we're like

Jonah—we just

want to run

away from all

our troubles.

Forgive us for

thinking that

we are in

control of our

lives. Help us to

learn to listen

to you.

Amen.

Read Jonah 1

Jesse spun his wrist down, and the cycle responded, jerking his whole body back as the engine raced through second and third and fourth. The speedometer said seventy in no time, and the grain fields spun by him in green waves.

On the road before him he kept seeing the old man, Fred, with the broom raised like a straw prison. The old man was no different from anybody else. Everybody tried to choke him, stifle him, keep him from doing what he wanted to do. Only the cycle gave him life, kept him free and strong.

It wasn't his fault, of course. Smashing that window was the last thing he had wanted to do, and he would have never done it if it hadn't been for the crazy man. The old man was responsible.

Still angry, Jesse kept the cycle racing until the needle nudged past eighty. Fence posts whirred past him as the bike climbed little hills and shot through the valleys behind them.

Suddenly the engine missed once, twice, then kept churning. Fear shot through Jesse's arms momentarily, and he slowed slightly, glancing down to check the plug wires.

When he looked up, Jesse saw the tractor and the truck right ahead of him at the bottom of a hill. Both lanes were blocked, and there was no way to stop. By instinct, he hit the brakes and the tires shrieked beneath him. The tractor was barely moving, but the truck was coming on strong in the left lane. There was no way, no way at all that Jesse could avoid hitting them if he stayed on the road. So he pulled the cycle into the ditch, swooping down to avoid the reach of the cultivator. Ditch grass came up around him to his waist, but he kept riding, still slowing the cycle, the throb of danger pulsing through his veins.

With both arms Jesse held the cycle as if it were a stallion. He could get out—he knew he could get out, because he was already around the cultivator. His arms shaking with fear, he hit the gas again and aimed the bike up and out of the ditch. He knew he could do it.

The front tire came up out of the ditch perfectly—a stunt man couldn't have done better. Confidence made Jesse hold his back straight and proud as he hit the shoulder. But he didn't see the rim of the road standing just above the gravel. The handlebars jerked out of his control and spun off sideways when the tire grazed off the lip of the blacktop and buckled back.

For a moment Jesse felt himself flying, the bike gone from beneath him. He curled himself into a ball, mid-air, so that his shoulders hit the pavement first, his arms up over his head. The blacktop seemed to be flying beneath him as his body sprawled out completely, then twisted up and around and flopped over and over again.

The last thing Jesse remembered was the sound of the bike's engine screaming somewhere off in the ditch grass.

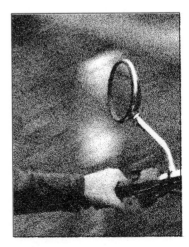

86

THE GREATEST MIRACLE

Prayer:

Dear Lord,

Ninevah's story

is our story. We

thank you for

forgiving us, for

taking us back

into your care

and love, even

when we don't

deserve it. In

Christ's name,

Amen.

Read Jonah 3

It might be fun to make a list of the Bible's most fabulous miracles. Elisha and the blind army has to rank as one of the strangest. Lazarus's return from the dead is probably the most touching (Jesus wept when he heard his friend had died). Water into wine at Cana is probably the most polite.

If we think of the plagues as miracles (and they are, I suppose), then the angel of death taking Egyptian firstborn males is probably the most terrifying. The sun that stood still for the warring people of Israel is probably the most astounding.

Christ's feeding of the five thousand (with only a little bread and a couple of fish) ranks as one of the most practical miracles. The violent earthquake that threw open the doors of the prison where Paul and Silas were kept has to be among the most exciting.

We could go on and on because the Bible is full of miracles: manna from heaven, water from rocks, the tumbling walls of Jericho, David's sling, Samson's strength, Elijah's fiery chariot, Jesus casting out demons, Jesus healing the crippled and blind and sick, Paul raising Eutychus from the dead. Each miracle seems to have its own peculiar interest.

Of course, some miracles are less spectacular than others. Reading through the book of Jonah, for instance, you might miss the incredible story of an entire city's conversion. Ninevah, the Bible says, was a big city—huge, in fact. God told Jonah to preach doom to the people, to warn them that their city would be destroyed in forty days—in less than a month and a half. Big Ninevah must have been a bad place.

The miracle was, of course, that the entire city confessed their sins. The Bible says that all the people in the city—both the rich and the poor— got down on their knees.

The Bible tells us that when God saw an entire city crying for their sins, he changed his mind. Even though he had told Jonah to tell the Ninevites they would be destroyed—even though Jonah himself had made that promise—God changed his mind and forgave every last one of them.

And in that act we see the Bible's greatest miracle—forgiveness. Most of the miracles are history, but not this one. God's greatest miracle goes on, long after we shut the Bible's covers. He is willing to forgive us, even when we forget him completely. Just look at the story of Nineveh. It's proof that God forgives far, far better than we can. God's mercy is our miracle.

87

FORGIVING AND FORGET-TING

Prayer:

Dear Lord, help us to forgive other people when they mistreat us. It's so easy for us to carry grudges, to spend all our time hating people who've been mean or pushy. Help us try to be as forgiving as you are.

Amen.

Read Jonah 4

Sandra's two friends, Michelle and Linda, pick her up one Friday night on their way to the mall. Sometimes they shop, but, like other kids, mostly they just like to hang out there.

They sit near the fountain in the middle, eating taffy, when who should show up but Gregg, Kevin, and a guy named Larry.

Everybody knows Gregg likes Linda, and Kevin and Michelle have liked each other since eighth grade. That leaves big-mouth Larry for Sandra.

Sandra's too tall for a tenth grader, and it bothers her. Sometimes when the girls walk around together she feels like a periscope. What's more, she doesn't have much for curves yet. The other girls catch boys' attention just by standing still. Sandra is sure that the guys think of her as a telephone pole.

The girls see the guys crowding around each other, talking. Everybody knows what's happening: they're trying to talk Larry into hanging around with Sandra. Sandra knows it better than anyone does.

"Go on," Kevin says. "It's just for tonight."

"You've got to be kidding," Larry says.

The girls can hear their conversation because they're not that far away. Besides, the boys want to let the girls hear.

"Just be nice," Gregg says. "We'll give you a buck apiece for the video games—"

Larry's big mouth echoes all over the mall. "I ain't going with that ugly beanpole," he says. Gregg laughs.

Sandra thinks immediately of suicide. But she pretends she hasn't heard, and so do her friends. Inside, she hurts. She hates Larry. She tells herself she will never forgive him.

Can you feel what Sandra feels?

Good.

Now imagine this: Larry knows he's a big mouth, and he doesn't always like to be. But in some ways he can't help it—the other guys expect it of him. When he gets home that night, he feels terrible about what he said, even though Gregg laughed his head off when he said it. He prays (I know that's hard to believe, but let's just say he does) and he asks God to forgive him. And God forgives him. Let's say that Larry even manages to mumble an apology to Sandra.

But does Sandra forgive him? Nope, not down deep. And can you really blame her?

What's the point? Look at Jonah. His preaching has accomplished everything it was intended to accomplish. Ninevah has repented of its sins. But Jonah's mad. Jonah wants God to destroy the whole city, just as Jonah had predicted.

The point is that God's forgiveness is a miracle. Even when we can't forgive, even when we can't forget, God can and he does. You can't help but feel sorry for Sandra. For that matter, you can't help but feel sorry for Jonah. It's just not human to forgive and forget so quickly.

And that's the big point—it's just not human to forgive. Only God can always forgive. That's the miracle.

88

THE FALL OF ISRAEL

Read 2 Kings 17:1–18

The whole story of this passage lies in two simple verses: (6) In the ninth year of Hoshea, the king of Assyria captured Samaria and deported the Israelites to Assyria. . . . (7) All this took place because the Israelites had sinned against the Lord their God. . . ."

"All this" means the end of the dream of a promised land for the ten northern tribes of Israel. Just as years ago they had suffered slavery under Egyptian whips, they were now hauled off to Assyria and chained in bondage once more. For many Israelites, the rich life of promise ended.

Ten verses (8–17) tell us exactly why. God didn't rob Israel of their promised land. He heard his people disregard him, saw their horrible idols, listened to them laugh at his prophets, and witnessed them sacrificing their children in fire. Then he said, "Enough," and sent in Shalmaneser, the king of Assyria, to haul the covenant-breakers into slavery once more.

In a way, something similar is happening today in North America. Of course, we know that the Jewish people are not THE chosen race anymore, but some Jewish people today are afraid that their race is going to disappear.

A man named Irving Howe, a well-known Jewish writer and intellectual, recently said, "History is pulling down the curtain on my kind of Jewish life." "A phase of Jewish history is nearing its end."

Why? Many Jews who once lived together in Eastern Europe came to this continent seeking freedom. Instead of staying together, however, they gradually lost their separateness in the American melting pot. Today many of them view religion—faith in the Yahweh of the Bible—as a silly remnant of their past.

Most of us know what the Jewish people suffered during World War II. Hitler tried to kill every last one of them. Only rarely in the history of civilization has any group of people suffered as heavily as the Jewish people did. Millions of them were slaughtered in Hitler's butcher camps.

Oddly enough, even the tyrant Hitler didn't do as much to destroy the unity of the Jews as does toleration in a country which accepts them. Today Jews are starting to look and act just like everybody else in America.

And that's exactly what happened to the ten northern tribes. It wasn't persecution that did them in. It was taking on the ways of their neighbors, worshiping their neighbors' idols, when their God had specifically commanded them not to. In America, many Jews have become indistinguishable from Americans; in Canaan, they had become indistinguishable from the Canaanites.

That's why God sent this Assyrian king. God's people no longer cared about him, his love, or his deliverance.

No longer were they his people.

89

THE POWER OF PREYER

THE
POWER
OF PRAYER

Prayer:

Sometimes

prayer seems so

silly, Lord—just

like we are

talking to the

ceiling. Bring

the Holy Spirit

into our hearts

to give us

confidence in

our prayers—to

give us faith,

like Hezekiah's

and Aunt

Sena's.

Amen.

Read 2 Kings 19:14–20

This is a true story.

One night a mother hears her baby coughing. When she touches the baby, she feels her burning up with fever. Full of fear, the woman shakes her husband awake quietly, so as not to wake their little four-year-old boy, who is asleep in the next room. Together, they watch the baby squirm and shake, delirious, her eyes swimming and rolling. "We got to get her to the doctor," Mom says.

Dad runs to the place on the hill to get Aunt Sena, the widow who often babysits for them. In bed, Aunt Sena jumps at the sudden knock at her door. "Sure," she says, "of course I'll sit with your boy while you go to the hospital." Aunt Sena sees the fear in her neighbor's eyes.

Mom and Dad take the baby to the hospital and watch as a doctor gives her some medicine so that she will sleep peacefully. Dad holds Mom close as they sit at the bedside, then sleep uneasily in their chairs, waiting for the fever's crisis to pass.

By morning, all is well. The baby seems to have recovered from whatever shocked her system. Her eyes are bright and clear, fresh with life. Mom and Dad go home just as the dawn spreads a glowing quilt over the fields outside of town.

It is still early, so they step in quietly, the door clicking shut smoothly behind them. Mom grabs Dad's arm and points. Aunt Sena is awake and on her knees at the side of the couch. She hasn't heard them come in. She is still praying for the baby.

Hezekiah was an Aunt Sena. Not all the kings of Judah were sin-filled Rehoboams. Hezekiah knew where his strength came from. Surrounded by the mighty powers of a huge Assyrian nation, Hezekiah went to the Lord for help and trusted in God for deliverance from what seemed an impossible situation.

He asked for deliverance, but he also asked for a demonstration of God's rule over all nations. Hezekiah prayed and was confident that God would come to the aid of his people.

When Mom and Dad came home from the bedside of their baby, they found Aunt Sena on her knees. Had she stayed there all night long and prayed? Maybe so. Maybe that's how much she believed in God's healing power.

What healed the baby? Was it merely a matter of the right amount and type of medicine given by a qualified doctor? Was it Aunt Sena's prayer?

Maybe it was both. Aunt Sena, like Hezekiah, believed that her prayer would bring deliverance to those she loved. Aunt Sena and Hezekiah believed in the power of prayer.

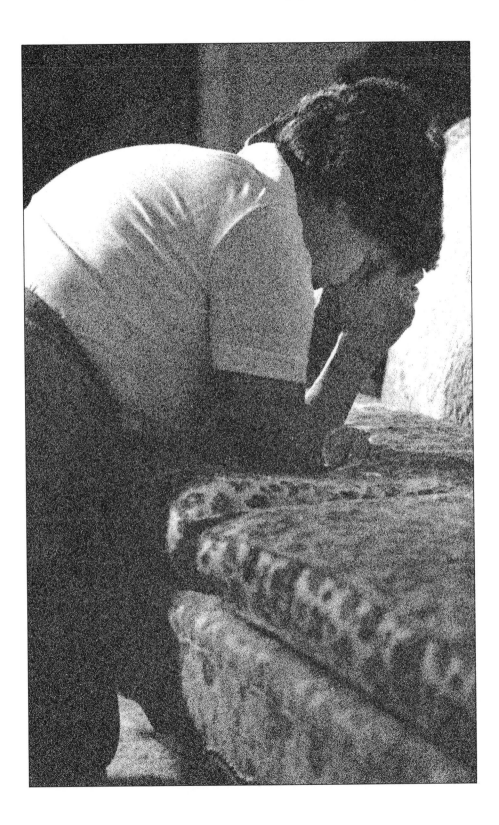

90

PK'S

Read 2 Kings 21:1–9

Some people call preachers' kids PKs. Usually that nickname is not a compliment. *PK* is a word people use to explain broken windows or smashed cars. "Johnny Vander Mop dumped me in the mud," a kid tells his father. "Johnny Vander Mop's a PK," his father grumbles.

There probably aren't more bad preachers' kids than there are bad bankers' kids (like me) or farmers' kids (like my wife). It's just that PKs—like the children of politicians or any people in the public eye—stick out a bit more. When a preacher's kid gets in trouble, people inhale a little deeper and don't dare look the minister in the eye.

Unfortunately, bad kids *can* come from believing parents— whether they be preachers or teachers or blacksmiths. The Bible tells us that Hezekiah, the praying king, had a bad boy named Manasseh. In fact, Manasseh, who took over the throne at the age of twelve, was probably the worst of all Judah's kings. Hezekiah was a strong believer. His son, Manasseh, was a wretched bum who abused his own son and then slaughtered him, practiced something like witchcraft, and actually put up an image of an obscene god in the great temple of God.

On top of that, Manasseh ruled Judah longer than any other king—he ruled for fifty-five years. All national leaders shape the lives of their people. When Hitler ruled Germany, people who thought they knew what was right and wrong did the most horrible things to Jews and other Europeans.

Manasseh had that kind of effect on Judah. He did nothing to bring his people closer to God; in fact, he pushed them away. Soon his people were looking and acting almost as evil as their king.

I suppose this story has a lesson for me and for each of us. My great-grandparents as far back as I can trace were firm believers in God. One of my grandfathers and one of my great-grandfathers were preachers. I might call myself a PGK—a preacher's grandkid.

But all the believing grandparents in the world won't make any one of us a child of God. It didn't work for Manasseh, it didn't work for the sons of Levi, and it won't work for us.

Each generation must make its choice of belief or unbelief.

Prayer:

Lord, we know that our parents' faith or our grandparents' faith won't save us. Give us faith to accept your promises and to believe in you. Amen.

91

TOO LITTLE, TOO LATE

Prayer:

Lord, we know that sometimes when we act like Christians it's only a show—like a new, clean coat over our bodies. Inside, we aren't any different than we ever were. Change us from within, Lord. Fill us up with your Spirit. Amen.

Read 2 Kings 23:1–7

Just about every year some hotshot riding a rubber tube drowns in Arizona's Salt River. Engineers control the flow of the river by raising or lowering the gates at a dam near the mountains. When the water is really rushing down toward the city of Phoenix, it swoops into corners and circles in powerful whirlpools that can actually suck people under. I know—I went down into one, but I came back up.

A whirlpool is like an upside-down tornado churning with water, not air. Edgar Allen Poe wrote about something like a whirlpool and called it a maelstrom. It's a dangerous thing, because it's like a drill boring down, down, down—always down.

God's people, the Israelites, were stuck in a maelstrom. For them, things just kept getting worse and worse. Down, down, down they went—chasing other gods, doing horrible things, forgetting the I AM. Their hearts were swirling with disobedience and sin.

Then along came Hilkiah, the high priest, with an old, worm-eaten book he had found while cleaning up the temple. "Check this out," he said to King Josiah. Josiah picked up the Book of the Covenant and didn't even recognize it!

But what the king read from that book bothered him all night long. It was obvious to Josiah that his people had forgotten the laws from the Book of the Covenant years ago and that they didn't give two bits for this Yahweh.

That scared Josiah. The book clearly stated that when people don't listen to God, they get in big trouble. Josiah was so frightened that his hands shook as he continued reading.

"Something's got to be done," he said. So he emptied the temple of all the pagan idols and shrines and altars. He made the people stop sacrificing children to the pagan god, Molech. In fact, he even brought back the Passover, a tradition that hadn't been practiced for years. It looked as if the nation was going to swim its way out of the dangerous maelstrom.

But Josiah's temple-cleaning wasn't enough to bring real faith back to the Israelites. It was a case of too little, too late. The people of the tribe of Judah might well have been living according to the letter of the law, but their hearts hadn't changed. They were not worshiping "in spirit."

Now only the I AM could rescue such a stubborn, sinful people from the power of the maelstrom.

92

HOPE

Read Isaiah 9:1– 7

Dear Mr. President,

I am ten years old. I think nuclear war is bad because many innocent people will die. The world could even be destroyed. I don't want to die. I don't want my family to die. I want to live and grow up. Please stop nuclear bombs.   Love, Karen

Some things don't change; some things do. Never before in history have so many children grown up knowing that hidden away somewhere are enough nuclear bombs to destroy every living thing. In the past, many kids have thought that they themselves might be killed in war, but never before have kids known that the earth itself could be destroyed. That's something new.

Psychologists try to study how kids react to knowing all about nuclear war. They look for ways in which that fear has changed today's children. If kids believe they will never grow into adults, that belief will very likely affect the way they act. It may make them unwilling to grow up and face a future they don't believe exists anyway. Just the thought of nuclear war makes growing up even more difficult than it used to be.

Movies like *The Day After* show us very clearly what might happen in even a little nuclear war. The initial blast would sweep away every living thing in a wide circle. Others, outside that circle, would die slowly and painfully from radiation. Some researchers feel that dust from a nuclear blast would block out the sun itself for weeks, destroying all sources of food. In a matter of days, all of the worst primitive ways could well return, making life for survivors a lawless nightmare.

Nuclear war is unthinkable. And yet we can't just block it out of our minds. The bombs are there. Hate grows between nations who have them. And more and more governments are racing to produce their own nuclear weapons. All of these facts affect kids today. No other generation has grown up with the fear that everything on this planet could be destroyed by one finger on the wrong button.

But some things don't change. Sin, for instance. The people of Israel followed their own desires and wandered away from God. So do we. So will people in the twenty-first century.

Another thing—God's rule doesn't change. He lives. He rules our lives, and he loves his people—those who love him and other people. That's the promise of Isaiah 9. Sure, Israel's going to suffer, but God's hand is still raised. He's not forgotten those he loves.

The bad news is that we live in a world of sin and death—and today, the possibility of nuclear war. The good news is that God's salvation is for all who live in his hand. "For to us a child is born, to us a son is given." And his name? "Wonderful Counselor, Mighty God, Everlasting Father, Prince of Peace." Real peace.

Wars may tear up the world, but God's love is the good news. That's a promise, a loving promise. That's hope, real hope.

Prayer:

Lord, please be with those you have chosen to lead governments and help them keep us from war. Thank you for the hope you've given us for a better life. Thank you for being our God. In Jesus' name, Amen.

93

THE MUSIC OF THE SPHERES

Prayer:

Heavenly Father, thank you for Isaiah's vision of hope. Thank you for showing us that one day, when Jesus comes again, he will bring perfect peace and harmony to his creation. In Jesus' name, Amen.

Read Isaiah 11:1–9

Hundreds of years ago—long before the invention of television and gymnasiums—people had less to do at night. Many of them spent hours watching stars. While stargazing may seem rather boring to you, these people found it enchanting.

With their faces up to the night sky, they came up with books full of strange ideas. A man named Plato knew stars move at different speeds, but he guessed it would be possible, once in a great while, for all of the stars to move together. At those special moments, imagined Plato, the entire universe would be in harmony.

Stargazers liked that idea and started thinking about what might happen if everything were in harmony in the universe. Some people guessed that the perfectly aligned motion of the stars would produce a musical note, even a song—the "music of the spheres." If you know the song "This Is My Father's World," you'll remember the first verse: "This is my Father's world, / And to my listening ears / All nature sings, and round me rings / The music of the spheres."

Although the idea of heavenly music created by the stars is not found in the Bible, it appealed to people so much that they painted it into their own picture of the first Christmas night. That night of all nights, they must have said, simply had to be one of those times when the stars themselves were singing.

And since the universe was in perfect harmony on that night, they continued, it doesn't seem possible that somewhere some ornery brother was teasing his sister or that somewhere soldiers were fighting. If the stars themselves sang beautiful music, all the earth must have stopped quarreling and been filled with happiness.

Maybe even the animals. An old Christmas myth says that on that night the mules and the sheep and the cattle standing around Christ's manger actually talked. Imagine that—the universe was in such perfect harmony that the whole world became a miracle of miracles.

The Bible says nothing about such harmony, so no doubt it's just an idea the stargazers dreamed up on a cloudy night. But it shows us how important people thought Christ's birth was to the entire world.

If you look at verses 6 through 9 of Isaiah's prophecy, you'll discover another reason people thought the earth was in perfect harmony on that night. They guessed that the prophet was talking about Christmas when he described a world of perfect harmony, perfect peace—the wolf tucking himself in next to the lamb, the leopard and the lion sleeping peacefully with the calf and the goat, and babies playing safely with cobras.

But Isaiah wasn't prophesying about Christmas. He was looking into the distant future—to the second coming. His vision of the wolf and the lamb is a picture of eternal peace, of a time when there will be heavenly music throughout the earth.

You can't help thinking that during eternity the stars will be singing along too. Maybe those stargazers weren't all wrong.

94

COMFORT FOR GOD'S PEOPLE

Prayer:

Thank you,

Lord, for the

comfort and

hope you've

given us in this

world. In all

those times

when we feel

most down

about things,

help us to

remember that

our comfort in

life and death is

that we belong

to you.

Amen.

Read Isaiah 40:1–11

Sure, Florida has Disney World and Epcot Center. Sure, California has Disneyland and movie stars and miles and miles of beautiful coastline peppered with good-time surfers—sun, sand, volleyball, and beach parties. Sometimes we northerners feel gypped. The Sun Belt has absolutely everything.

But I know what neither Florida nor California has—and what's more, neither will ever get it. You want to know what it is? Hot chocolate. That's right, hot chocolate.

I'm not stupid. Of course, suntanned southerners *have* hot chocolate; they can buy it at the local Safeway. But they don't have chocolate on a snowy day. No, sir. They can't know what a cup of hot chocolate is after a night of ice-skating, a day of tobaggoning, an afternoon of working outside when the temperature barely peaks above the single digits.

I remember winter nights we spent skating miles and miles down the sharp turns of an ice-covered river. On both sides the trees leaned in from the banks, jet-black skeletons in the moonlight. Sometimes sweat would break out beneath our stocking caps, but by the time we'd quit, our red noses would shine like gum balls, and our apple-cheeks would be nibbled with frost.

That's when hot chocolate was comfort—real comfort. We'd hole up in someone's family room, long wool socks pulled halfway up to our knees, and hold that hot chocolate in both hands. That was real comfort. Hot chocolate went down into the chest like a warm swarm. It takes a load of snow to appreciate the comfort of hot chocolate.

Comfort on a winter's night is a cup of hot chocolate—at least that's what it is to me. To my little son it's Curious George, the beat-up monkey that he's taken to bed for several years now. Maybe to some of you it's the memory of a warm sleeping bag and a dry tent on a cold, rainy night. Maybe it's just your own bedroom, a place where no one bothers you.

Comfort comes in many forms, I guess. What's more, we all need it. Maybe the folks in the Sun Belt don't know about *real* hot chocolate, but they probably know what comfort is.

Isaiah told the hurting people of Israel about comfort, but he had more on his mind than hot chocolate. Israel had been apart from God for a long time. His warmth was hardly a memory for them. But Isaiah told them there was still hope, hope that would warm itself into the deepest comfort that anyone could ever hope for—the comfort of knowing that someone is on his way to take them back again, back to their God.

This rescuer would be nothing to sneeze at. He would be so powerful that he'd cut through mountains, raise valleys, and level foothills. Isaiah said this comfort-bearer would show Israel, once again, the glory of the Lord. That's warmth for the soul.

95

JESSE'S ESCAPE (8)

Read Isaiah 53

Jesse had to work to open his eyes. He knew they were closed, but it took strength and will to open them.

"Jesse, your father's outside."

Jesse struggled with his eyes again, opened them, and saw someone strange in front of him.

"Who are you?" Jesse asked. The man's hand was over his arm.

"You're alive," the man said. "Thank God for that."

Slowly things came into focus. He was in a hospital, and a man with a beard and a mustache stood beside him. The smell of antiseptic burned in his nose.

"Your father's outside. You've been out all day. He flew in as soon as he found out where you were—"

"Who are you?" Jesse asked.

The man backed off. He smiled and stood there with his hands on his hips. "I know about your running off," he said. "Your father told me all about it. I know it all—"

"Who are you anyway?" Jesse pulled his right arm out from under the covers. Pain shot through his shoulder; his skin felt tight through his back.

"Hurts, doesn't it?"

Jesse's back felt as if it had been skinned. The soreness inside wasn't as painful as the torn skin outside. He raised his arm slowly to the wraps over his head.

"My name is Pastor Chuck," the man said. "I work here."

"I ain't seeing my old man," Jesse said. "You can tell him to get lost. I ain't seeing him no matter what—"

The man grinned. "Pretty tough kid, aren't you?—riding a motorcycle like that, running away? You got guts, don't you?" The man named Chuck sat back in the chair at the side of the bed. "Man outside must have beat you bad to make you take off the way you did—"

"He never beat me," Jesse said.

"He didn't? I thought for sure he beat on you to make you take off like that—" He picked a magazine off a table and pretended to shuffle through the pages. "Born and reared a Christian, weren't you, Jesse?" he said. "You know about suffering, don't you?"

It made Jesse feel uncomfortable to have him there. He wondered what the man was going to say next.

"You know how much Christ had to suffer for you, don't you, Jesse? It's a mighty good thing for me and you that he didn't just take off and run away from it all."

"I don't have to listen to you," Jesse said.

"You're right—you don't." The man got up from his chair. "You know what scares me though? What scares me is that I could be showing your father a dead body instead of one that's only a little scraped up."

He turned toward the door. "That scare you, Jesse?"

Jesse tightened his lips when the man left. He tightened his lips, trying to avoid the horror of thinking that he might not have been here—that he might not have been in a hospital or anywhere else. But it was a thought he couldn't avoid.

Prayer:

Dear Lord, thank you for suffering instead of running away. Thank you for taking our sins upon yourself, for taking our place. Thank you for dying for us, because your gift has brought us life and hope. Amen.

125

96

TO TELL, OR NOT TO TELL

Prayer:

There are times, Lord, when we know we should say something, times when we see things that shouldn't be happening. Give us the wisdom at those times to know what we should do, and give us the strength to do it. Amen.

Read Jeremiah 20:7–18

Doug likes Ken a lot. So do most of the other guys in sixth-hour gym class. Ken's got style. He snaps towels like a fiend, and he's good in lots of sports. When he comes out of the shower, he struts around like a TV star. He says he can't stand the principal, and all the guys laugh.

One day in the mall Doug sees Ken heist a fishing reel—maybe worth thirty bucks, who knows? Ken just jams it in his jacket, the one he wears with the sleeves rolled up and the zipper half down. Just flicks it in there as if stealing it really isn't that big of a thing.

Once they get out in the parking lot, Ken hauls it out. It's a beauty—open-faced, lightweight, really expensive. And he got away with it! Doug can't believe how simple it seemed. Ken just dropped the reel in his coat pocket and walked out.

When Doug gets home that night, it starts to bother him. He's seen guys lift candy and cigarettes, but he's never seen anybody heist a fishing reel. He knows it's wrong. He knows that a guy can get in real trouble stealing something that big. What Ken did bothers Doug, bothers him a lot. So at supper that night, he just doesn't say much.

"What's bothering you, Doug?" his father asks.

"Nothing," Doug says.

But that night he lies in bed, wide awake. The more he thinks about it, the more he hates what Ken did—stealing like that.

Doug's got only a taste of what Jeremiah had. Jeremiah knew very well what he had to tell the people of Judah. He had to tell them that God would destroy them, just as he had destroyed the tribes of the northern kingdom a hundred years earlier. But Judah didn't want to hear the warning. They didn't want to hear because they didn't want to listen, or obey, or behave. "I wish I'd never been born," Jeremiah said. He knew the people were going to hate him for saying what he had to say.

It's almost eleven o'clock, and Doug figures he's got three options: he can tell his father, he can tell Ken what he thinks about stealing, or he can just keep his mouth shut.

Jeremiah didn't have a choice. "If I tell myself I'm going to keep still," Jeremiah says in verse 9, "then my heart will burn up. I won't be able to take it, because I know what I have to do. God himself has told me what I have to say."

Jeremiah had to speak. What about Doug?

97

TAKING IT

Read Jeremiah 21:1–10

"There are no atheists in a foxhole."

Maybe some of you have heard that line before. It makes a lot of sense. Soldiers, crouched in a foxhole, waiting for the enemy to attack, know they could die at any moment. Staring death itself in the eyes is enough to make anyone think seriously about what's important.

King Zedekiah was the last king to reign in Judah before the destruction of Jerusalem in 587 B.C. Not once in all his years as king had he shown any interest in God. Not once. But now the enemy, Babylon, was pounding on the gates of the city. Zedekiah didn't know what to do, so he called in Jeremiah in a last ditch effort to get help—as silly as praying to do well on a test you haven't studied for. "Quick, bring in a little God here, will you?" he might have screamed. "I've always been a believer, you know."

Jeremiah watched the king's hands shake in fear. If I were Jeremiah, I probably would have laughed—an I-told-you-so kind of laugh. "So you finally want my advice, do you?" Jeremiah said. "Here it is: just take what you have coming to you. Get on your knees before God and at least escape with your life. Take your punishment and repent."

Judah's God was sending the Babylonians to teach Judah the lesson it deserved. Jeremiah told King Zedekiah simply to take it and repent.

One day a student of mine stayed after class. He told me he didn't have an essay done, one that was supposed to have been in a couple days before.

"What happened, Bob?" I asked.

Just like that he broke into tears. He wasn't a tall kid, but he had huge arms, because he was a gymnast and a good one. He had arms that could have been in magazines. Big muscles hung like huge cables when his hands were on his waist.

I wasn't used to seeing a big guy like that cry. "What is it?" I said.

Sobbing, he told me about his parents fighting—how it was tearing him up inside—how he just couldn't study.

"It's okay, Bob. Get the essay done when you can," I said.

Two weeks later one of the guidance counselors, really disgusted, dropped by my room. He asked me why I let Bob out of his assignments.

"He's got this problem at home—"

"You can't let him do that," he said. "He's been pulling that since he was a freshman. It's true, you know—his parents have trouble. But he's been using that like a crutch for years. You're just hurting him when you let him out of responsibility."

That counselor was really mad at me. Teachers had been patient with Bob for too long. Now it was time for him to face up to his responsibility, to take his punishment and live in a new way.

God was patient with Judah for four hundred years, but finally the people had to be taught their lesson. Jeremiah's lesson for the king in the foxhole was simple: take God's punishment and repent.

98

REAL ESTATE

Prayer:

Lord, sometimes it's easier to say we believe in you than to act like it. Give us Jeremiah's certainty. Help us build a faith as strong as his. Amen.

Read Jeremiah 32:6–12

Plunked right in the middle of all of Jeremiah's weeping over Judah's destruction, we find a real estate deal. That's right. The whole nation is falling apart, dreams are exploding right before people's eyes, and in the middle of it all, Jeremiah's buying up land. Somehow, it seems so out of place.

Of course, real estate is big business. Today, lots of people have made thousands and even millions of dollars dealing in land. From Los Angeles to Calgary, cities sprawl farther and farther into the country. Farmers who once thought themselves miles from cities suddenly stare up and down boulevards lined with high-rise apartments and Burger Kings. When they sell their land, some become instant millionaires.

Big money always prompts big swindles. In some areas, land sharks sell "city" lots in cities that turn out to be nothing but stakes pounded in desert waste where roads are supposedly plotted. "Going to have a city of thirty thousand, sure as shooting," the salesman says. More than once, land buyers have been swindled into believing their money was well spent. More than once, people have given up lifelong savings only to find nothing more than spiders and snakes where the salesman swore there would be a library.

Jeremiah's cousin, Hanamel, sounds like a guy who would wear a white tie on a black shirt and smoke a big cigar. "I got this parcel of land here, Jeremiah," he says. "It's a steal, see? Take you ten years to come across another deal like this."

Jeremiah knows Jerusalem is going to be crushed by Babylon's army. What's more, Jeremiah isn't even a free man. King Zedekiah has stuck him in prison for forecasting depressing things.

What good is a piece of land to a man who can't even use it?

Furthermore, it's obvious *why* Hanamel wants to get rid of his property. Just a matter of time and it's not going to be worth a plugged nickel anyway. Once the Babylonians take over, it won't do him any good. Maybe he can make a few shekels on it yet—if he can sell it to his cousin.

But there's more to the story. Hanamel's telling his cousin Jeremiah to put his money where his mouth is. After all, Jeremiah has been preaching two sermons: first, that Judah will be destroyed; second, that it will be restored. "If you really believe we'll ever live here again, Jeremiah, you'll buy this land, see?" Hanamel might have said.

Jeremiah knows the truth. God has spoken to Jeremiah as a believer, and Jeremiah has cried a bathtub full of tears because he knows it all, the whole sad story.

So Jeremiah takes his cousin up on the offer. Jeremiah is no speculator, out to make a quick profit on somebody else's loss. But he knows the truth. He buys the land. He puts his money where his faith is. He buys to show that he believes what God has said.

99

MAKING DISCIPLES

Prayer:

Our Father, make us your disciples. Give us the desire to do your will and be your witnesses in a world that doesn't honor you.

Amen.

Read 2 Kings 24:10–17

Pick up the Bible and open it to 2 Kings. Put your finger there and page back to Exodus 15, holding the wad of pages that separate the two books between your fingers. In my Bible, that stack of pages amounts to a little more than a quarter inch. Not much.

Exodus 15 tells how Pharaoh and posse, trying to recapture the Jews, were drowned in the Red Sea. Second Kings 24 describes the Israelites' return to captivity, this time under Nebuchadnezzar. From slavery to slavery—not more than a quarter inch of pages.

How soon they forgot.

God chose the Israelites to be his people for two reasons: he wanted them to witness to the honor of the only true God and he wanted them to carry out a very special role in the history of the world.

During the years between the reigns of King Solomon and King Jehoiachin, the Israelites wandered farther and farther away from God. By the time of Nebuchadnezzar they didn't look any different than a hundred sin-sick pagan tribes around them. As witnesses, they had failed miserably.

God's chosen people didn't care about him; most of them didn't even know his name. "Yahweh?" they might have asked. "Is that somebody's old grandfather or something? Never heard of him."

God knew his people needed discipline.

Nobody *likes* discipline. I remember one night my mother drove me to my geometry teacher's apartment. That day my mother had received a failure notice in the mail—a sweet little letter that said if I didn't watch it, I was going to flunk geometry. My mother didn't like her son failing anything, so she stuck me in the car and pushed me out at my teacher's apartment. She was disciplining me.

Everybody knew the geometry teacher was a loser. He wore white socks, black shoes, high-waters pants, and huge flowered ties. He hated sports, and he had a body like a chimpanzee.

My mother didn't care.

You think I wanted to talk to that teacher all by myself up in his dumb apartment? No siree. But something had to be done—that's the way my mother saw it. When she shut off the car's engine, I knew I had no choice. I had to visit this guy. She watched me climb every step of the stairs.

Later, when the grades came out, I had passed geometry with a C.

Discipline—the word has the same root as *disciple.*

God disciplined the Israelites, threw them back into a captivity just as horrible as what they came from years ago in Egypt. Why? Because he wanted to make them disciples.

God hadn't forgotten the other reason he chose the Israelites. He still had them marked for a special mission—to be the ancestors of Jesus Christ.

100

PRINCIPLES AND POTATO CHIPS

Prayer:

Dear Lord,

thank you for

the witness of

Daniel. Help us

know when to

say no to the

world. We know

that it's terribly

easy to give in.

Forgive us when

we do. In Jesus'

name,

Amen.

Read Daniel 1

I love potato chips. I know I shouldn't. My wife says they aren't worth a thing nutritionally—just all sorts of salt laid on all sorts of grease. But I love them anyway.

People who make potato chips probably disagree with my wife, but I think she's right. Potato chips don't do a lot for you—no matter what name is on the bag. But even knowing that chips are junk isn't enough to keep me away from them. You just can't beat a handful of chips with a hot dog.

Daniel didn't eat things like potato chips. In fact, when you read today's passage, you get the impression that Daniel was some kind of health food nut who wouldn't touch a candy bar or a Twinkie, the kind of guy who makes you nervous because he's so uptight about his health. "Junk food!" he'd say, turning his head, one eyebrow cocked way up in the air. That's the impression you get.

But for Daniel, not eating the king's food was a matter of principle. He was more concerned about his spiritual health than his physical health. Nebuchadnezzar wanted Daniel and his friends to become experts in Babylonian language and literature; he wanted them to adopt Babylonian culture. But Daniel knew that becoming Babylonian meant giving up his allegiance to God. So for Daniel, not eating the king's junk food was a necessary part of keeping his soul clean.

One more thing. Daniel was worried that if he took everything the king offered him, he would become a slave to the king's rule. After all, you can't stay free of someone if you take everything he offers you.

And he was a smart character, this Daniel. When Ashpenaz said he was worried that Daniel and his friends would look like scrawny wimps next to the rest of the muscle-bound Israelite slaves, Daniel put a hand up to the guy's ear. "Try it for a couple weeks," he told Ashpenaz. "Check it out. We'll be all right."

Likely as not, Ashpenaz didn't mind. Whatever food and wine Daniel and his friends didn't take, he could sell on the side and make a little pocket cash. Ashpenaz put Daniel's idea to the test, and after ten days the vegetarians were just as healthy as the guys on the king's rich diet of meat and wine.

Daniel was wise. Not merely bright, or sly, or quick to make a buck—but wise. That means he had principles based on the Word of God.

Daniel didn't eat potato chips. He was smarter than that. While he did care about his health, he cared much more about keeping himself close to his God. If that meant giving up meat and junk food, then there was no choice—no matter how much he might have liked a fried pork chop.

God had big things in mind for Daniel.

101

TRIAL BY FIRE

Read Daniel 3

There are two ways to read this famous story. One of them isn't quite as good as the other.

Nebuchadnezzar wants to unite his people under one god, so he builds the statue. The men with the funny names—Shadrach, Meshach, and Abednego—refuse to bow. The king screams at them, warns them that they will burn, just as he has ruled.

Reading one: There stand three men, shoulders back, heads up in front of a crowd, full of confidence that nothing will harm them. They know God will save them. The men who haul them into the furnace burn like paper, but the three men stand there, unsinged by the flames, their robes hanging gently at their sides.

That's one way to read the story. It's not the best way.

Reading two: Shadrach, Meshach, and Abednego are confident all right, but they're confident of something more important than being saved from the fire. "Our God is able to save us from the hottest furnace in all the world," they tell the king. "He can deliver us."

Notice the change. "He *can* deliver us," they say. Read verse 18 again: "But even if he does not [rescue us], we want you to know, O king, that we will not serve your gods or worship the image of gold you have set up."

There's the difference. Shadrach, Meshach, and Abednego, likely as not, were not as confident of coming out alive as we might think they were. It's possible that they stood there before the furnace, hugging their friends and families. They didn't know. Think of the whole story that way—they really didn't know what would happen to them. They didn't just walk in as if a stroll in the kingdom's hottest furnace were some cakewalk. They *didn't*

know what God would do.

I prefer the second reading. You know why? Because in this second reading, Shadrach, Meshach, and Abednego have a different kind of faith. Even though they may not have walked into the furnace with the confidence of accomplished musicians walking on stage, they are completely faithful to a God whose ways they aren't always smart enough to know.

"Even if he doesn't save us," they tell Nebuchadnezzar, "we still know that he is the true God."

Daniel's three friends are confident before Nebuchadnezzar because their faith in God is immense. It's not simply the faith that they will not be incinerated; it's the faith that they are doing right. Even if they are burned to a cinder, Shadrach, Meshach, and Abednego know—really know—that their God will save them for eternity.

In the first reading, Daniel's friends have confidence that they know exactly what God will do. In the second, they have faith that whatever happens to them, it will be for the best.

I like the second reading.

102

SPOTTEN

Read Daniel 5

One of the few Dutch words I know is *spotten*. (I'm no language expert, but I think it's pronounced "sput-tin.") It's a great word, one that has no equal in English.

Even though my ethnic background is Dutch, for three generations no one on either side of my family has spoken the language of the old country. The only Dutch words my parents ever used were words that just couldn't be said in English.

Right off the top of my head I remember only four. First, my mother's favorite, *benauwd* (pronounced "bin-out"), which is the cramped feeling Jonah must have had when he was locked up tight in the belly of a whale. Second, *zanik* (pronounced "zah-nick"), which is what my children do when I tell them we can't go to McDonald's like we had planned to do. Third, *brom* (pronounced "brrrrum"), which is the kind of grumbling *zaniken* kids do when they grow into unhappy adults.

And then there's *spotten*. It means to take something really serious and make it silly—like singing "Jesus Loves Me" with a clothespin on your nose, or saying Daniel's three friends had asbestos skin. Some people who are reading this may think that what I've just said is *spotten*. If they do, they'll probably write me a letter and *brom* about it. Maybe they're right.

But in today's story, it's Nebuchadnezzar's grandson Belshazzar who is guilty of *spotten*. He and his party took the gold goblets from the temple and used them for getting drunk. That's *spotten*—taking something very serious and making silliness out of it.

In the middle of all their *spotten*, a mysterious hand appeared on the wall and wrote out some words nobody knew. Daniel translated, because God had given Daniel the ability to interpret things like that. All around Babylon Daniel was known for his wisdom, his ability to know things other people didn't know.

Daniel translated the king's bad news. "God has numbered your days, Belshazzar," he said. "You've been judged for what you are, and you've come up short."

No doubt God was angry with Belshazzar for lots of reasons, not just because he used the temple goblets. But Belshazzar's silliness—his mockery—must have deeply offended and angered God. The king had taken something holy and made a joke out of it. God doesn't like it when people—including us—mock him by making fun of things we ought to respect and take seriously. *Spotten* is wrong.

And that's enough to make anyone a little bit *benauwd*.

Prayer:

Holy God,

forgive us for

sometimes

making jokes

about you and

your Word. We

really don't

mean to mock

you. We love

you and honor

you as King of

kings and Lord

of lords. Fill us

with awe in

your presence.

In Jesus' name,

Amen.

103

THE DEN OF LIONS

Read Daniel 6

He heard her walk up behind him. He was looking out over the city, toward the den of lions.

"It's your pride, Darius," she told him. "You've been trapped by your own men, and you're just angry—"

He had left special orders that he not be disturbed that night. He didn't want to see anyone—not even a wife. "It's not that," he said. He kept his back to her, putting his hand on the torch base at the window. "It's more than that—"

"What else could it be?" she said.

He felt her come closer until she stood right behind him. It angered him to have her—to have anyone—in the room.

"Certainly it's not the man himself," she said. "Everyone knows Daniel is wise, but the death of just one man can't be bothering you—"

"Don't say it—don't." He took his hand from the torch and held it behind him, outstretched. "For some reason, I can't believe that Daniel could be dead. He's not dead."

"What on earth could stop those lions from ripping him apart? You're a fool to think he could be alive." She pointed out the window toward the darkness. "Look out there—all of this is yours. From the dark ridge where the horizon stops the stars—all the way behind us. Nothing should make you sad. You're the king."

He turned away from her and went quickly to the other side of the room. "All night I've been up. My heart is on fire in my chest. There is something about this Daniel—"

"What, Darius?" she asked. "Whatever is so great about this man who refuses to bow to your rule?" She followed him, stood there behind him again. "He doesn't honor you as highly as he does this God of his—"

"There is something about that man that I don't see or feel in anyone else. He has some kind of strength—I don't know what to call it—what name there is for it—"

"Darius, must I remind you that he brazenly refused to worship you alone? That man is a traitor!—"

"Stop it!" He spun around. "He is, of all my men, the most loyal, the wisest. No one else is like Daniel—"

She took his hand. "Look," she said, pointing out toward the eastern sky. "Look how the morning starts in streaks that rise from the darkness of the night."

Quickly he tugged himself away from her and looked out at the first rays of morning. "He will be there. I know he will—"

"Don't be crazy, Darius—"

"He will be there. I know it. He will be alive. He has this God. I know he will. He will be there—" The sound of his running feet echoed down the long marble hallways.

When he left, she stood there at the window, happy this man Daniel was dead in the den of lions.

104

GHOST CITY

Prayer:

Thank you,

Lord, for giving

us your story.

The way of life

with you is so

much more

clear when we

read the Bible.

Your Word

speaks to us so

clearly. Thank

you for such a

great gift.

Amen.

Read Lamentations 1:1–9

(This time, read what follows before you read the passage, okay?) Imagine that you are an old man and that you've lived in the same city your whole life. You've always attended the same church, shopped in the same shops, and played in the same parks. You can't imagine living anywhere else.

Now imagine a little more. The church where you've been going is, in your mind, the very house of God. He doesn't live in some other province or city; he's always lived right there in your church, in a special room that very few people ever get into. That's the way you've always thought about your church and your town—the place where you live, but also the place where God dwells. He's there, and there only.

Now imagine that your city is destroyed. One day a bomb hits and everything is wiped out. Recently, a movie on TV scared viewers by picturing life after nuclear war. One of the images I remember best from the movie was the rubble that was once an entire city, a huge graveyard of uneven hills of brick and stone and dust, ghostly rubble as far as you could see, no sound but the whistle of wind through the debris.

Think of Jerusalem that way when you listen to Lamentations. Think of that old man, looking over the destruction of the city where God lived, remembering, then wondering what went wrong.

Jerusalem lies deserted and ruined, dead but without a decent burial. Once she was queen among nations; now she is a widow—once a princess, now a slave girl. She's mocked and beaten and dirty.

It's impossible not to feel pity for the city where God lived. But why has it happened? Why is her glory gone, her home a shambles, her spirit and strength broken?

Because Jerusalem, the city named as a "foundation of peace" has not even considered her own future (v. 9). She has rejected all of God's promises by refusing to live the kind of righteous life that she should. She has sought her own way, apart from the love of the God who dwelled there—right in the middle of town.

Look around with Jeremiah, the "weeping prophet." See what has happened to her, this city that David made into a great home for his God. No pilgrims come to the temple anymore. No one says, "Come, let us go up to the house of the Lord." The streets are desolate now, and everything is ruined. God is gone from the temple, and the only sound is Jeremiah's weeping.

Read Lamentations 1:1–9 and listen.

105

JESSE'S ESCAPE (9)

Read Ezekiel 37:1–13

A half hour passed while Jesse waited for his father to come into his room. It angered him that the two of them—his father and that crazy preacher—let him lie there alone for all that time. He wanted to get it over with. Besides, his whole body felt as if it had been dropped from a third-story window. Everything hurt.

It reminded him of a song he had learned at a Bible camp four years ago—when he was just a little kid. He could still picture the counselor singing it during devotions. "Leg bone connected to the collar bone; collar bone—" Jesse couldn't remember all the words.

But he sure remembered the counselor. That guy—Jack, his name had been— could turn a double play better than any shortstop Jesse had ever seen. While watching Jack, Jesse used to pretend he was a sports commentator: "A flat liner skips twice off the ground on its way through the box into center field. Jack scoops it up, leaning way over to the left, turns on a dime, hits the bag with his left foot, jumps to avoid the runner, and throws. His arm uncoils like a tightly wound spring, and he gets the runner on his way to first." Incredible. And from a preacher no less.

The kids listened to Jack because they liked the way he fielded ground balls. Soon they realized they liked him too. Jack taught them the "bone" song, more for fun than anything else. First they'd sing it, then he'd get serious. "Friday night, I want some of you to give a testimony at the bonfire," he told them. When Jack said something like that, you took him seriously, whether or not you wanted to do what he said.

"The song's wrong," he told them one night, after they had it down cold. "The song doesn't say it like the Bible does. The Bible shows us that God can put us all back together," he said. "But the guy who wrote the song didn't care about that." Then he read that Bible passage. Crazy business— leg bones, and all that.

Jesse played third base for the camp all-stars when they challenged the counselors on Friday afternoon. Everyone was there. Jack beat them single-handedly. Jesse even thought about asking for the man's autograph. That's how much he thought of him.

Friday night came. The bonfire was something most guys hated because they knew what was expected of them. It wasn't at all cool to get up there and say how much you loved Jesus—even if in your heart you knew you did.

Jesse never forgot how Jack waited for him to give a testimony. In the flickering light of the fire, Jesse could see Jack's eyes ranging over the guys in his cabin, the same way they ranged over the infield. Confident eyes, just waiting for the big play.

Two of the guys did speak. Two out of eight. Not Jesse.

He wondered where Jack was today. He wished he knew. Jack, the preacher with great hands. Right now he'd like to talk.

106

GOD'S WAY

Read Nehemiah 2:1–10

Sanballat the Horonite and Tobiah the Ammonite had more to be angry about than their weird names. They were really upset when they found out that King Artaxerxes had allowed that Jewish man, Nehemiah, to go back to Jerusalem and rebuild the wall. "The height of stupidity," Sanballat probably said to his buddy Tobiah. "The king's actually allowing his own enemies to rebuild their fortress in Jerusalem. He must be mad."

Just exactly why Artaxerxes allowed Nehemiah to go back to his father's homeland isn't immediately clear. Old Sanballat was right; letting the conquered people rebuild was like allowing them to walk away from captivity.

So why did Artaxerxes do it? For the answer to that question you have to look farther back into biblical history, back to the book of Esther. Esther is a great story—almost like a short novel—about how a beautiful Jewish girl became queen of Persia. But there's something very odd about the book. In the book of Esther the word *God* isn't mentioned once. That's right. Not once. Of course, that doesn't mean the book doesn't teach us something about God. It does. Even though the word *God* appears nowhere in the book, the story of Esther shows how God controls all things.

But back to Nehemiah and the grumpy Horonite, Sanballat. Why did King Artaxerxes allow Nehemiah to go back and rebuild the wall of Jerusalem? Perhaps because Artaxerxes was the stepson of Esther. It's not so hard to imagine that Artaxerxes may have had a special place in his heart for his stepmother's people. Maybe that's one reason why he allowed Nehemiah to return to rebuild Jerusalem for the Jews.

Another possible reason might be that the king respected and trusted Nehemiah as a valuable advisor. Any king worth his salt knows that when you have the loyalty of a great man (or woman), you have to give him some freedom in order to keep him. If that's the reason, Artaxerxes' plan worked: twelve years later, Nehemiah returned to serve King Artaxerxes.

It really doesn't matter all that much why King Artaxerxes allowed Nehemiah to return to Jerusalem. What does matter is that we see that God was behind the scene, working hard to keep his covenant promises to his people, to see to it that the faithful few who still worshiped him would survive and would one day be blessed by the birth of the Messiah.

Poor Sanballat the Horonite! He just didn't understand that God has ways of getting things done. We don't always understand just what God is up to, either. But we do know this—he will get his way. He always does.

Prayer:

Lord, sometimes we really don't know why things happen as they do. But we thank you that you are always in control of everything, no matter what happens. In Jesus' name, Amen.

138

107

BUILDING WALLS

Read Nehemiah 4

Nehemiah worked up a thick sweat trying to get the wall around Jerusalem rebuilt, and it's easy to understand why. As long as there was no wall to protect the city, an enemy army could swoop down and wipe out the Israelites with no problem. If the mad dogs around them were to stay off Israelite property, Nehemiah knew the wall had to be rebuilt.

In fact, the wall was so important that Nehemiah had his men working constantly. Things must have really poked along with a whole crew of one-handers, but they had to get that wall up, brick by brick, no matter how long it took—sword in one hand, trowel in the other.

Walled cities still stand here and there throughout North America. There are probably a hundred or more forts around too—some of them pretty much intact from the days when they stood alone on the plains or in the forests. Back in those days pioneers from miles around would hightail it behind the wall at the first sound of enemy fire.

Walls meant protection to soldiers and settlers back in the "olden days." They meant protection to the Israelites too. Stout protective walls were the only way to live.

But there was another reason Nehemiah cracked the whip the way he did. He remembered what a few survivors had told him about great Jerusalem. "Those who survived the exile and are back in the province are in great trouble and disgrace. The wall of Jerusalem is broken down."

Building the wall was also a way to rebuild pride. The wall, Nehemiah knew, would give the Israelites a new will to live. Without the wall his people were sitting out in the middle of nowhere like some wounded animals waiting for the next predator to catch the scent of blood. The wall would keep them safe and pump them full of pride.

And Nehemiah knew one more thing. He knew that if the people rebuilt the wall themselves, they would be proud of their work. Each of them would point to his or her section: "See that wall there—took me most of two weeks, but I did it." That's what they would say.

Once I walked through a brand-new Christian high school where teams of parents in grubby clothes were slapping paint on the hallway walls. They painted in bunches all through the corridors and sang hymns as they worked. Volunteer paint crews saved that school a lot of money and also gave a whole lot of people the chance to take pride in their building and in what would go on in its rooms the following September.

Nehemiah knew the rebuilt wall of Jerusalem was more than a way to stay alive; for the Israelites it was a reason to live.

108

GREAT AND DREADFUL

Prayer:

Thank you that we do not have to be afraid of judgment day. Thank you, Son of Righteousness, for taking away our sins and healing us. Amen.

Read Malachi 4

You might think of the Bible as an old, old book. Well, it is. Yet, at the same time, it's quite forward-looking. Much of the Old Testament stands up like a giant highway sign pointing at something big just up the road a ways. By now, I shouldn't have to say what—or whom—it points at.

The very last words of the Old Testament do the same thing. Like just about everything that has been said before, the words of Malachi stand up and point at Christ. A messenger—who Malachi calls Elijah in verse 5—will prepare the way for Jesus. That messenger will be John the Baptist.

"Surely the day is coming; it will burn like a furnace," says Malachi. Seems like an odd thing to say, doesn't it? Christ's coming will burn? What's Malachi trying to do—scare us?

Maybe so. What's coming is Christ and his new gospel of justice and love. And God's justice can be good or it can be bad. It all depends on where you sit.

Christ's coming won't be a holiday for everyone. "All the arrogant and every evildoer will be stubble, and that day that is coming will set them on fire," Malachi says. The bad guys are going to get themselves scorched right to the ground by God's justice. If you're one of those who have spit on the lowly and the oppressed, it's not going to be pleasant.

But what of those who have been faithful, who have worked hard to help the victims of society? What of those who have spent all their born days trying to love, to serve, to do righteousness in a world that hasn't always taken kindly to it?

"You will go out and leap like calves released from the stall." That's the other side. Nobody likes to be penned up for long, not even a calf. When God's justice comes, all of those who have given of themselves, all who have listened to God will take off into the pastures of freedom and kick up their heels in joy. All the gloom will turn into glory.

The two sides of God's justice are something like fire. My young son is afraid of fire. In school his teacher has to talk about rather unpleasant things—bodies rolling around in blankets, people coughing—in order to warn the kids to stay away from flames. Fire scares him, he says—with good reason.

But he loves roasted marshmallows. What's more, he loves hamburgers and hot dogs and bratwurst—in fact, most anything cooked over a fire. Fire also purifies and cooks; it works for us as a servant. If you want to get something squeaky clean and pure, you put it in boiling water or hold it over a flame.

Christ's coming will have two simultaneous effects, Malachi says. It will free forever those who have been in slavery; those folks will dance. But it will destroy those who have been the slave-masters; they will be trimmed to stubble.

For God's own people, this Christ who is coming will rise with healing in his wings. That's nothing but good news.

109

JUST THE PLAIN AND SIMPLE FACTS

Prayer:

Dear Lord,

thank you that

we know that

the story of

Jesus is true and

happened

exactly as the

Bible says it did.

Thank you for

coming into the

world to save us

from sin.

Amen.

Read Matthew 1:17–24

Howard Cosell may well be the undisputed champion of hype. He seems to love to yak about the best screen pass, the safety with the quickest feet, or the quarterback who throws best against the grain. Everything is the greatest ever. To me, it's all just dumb football hype. But I suppose it's not so dumb to those who love football.

If the disciple Matthew had been blessed with Cosell's gift, his story of Christ's birth wouldn't read at all like it does. Matthew could really have hyped the story if he'd wanted to. He might have told it in a way Hollywood would appreciate . . .

Joseph was a young man in love. One day, very unexpectedly, he discovered that his fiancée was already pregnant—and he knew very well that he was not the father. Joseph stomped around, kicked tables and walls, threw a fit. That's probably how some movie director might stage that scene.

But Matthew says Joseph was an honorable man. He didn't blow a fuse. He planned to end their relationship quietly, not making a big deal out of Mary's pregnancy—even though by law he could have. Matthew takes a real low key on Joseph.

One night Joseph was confronted by an angel in a dream. A film director might call for some dry ice to create plenty of smoke, then slowly rotate a spotlight through the steam over the bed. A little eerie music— some high notes rolling up and down.

Matthew tells us only that it happened. No special effects. No hype. No Joseph scared to death.

So what happened once Joseph awoke from the dream? Holly- wood would certainly expect a dramatic reaction. Did he sit there in pain wondering what he had

seen? Did he ask himself over and over whether he only imagined the dream?

Matthew says only that Joseph did exactly what the angel told him to do. Nothing less, nothing more. Just the facts.

Matthew isn't interested in hype. He's interested in proving this new baby Jesus to be the Messiah the Jews were awaiting. That point doesn't take any hype, and it doesn't take any special effects. All we need are the facts.

And that's what Matthew gives us—three lists of fourteen generations, an angel's announce- ment to a man from the house of David, and a name for a baby— Jesus. Those, he says, are facts.

And that—like it or not, Howard Cosell—is the absolutely greatest story ever told. It's no hype.

110

NO BIG DEAL

Prayer:

Lord, forgive us for sometimes being bored by the most exciting story ever told. May the gospel always be good news for us. In Jesus' name, Amen.

Read Matthew 2:1–6

Rebecca has just become a Christian. All year some friends on the volleyball team have been talking to her about Christ. Through them Rebecca has become a believer, and she's really excited about it. For the first time in her life, she claims, she feels strong and confident. She knows she's no better volleyball player than she ever was, but somehow the whole world suddenly seems different. She says other people matter to her now. Before she cared only about herself.

For the first time in her life, Rebecca realizes that her own parents don't really believe. It's not that they're atheists or anything, but she knows very well that God doesn't mean much to them. She also knows her parents are worried about her. They wonder why she's always reading her Bible and forever talking about Christ.

One Sunday morning Rebecca walks to a church not far from where she lives. Her mother stays in bed, and her father heads for the handball court in the park. But Rebecca is a Christian. She goes to church.

Walking alone down the street, Rebecca is excited about church. She expects that everybody there will feel exactly like she does about Christ. She's sure they will be full of joy and love, people who are excited about being Christians.

But that's not what she finds at the church down the block. The people seem healthy all right, but they don't smile and they don't seem turned on about the Lord. They sit quietly in their pews, sing when they're told to sing, and pray when everybody else does. Some of the kids look bored stiff, and some of the parents sleep during a long and tiring sermon. When it's over, Rebecca tells herself that there's something wrong with that church. Next week she'll go elsewhere.

Rebecca's story is sad, but it's not unique. Way back at the birth of Christ something very similar occurred. Wise men from the East, men we can assume weren't even Jews, saw an incredible star and headed immediately for Jerusalem, positive that something really big had taken place. We might imagine them hurrying along on their camels, eager to get to the place where the people would be celebrating.

When they arrived in Jerusalem, they found that everything was business as usual—no dancing in the streets, no ticker-tape parades, no national holidays. Even though people must have seen the star, no one seemed to care. In Jerusalem, it was no big deal. The religious leaders knew the Scriptures all right; they knew where the child would be born as well as the Eastern wise men did. But they didn't care. Even though they knew, they just shrugged their shoulders, as if the star meant nothing at all.

It's a scary story, really—especially if you're like me, a person whose grandparents were Christians. The people who should have been excited didn't care. The whole story of the Messiah's coming to earth was old hat to them. Familiarity had led to apathy.

They'd seen the star all right, but it was no big deal.

111

TWO KINGS

Read Matthew 2:13–18

Our world has seen its share of evil kings and wicked rulers. Do you know the name of the king who the Bible says "did more evil in the eyes of the Lord than any of those before him"? Among other things, this loser married someone whose name will live forever as a symbol of sin. She once persuaded her husband to have their neighbor killed so they could take over his vineyard. Her name was Jezebel and her scoundrel of a husband was called Ahab.

Who would you say was the most evil ruler of the twentieth century—so far at least? Many people would pick a crazed wallpaper hanger who sent millions of Jews to their deaths in his concentration camps. His name, as you know, was Hitler.

King Herod, in our Bible story for today, ranks right up—I mean, right down—there with Ahab and Hitler. King Herod was a butcher. He had his own sons killed so that he could remain king. Then, when the wise men told him about Jesus, he ordered all the little boys around Bethlehem murdered in cold blood. It's hard to imagine people as evil as King Herod.

King Herod ruled by intimidation. He slaughtered innocent children, even his own. He had no fear of God—no belief whatsoever, except a belief in his ability to rule. He cared about nothing or no one but himself. King Herod was a brute, a son of Satan's power. He was king all right, but by the time of Christ's birth, he was also a bitter old man, insanely jealous, fierce, and cunning. He was a man without any sense of good. Oddly enough, he was called "Herod the Great." Some people must have considered him good at being a king.

But God saw to it that Herod's wicked plan didn't work. Another king, a baby king, escaped safely from Bethlehem.

King Jesus would shed blood in order to rule, just as King Herod did—but it would be his own blood, and it would be spilled so that others could live. Love and peace would reign in Jesus' kingdom, while intimidation and murder strengthened King Herod's rule.

Some things don't change. It was difficult for the Jews to imagine how a baby could be king, how someone could rule by love and self-sacrifice.

It is just as difficult today.

We expect our leaders to be tough and strong, to carry big sticks even if they speak softly. It's hard for us to think of Christ as king, this baby in a manger full of straw, this infant wrapped in rags and lying in a barn.

But he was—and he is. And he is not just king of Israel, but king of all of our lives. He came to save us from people like Herod, from the treachery of men and women who give themselves to evil. He came to save us from sin and death.

Through him we have life and joy forever.

112

CARPENTER'S SON STUNS TEMPLE CROWD

Read Luke 2:41–52

[Special to the *Jerusalem Gazette.*]

Temple officials are still shaking their heads today, in the wake of the visit of Jesus, the twelve-year-old son of a Galilean carpenter from the town of Nazareth, who left everyone just about speechless in nearly three days of discussions.

Young Jesus created quite a stir in the temple by asking sharp and pointed questions of the scholars and men of faith who regularly meet there for discussion. Reportedly, however, it wasn't only the questions that stunned the elders; it was his answers as well.

"Such a sharp mind that boy has!" remarked Levi, a longtime frequenter of the temple discussions. "There were times when his questions pinned the most brilliant of the old men."

Equally amazing to some observers was the story of the boy's relationship with his family. It is commonly thought that the parents of this Jesus had come to Jerusalem for the Passover a few days past. The boy, however, stayed on alone—apparently without his parents' knowledge.

For more than a day, no one appeared to notice the boy's absence. Police in Jerusalem admit that a carpenter named Joseph filed a missing-child report with their office on Tuesday. But it wasn't until Wednesday that the brilliant child was located by his parents.

Bystanders claim a strange conversation took place when the boy was discovered in the temple. The boy's mother reportedly asked him why he treated them so poorly.

Standing before twenty or thirty wise men, Jesus replied to his mother's question with a question, "Why were you looking for me?" And then, "Didn't you know I had to be in my Father's house?" Several of those present remember the exact words of the boy's reply.

Temple officials are still scratching their heads over the implications of the final comment.

"Does it make any sense that he would call the temple 'his Father's house?' " asked Jehozadak, a leader of the daily temple discussions. "What kind of boy is this anyway?"

Most of those who overheard the boy's discussions with the elders admit that rarely is such a fine, discerning mind on display in the temple debates and discussions. By the time his parents found him with the elders, a group of people had gathered outside the temple. News of the child had spread all over the city.

"That boy will be heard from again—you can mark my words," said Jehozadak. "Not in all my born days have I seen such brilliance—and he is still only a boy."

113

Prayer:

Thank you,

Jesus, that like

the water of

baptism, your

blood washes

away all of our

sins. Help us to

remember what

it cost you to

make us

blameless in

God's sight. In

your name,

Amen.

Read Mark 1:1–11

No matter how you look at it, John the Baptist was one strange character. If he were around today, people would write him off as someone whose mind had permanently gone fishing. But back then he could draw a crowd. Mark says that people came way out to the desert just to hear him preach.

Some of today's famous preachers have immense churches, manage huge financial empires, are chauffeured around in big cars, and wear expensive suits. Not this character. Mark says John ate locusts and wild honey. What's more, he must've looked like something the cat dragged in—hair and beard flying and body swathed in camel's hair.

But the man was famous for at least two reasons: first, he knew how to preach—hundreds, maybe thousands, came out to hear him; second (and this is much more important), his job had been waiting for him for a long, long time. Mark even quotes from Isaiah to explain how John the Baptist accomplished a task that people several generations back knew would have to be done.

What exactly was his job? It consisted of just one very significant task: he had to roll out the red carpet for the Savior. He had to clear the air, get the whole nation of Israel ready for the gospel of Christ. Isaiah says he had to do some bulldozing to "make straight paths" for Jesus Christ.

Mark, unlike the other gospel writers, seems most interested in Jesus' ministry. While the others remember Jesus' earlier years, Mark concentrates on the three-year period in which Christ preached the gospel on earth. So Mark starts his Gospel with this John the Baptist and the way he handled Christ's commencement.

Some of us think the word *commencement* means the end. After all, kids graduate from grade school and high school at cere-monies called "commencements." But the word *commence* means "to begin." When kids finish high school, after all, they certainly do "begin" another period of their lives.

This strange man, John the Baptist, did two things to make straight paths for Jesus Christ. First, he preached that people need to be forgiven for their sins; hundreds responded to his message and were baptized. And second, he baptized Jesus Christ at Christ's own commencement, the day that marked the beginning of his life of preaching on earth.

There will never be another commencement like this one. Right there, as John and Jesus stood in the Jordan River, the heavens opened and God said he was well pleased with Jesus, his beloved Son.

What a beginning!

TEMPTA-TION AND SIN

Read Luke 4:1–13

My wife just had a garage sale. Once a year she checks over the kids' clothes, picks out what no longer fits, and prices everything with little pieces of masking tape. Then she cleans the garage. (I like garage sales—*she* cleans the garage.)

Tons of people showed up for our garage sale. Some even came a half hour before the ad said the sale was supposed to start. They figured the early bird would get the best bargains, I suppose.

When my wife tallied up all the sales, she started to wonder about a couple of things—our daughter's overall skirt, for instance. She couldn't remember anyone paying for it, but it was gone. Somebody must have picked it off the table and taken off without paying. Things like that happen more often than we care to admit.

Why? It's not because the people who come to garage sales are poor. And it's certainly not because my daughter's overall skirt cost too much. People steal things for another reason—just plain sin. There's something very exciting about being able to get away with something, especially if you come away with something you like. Sin starts with temptation.

Jesus was tempted by Satan, just as Adam and Eve were tempted way back in Eden. Jesus hadn't eaten for forty days. He must have been starved. Satan came around and told him to make himself some bread. If Jesus had obeyed Satan, he would have been sinning.

Next, Satan offered Jesus all the kingdoms of the world. Jesus Christ knew very well what his mission on earth meant. He knew that he would have to die to save the nations of the world. So taking those nations without having to die must have been quite a temptation for him. But again

Jesus said no to Satan's smart offer.

Finally, Satan told Jesus to pull a dramatic stunt so that his fame would spread throughout the land. Few people knew who Jesus was yet. So Satan's proposition—quick headlines—must have been very appealing to Jesus. But again he said no.

Jesus Christ was both human and divine at the same time. How can that be? It's impossible to explain. Yet he *was* both, and his temptation proves it.

Jesus had to be human to suffer in the place of sinners—you and I and the person who stole my daughter's overall skirt. But he had to be God in order to conquer death and Satan. And that's just what he did.

Both God and man, Jesus Christ is our only Redeemer. Hard as it may be to understand, that's the simple truth we need to know in order to believe in him.

115

SIGNS AND WONDERS

Prayer:

Thank you, Lord Jesus, for your wonderful miracles. Thank you especially for the biggest miracle of all— that you came to earth to live and die for all those who believe in you. In your name, Amen.

Read John 2:1–11

Being the mother of Jesus couldn't have been an easy job. Long before he was born, Mary knew who her child would be. No doubt, she spent hours watching him play, wondering how to handle this child who was more than human.

For instance, do you think she wanted to scold him for hanging around the temple while the rest of the family headed back to Nazareth? How do you think she felt that day when he told her she should have known he was in "his Father's house"? Mary was human—just as human as you and I. So knowing that Jesus was the Son of God probably wasn't enough to keep her from acting like any other mother in the world.

Jesus' first recorded miracle occurred almost at Mary's request. It happened at a big wedding celebration, a gala event that had everyone smiling. Sometimes people accuse Christians of being sour. Maybe some are, but they shouldn't be. Christ's presence at this wedding shows very clearly that he liked a good time too.

But it was Mary who brought it up. "Jesus," she said, "they have no more wine."

Now why would she tell him that? Was it just a matter-of-fact statement: "Oh—it's too bad all the wine is gone, isn't it?"

Or was she being a little sly? Was she guessing that Jesus could do something about the shortage of wine if he really wanted to? We don't know for sure, of course, but listen to what happened.

"My time has not come," Jesus told his mother, as if to say, "This is not the time to work a miracle."

But Mary seemed to know something, at least more than we do when we read the story as John remembered it. She knew something all right, because she left her son's side right away and walked over to some servants standing near six big pots of water.

"Do whatever he tells you," she told them. You bet—Mary knew. She'd always known about her son.

It was Christ's first public miracle: water into wine at the wedding in Cana. The miracle was like a road sign, pointing at a destination, pointing at the man who pulled the miracle off, at Christ himself, who would later tell the people, "I am the Way." It was the first sign that this man Jesus was more than human. Through this miracle he proved that he had power over nature, that he was more than just a carpenter's son. People couldn't help but follow.

What did Mary have to do with it? Well, Jesus was, after all, Mary's son. And she knew what her son could do.

116

JESSE'S ESCAPE (10)

Prayer:

Dear God, help us be peacemakers in your world. And give us your peace in our hearts. In the name of the Prince of Peace we pray.

Amen.

Read Matthew 5:1–14

They came in together, his father and the preacher. His father looked beaten and worn. He stood there at the bedside, his fingers curved on the edge of the blankets, as if he were ready to play a piano.

"I'm sorry, Jesse," he said. "Really, I am—for everything. Your mother and I want you back home with us."

But Jesse didn't want to talk, didn't want to say anything at all. He wished he could snap himself awake from a bad dream.

"We've been worried sick about you—," his father said.

Jesse twirled the straw in the glass of water on the tray over his bed.

"You aren't hurt bad, are you?" Jesse lifted the glass and took a mouthful of water. "Just scratched up kind of—"

"It could have been worse, son—"

"I ain't scared of dying," Jesse muttered.

The preacher cleared his throat. "Only one person I know of that wasn't scared of dying—and even he asked God to get him out of it: 'Take this cup from me, Father,' he said." The preacher said it without emotion, as if he were reading. "You got to tell the truth, Jesse. We can get somewhere here if you decide that you're going to talk straight and not hand us all this garbage."

His father stared down at the blankets. "I want to start over new, Jesse. I want to start over as if there never was a bad time between us—"

Jesse winced as he reached to return the glass to the tray. The road burns over his shoulder pulled tight and hurt bad. "No way do I want to go home with this man," he thought. "No way."

"Seems you don't have many choices, Jesse. Going home's about your only option. Your

motorcycle's junk—" That preacher said things so matter-of-factly, as if he were reading the news.

"Jesse," his father reached for his arm, held it right at the elbow. "Please—you're our son."

It was the weakness in his father that seemed new to him, his nervous fingers, the shaking in his face. No yelling.

"Maybe I *do* have to go home," Jesse said uncertainly. "Maybe I got no choice. But it's not what I want—"

"It's not what you want to do that counts, Jesse," the preacher said. "It's what you have to do." He got out of his chair and stood there next to them. "You ain't a kid, Jesse. This whole running business made you into something you weren't before." He nodded toward Jesse's father. "He's changed too," he said.

Jesse felt as if he couldn't move right then, the two of them standing there and his back and arms full of pain.

"What's great about God is he gives us tons of second chances, but he sure wants us to take them when we got the opportunity. You understand, Jesse?"

Jesse waited and waited in the silence. Then, slowly, very reluctantly, he nodded his head.

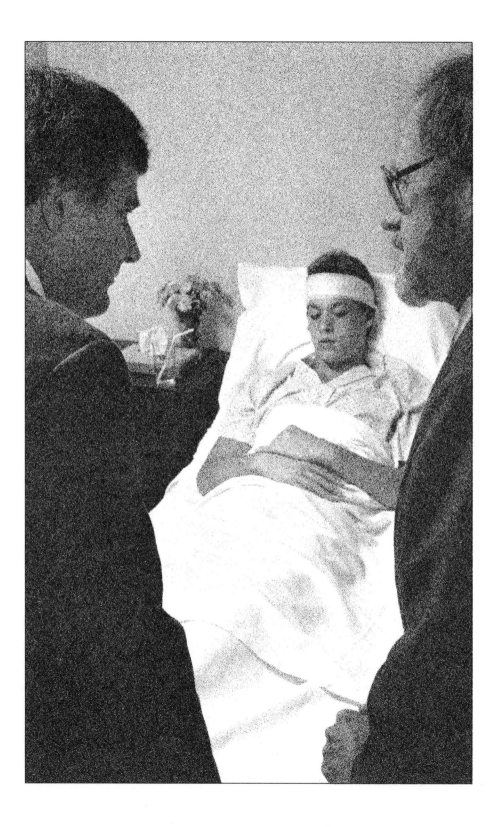

117

WISHES AND PRAYERS

Prayer:

Thank you for teaching us how to pray, Father. May our prayers always praise you for what you have done for us. In Jesus' name, Amen.

Read Matthew 6:7–15

Here's what Sarah says: "Uncle Marvin sure does pray good. Everyone likes the way he does it. He's got a great way of using words like *beseeches* and *behooves*. And he can throw in some Bible verses and even quote from some of our favorite hymns."

Sarah's Uncle Marvin may be good at praying, but if he is, it's not because he knows how to dress the prayer up in nice words. If he's good at praying, it's because he follows Jesus' instructions on how to pray.

What are those instructions? First, don't make a show of it. Second, don't babble on and on, thinking the longer you pray, the more God will be impressed. And third, pray in a pattern like the Lord's Prayer (which was really the Disciples' Prayer, since Jesus gave it to them as a model).

How does the Lord's Prayer work? We begin by honoring the Father: "Hallowed be thy name." Then we ask that the Father's rule on earth will be advanced: "Thy kingdom come." Next we ask for our physical and spiritual needs: bread and forgiveness. That's the pattern Jesus gave his disciples in the prayer he recited to them as a model. It's not very difficult to pray good prayers. Uncle Marvin probably does it—but, likely as not, so does Sarah.

Ralph Waldo Emerson was a writer who thought that he was just as divine as Jesus. In fact, he thought that everybody—even Sarah and her Uncle Marvin—could be divine.

This man Emerson also thought that every time he wished something, that wish was already a prayer. Think of it this way: it's about 150 degrees outside on a Saturday afternoon, and you're doing some huge lawn with an antique hand-pushed mower. The guy who owns the house isn't home, and you're so thirsty you could inhale an entire swimming pool. "Oh, man," you say to yourself, "I'd give anything for a can of pop."

Emerson didn't take what Christ said about prayer very seriously, because he didn't take Christ seriously. Christ said very plainly that a good prayer takes more than a wish. God must be honored in our prayers.

118

Prayer:

Lord God, we

know that you

have authority

over all things

and all people

everywhere. You

are our

authority.

Thank you for

loving us.

Amen.

Read Matthew 8:5–13

When I was a boy, I used to love to watch TV shows about war. One of my favorites was a show called *Combat*. The hero of that show was a brave troop commander who led his men into dangerous battles with the enemy. His men listened to his authority.

Today, some people would say that *Combat* was a bad show, because it glorified war, made it seem exciting and noble. It did, of course. They're right about that.

Just recently, a show entitled *M*A*S*H* finally ended. Those people who hated *Combat* probably loved *M*A*S*H*, because *M*A*S*H* didn't make war seem exciting and noble at all. *M*A*S*H* made war seem as ugly as it really is.

A big difference between the two shows was the way in which they viewed authority. In *Combat* the commander's rule was law—nobody questioned it. In *M*A*S*H*, the commander was usually kind of silly. Hawkeye Pierce, the leading character, didn't give two cents for authority other than his own.

If we assume that the popularity of these two different shows tells us something about the values of the people who watched them, then we can see very easily that values change. For instance, *Combat* watchers liked to see commanders exercise sharp and strong authority over their troops. To *M*A*S*H* viewers, on the other hand, military authority wasn't important. They laughed when Hawkeye shrugged off commands from his officers.

The centurion in this Bible story could not have starred on *M*A*S*H*. To this soldier, authority was of highest importance. Look at the way he talked to Jesus. "My servant is sick," he said. "Just say the word and he will be healed."

The centurion would have served well in the old TV show *Combat* because he recognized authority when he saw it. He himself was in charge of troops. He probably knew that a commander without authority isn't a commander at all. Furthermore, troops without a leader aren't worth much.

The centurion undoubtedly understood Jesus' great authority. Lots of Jewish people—the religious leaders especially—asked Jesus where he got his authority. The centurion didn't question him a bit. He had no doubt whatsoever that Jesus had authority over natural things, over the powers of darkness, and even over death. This man, who constantly exercised his own authority, recognized authority when he saw it in Jesus.

The centurion was right. Jesus' miracles demonstrated over and over again how he had authority over everything in the world—over water, over sickness, over storms, over death itself.

And look what Christ said to the centurion when he saw such faith: "It will be done just as you believed it would." That's Christ's answer to real faith in *his* authority.

119

TWO VIEWS

Prayer:

Dear Lord, we

praise you for

being able to

forgive all of

our sins. Please

give us the kind

of faith which

trusts and

obeys.

Amen.

Read Luke 5:17–26

"My name is Marabis, and I come from Jerusalem, where I am highly respected as a teacher. You ask me what I think of this man who calls himself Jesus, and I will tell you what I saw this morning—in no uncertain terms, I will tell you.

"This man called Jesus was teaching many people, teaching them things that must be called into question. There is no doubt he is popular with the people. He performs many strange tricks which the people rather unknowingly call 'miracles.' And they love him. That fact I do not question.

"Today when all of us were there listening to him talk, suddenly from the ceiling a man was lowered into the house, a crippled man. It was such a strange sight that we almost laughed.

"But then Jesus said something most awful. 'Friend,' he said, 'your sins are forgiven.'

"I tell you, I was born and reared on God's Law. I have spent my life learning the ways of God. I know much of what is in the Holy Book by heart. And never—not in all my years in the temple of Jerusalem, the greatest temple in all the country—have I heard such an outrage. This man considers himself Almighty God! Nothing less. Now I ask you—who alone can forgive sin? Don't we all know, and haven't we all confessed, that only God can do such a thing? Then who is this man who upsets so many of our people with his 'miracles' and his blasphemous teaching? He is a fake. Believe me, I know. I have been studying for years, and I know he is evil."

_____

"My name is Aramen. I will tell you what I know. I was one of those who lowered the crippled man into the house where Jesus was teaching. All around him stood the big-shot teachers from Judea and Galilee and even from Jerusalem. There they stood, ready to jump on his every word.

"We lowered our friend down through the roof because we knew that Jesus could heal him. He's done it before. Everyone knows he does these miracles.

"There we stood, our arms aching, while our friend on the stretcher swung in front of Jesus. And then Jesus said, 'Your sins are forgiven.' And he looked around him. All the big shots were grumbling—like a murmur throughout the house. We could hear it, even on the roof.

"And then Jesus said to our friend, 'Get up and walk.' That's all. Just 'Get up and walk.' And you know what happened? Our friend did just as he was told.

"I know. I saw a miracle. I was there. I saw it. This Jesus is more than just a man. Believe me."

120

HOG WILD

Prayer:

Keep our

perspectives

clear, dear Lord.

Help us

remember that

nothing means

quite so much

in the world as

our devotion to

you and your

kingdom. In

Jesus' name,

Amen.

Read Mark 5:1–17

Just now I checked the latest prices for pork on the hoof. A friend of mine who buys and sells hogs throughout the Midwest claims that if those hogs Christ sent the demons into weighed in at about 220 pounds a piece, they'd bring about $110 per pig today on the market. You don't have to be a mathematician to figure out that their owners lost more than their shirts when Christ sent the whole herd scampering off the cliff.

"We're talking big bucks," my friend said over his business phone.

If you haven't figured it out yet, the sum total of the owners' loss was better than $200,000. It's hard to write off that kind of cash.

So it's not surprising that this story doesn't have a particularly happy ending. The people of Gerasenes would have preferred a naked lunatic, too strong for an entire police force—a wild man possessed by demons—to such immense financial loss. For them, asking Christ to leave was a matter of good business sense, a matter of priorities. "Please, Jesus," they said, "why don't you just leave and let us alone? We'll keep our lunatics, *and* our money, if you please—"

Money, then as now, is all-important to many people. Some of those pig owners probably would have agreed with a current expression: "Money may not be everything—but it sure is a long way ahead of whatever is in second place."

But that cannot be the attitude of Christ's people. The first commandment says, "You shall have *no* other gods before me." People who want to be called Christians have to give some things up—that's all there's to it. They have to face the fact that the love of money often destroys our love for God. As Paul warned his readers, "The love of money is the root of all evil."

An old gospel song claims, "I'd rather have Jesus than silver and gold." Of course, loving God more than money is much easier to sing about than to do. Putting God first means we won't have all the things TV commercials tell us we can't live without. Putting God first can be tough in our world.

Putting God first means saying (or singing), "I'd rather have Jesus than silver and gold" and meaning every word. That's the kind of obedience and devotion God demands of his people.

121

AN ALMOST MISTAKEN IDENTITY

Prayer:

Dear Lord, we thank you for coming to this world to redeem us from our sin. Help us to recognize your hand in our lives today, as well as yesterday. Help us live for you. Amen.

Read Luke 7:18–23

See if you can figure out this riddle: One night as a man and his son were driving along, a drunk smashed his truck into their car. Both dad and son were badly hurt and taken immediately to a hospital. Nurses and doctors in the trauma ward scrambled to care for them, but the boy needed surgery.

A surgeon was called in, informed of all the complications, and appraised of the boy's general condition. As the trauma staff watched, the surgeon entered the operating room, took one look at the boy, and stepped quickly back, as if shocked. "I can't operate on this boy," the surgeon said. "He's my own son."

How is that possible?

One of the men is the stepfather, you say? Sorry. It's just a case of mistaken identity? Nope. Give up? Come on, it's not that hard.

Here's the big clue: the surgeon is a woman. That's right— she's the boy's mother.

Maybe you guessed the answer without any clues, but lots of people have trouble with that story. They automatically picture a surgeon as a male in a white smock. Their unexamined—and outdated—ideas don't let them recognize what is really very simple: women can be—and often are—surgeons.

Many of the Jews of Jesus' time had that same kind of problem in recognizing their Savior. Even John the Baptist had his doubts. Jesus just didn't look and act like people had always imagined the Messiah would look and act.

Don't be too quick to blame John the Baptist for sending a message full of doubt to Jesus Christ. John may have been specially designated to prepare the way for Christ, but he was also very human. Let's not forget that he was sitting alone in prison, no doubt wondering what on earth he was doing there while Jesus was out on the streets, seemingly forgetting all about the very man who had recognized him first.

"Are you the man we've been waiting for," John asked, "or should we keep our eyes out for another one?"

For thousands of years the Jews had looked forward to a Messiah who would establish God's rule. The problem was, they had this vision of what "establishing God's rule" would look like, just as most of you probably had a mental image of what a surgeon would look like.

Many Jews believed the Messiah would build a big capitol that would stand at the center of the world, that he would rule all the nations and bring everyone under God's power. Many Jews expected a king on earth, a real king with castle guards and a big army.

Jesus Christ was—and is— King, but he's not *that* kind of king at all. I'm fighting a war against sin, he told John, and he pointed at the lame who now walked, the blind who could now see, and the sick who were now healthy. That's the battle he was fighting.

John had trouble recognizing what the Messiah was because he was sure the Messiah would be doing other things. Even John had to learn something about this Savior.

Jesus would rule all right, but not with a sword.

122

FEEDING FIVE THOUSAND AND ONE

Prayer:

Thank you for choosing all kinds of people to be in your family, Lord. We're not all like Peter, and we're not all like Philip. Help us to be your children, no matter how we differ from each other.

Amen.

Read John 6:1–13

Sometimes Jesus was so human. As the huge crowd of followers swarmed after him and his disciples, Jesus thought about their physical needs. He turned to Philip and asked a serious question—but in a way, he was just kidding around.

"Where in the world are we going to get enough food for all these people?" he asked. Jesus knew very well where the meal would be coming from, of course—so it was a test question, maybe a little tease. If I were an artist drawing Christ's face at just that moment, I'd probably give him a little smile.

Philip was a real character. Likely as not, he didn't say much. If you want to picture him somehow, try this: lean him up against a tree, poking a piece of grass between his teeth, always listening. Sure, he was a believer, but he was no Peter. Fiery, energetic Peter was the rock on which Christ would build his church. Philip was a different kind of rock—sturdy, immovable, stable.

Philip seemed to be the kind of guy who liked to put on the brakes about things. At another point, Christ was telling his disciples how he had come from and would return to the Father in heaven. It was Philip who told him he wanted proof: "Lord, *show* us the Father and that will be enough for us," he said. Philip needed convincing before he'd really believe. Maybe he was a little like the disciple called "Doubting Thomas."

Philip was naturally skeptical about things. It took quite a bit of fuel to get his engine running.

Think of him this way: stand half a glass of water on the counter and ask Peter, then Philip, how much is there. Peter, grinning, would say the glass is half full. Philip would shake his head and rub his chin. "That glass is half empty," he'd say.

But in spite of his skepticism, he had something of a sense of humor. When Christ asked him where they could buy all the food, Philip said jokingly, "Eight months wages wouldn't buy enough bread for each one to have a bite!" Then he pulled a long, lazy smile across his face.

Philip reminds me of some heavyset guy with a green seed cap, sitting on an old church bench parked in front of a country store, watching time pass. "Hey, Ed—what you up to?" somebody yells. "Trying to hold this thing down," Ed says, both hands slapping the bench beneath him.

Everyone knows the story of the feeding of the five thousand. Jesus pulled off another astounding miracle. With only five loaves and two fishes, the disciples were able to feed five thousand people and still had bushel baskets left, filled to overflowing.

Sometime during that big picnic by the Sea of Galilee, I just know that Jesus must have looked over at Philip, given him a quick glance. And Philip the skeptic sat there, likely as not, with his mouth wide open, amazed at what he was witnessing.

123

A. E. Houseman once wrote a poem about a boy whose ability to run was the pride of his hometown. One day the young athlete died unexpectedly. The poet said the boy was fortunate to die young. If he hadn't, he undoubtedly would have lived longer than his name, long enough to realize that people had forgotten him as their hero and had picked up someone else instead.

NO FLASH IN THE PAN

The artist Andy Warhol once said that in the future everyone will be famous for five minutes. That's an odd thing to say, but when you think about it, you can see he's already been right about lots of people. Just in the last few years, how many beautiful Hollywood sweethearts on how many sexy posters have suddenly disappeared completely from the TV screens that made them rich and famous overnight? How many great running backs have just slipped between the cracks not long after their pictures have smiled from the cover of *Sports Illustrated*? Popularity is a fickle thing. It comes and goes. Think how hard it must be to live in the shadows if you love the bright lights.

In today's reading, Jesus is concerned about being little more than a flash in the pan. That's why he sends the disciples out across the lake and dismisses the huge crowd they have just fed. Free food always creates an instant crowd, but Christ doesn't want to be a media star. He doesn't want his name in flashing lights. He wants souls burning with faith. He wants hearts, not headlines.

That's a lesson Peter will have to learn on his own. Even though he is tired after rowing fiercely for several hours and getting nowhere, Peter—always the excited type—sees Christ and begs to perform miracles himself.

Prayer:

Lord, it's easy to believe in you when everybody else around us does too. Give us faith to follow you even when it's not the popular thing to do, even when we are afraid. In Jesus' name, Amen.

For a moment he does—he walks on water. But then, losing faith, he sinks.

It will take more than swelling excitement to follow Christ; even for Peter the rock it will take more. It will take a lifetime of faith firmly grounded in obedience to the Savior.

124

CHURCH SCHOOL

Read Luke 9:18–22

Let's be honest, church school isn't the most terrific hour in any kid's week. It's a chore to answer the teacher's questions and to have to hear about things you already know. A good ball game is lots more exciting; just talking with friends is much more fun.

In today's passage, the crowds are gone from view. Things are quiet. After all the excitement of thousands of people and the thrills of incredible miracles, things have settled down. So Christ turns to his disciples and has a little church school class. "Who do the people say I am?" he asks.

The disciples list some old heroes of faith, including John the Baptist. It's not a bad list for Christ to be included in, but it's not really the answer he's looking for.

"Okay," he says, "who do *you* say I am?"

It's Peter who replies. "The Christ of God," he says. To Peter, Christ's question has only one correct answer. Jesus is in a class by himself, and Peter's answer is the greatest confession of faith he can make. To the Jews, *Christ* means "the anointed one," the Messiah appointed to a very special office by none other than God himself, the one specially born to restore a lost people to their heavenly Father.

To the Jews, the Messiah is unique, the greatest person ever— greater by far than any hero who had lived or would live.

If you've ever been to Mount Rushmore, you'll probably never forget it. You can't help but be impressed by the sheer size of what that sculptor, Gutzon Borglum, accomplished. From miles away you can see the four sixty-foot-high faces standing alone above the hills and looking into the sun.

George Washington is there because most Americans call him "the Father of the Country." Thomas Jefferson, the man who wrote the country's Constitution, is next to him. Then comes Theodore Roosevelt, the president who brought the US into world affairs at the beginning of this century; and finally, Abraham Lincoln, the man who guided the country through Civil War in a quest for real equality for all citizens. If you're a US citizen, it's almost impossible not to be affected by standing there at the foot of that mountain. These men are certainly real heroes.

But take the greatest politicians; throw in a few famous athletes—Babe Ruth, Bobby Orr, Chris Evert Lloyd, and Jesse Owens; add some real intellectual power like Sigmund Freud or Albert Einstein; then, for spiritual leadership, toss in maybe Billy Graham, Mother Teresa, and Martin Luther King, Jr. Mix up the whole group, all the heroes you can muster from ancient civilizations to the present, and you still come nowhere near to Jesus, the Christ of God.

There are lots of heroes, but only one Savior. That's what Peter confessed to his Master on that quiet afternoon.

Prayer:

Dear Lord, help us to say with our mouths and with our lives that you are the Christ, the Son of God, our Savior from sin. In his name, Amen.

125

JESSE'S ESCAPE (11)

Prayer:

Dear Lord, we know that it takes a great price to be a real believer. Following your word is not always fun or easy. Give us the strength to follow you. Make us strong and willing disciples. In Jesus' name, Amen.

Read Luke 9:57–62

Jesse figured the judge would be an old man in a robe, sitting behind a huge desk way up front in a high-ceilinged chamber. But the hearing room was small. There were just enough chairs for Jesse, his father, some guy from the church where he broke the window, and the janitor couple, Fred and Deb. The judge was young, heavyset like a football player.

Jesse's father sat next to him with his legs crossed, as if the whole story was like a burden they simply had to bear.

"We found him in the church that morning, sleeping there as if he owned the place," Fred told the judge. He used his hands a lot when he talked. "I tried to be gentle with him, but the boy wouldn't respond. It was like he was mad or something, judge."

Jesse looked at his father, but his father stared at the floor.

"When we tried to get him out of there, he grabbed my broom, see—like this—" Fred got to his feet and put both fists together as if he were holding a baseball bat. "The kid was plum crazy, I'm telling you—" Fred stood there with his hands up in front of him, as if he were wielding a weapon. "First he swings it at us, see?—and then he sees the window over there and flings it—just flings it—right through the window."

"That's not true," Jesse said, but his father grabbed his arm. "That's a lie—"

"You just control yourself, son," the judge said, pointing.

"But it's not true—"

"Be quiet, Jesse," his father said.

"You didn't threaten him, didn't provoke him, Mr. Bedlow?"

Fred sat down slowly. "We were innocent. We just came in to clean up the church, and this kid was there threatening us with this broom."

"He's lying—"

"What we have here is your word against Mr. Bedlow's, Jesse. I've got two different stories, and I've got to determine which is closer to the truth." The judge leaned back in the chair and patted the armrests. "Maybe someone else would like to say something?" He waited.

"I would like to say something, judge," Deb said. Her voice squeaked out nervously. "I—I love my husband, your honor, but I got to tell the truth here, and it's not the way he says it was." She dropped her head quickly, raised her handkerchief to her eyes. "He's a good man, but it's not the way he says it was."

Fred sat watching her at the edge of his chair.

"I love my husband, but God wants truth. The boy's right. Fred wouldn't talk to him—wouldn't hear him. It was my own Fred that threatened with that broom. What happened after that was an accident. I'm sure of it."

She stopped right there and looked at her husband, nodding. Fred's eyes burned with anger, but she took his hands in hers.

Jesse never guessed she would have done what she did. He couldn't believe someone would do that because of God wanting the truth.

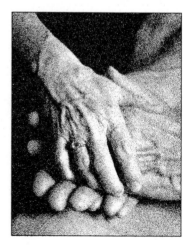

126

TRANSFIG-URATION

Prayer:

Lord God, your glory is greater than anything we can imagine! All praise to your holy name. Amen.

Read Mark 9:2–13

"There were twelve disciples Jesus called to help him: Simon Peter, Andrew, James, his brother, John . . ."

We used to sing that song over and over again when I was a boy. One reason, I suppose, was to help us remember the names of the disciples. They're all there in the song.

By singing about them so much, my classmates and I came to really respect the twelve disciples. "The disciples"—even the phrase sounds like some kind of religious Hall of Fame. And these *were* important men. It was their special privilege to be right there beside Christ during his ministry.

But it's important to remember that in spite of their special role in Christ's ministry, the disciples were real flesh-and-blood men. If you read the Bible closely, you'll see that even the disciples didn't always know what was going on with this unique man they followed.

Imagine what Peter, James, and John thought of this transfiguration. Specially chosen by Jesus to accompany him, they were present at the most spectacular scene they had ever witnessed. First, Christ appeared to light up. Then, there at his side, stood two old heroes of faith, Moses and Elijah.

Peter, never at a loss for words, thought he had to say something—that's what Mark tells us in verse 6. So he suggested putting up three tents, thinking Elijah and Moses were going to be around for a while, like out-of-town company. Peter didn't really have a clue as to what was happening right before his own shining eyes.

What did he see? An amazing event—that's for sure. An event that was more than a dream or a vision. But what did it all mean? Here's what we believe. We all know that Christ's stay on earth meant a great deal of suffering. Remember how the herdsmen at Gerasenes told him to leave when their pigs went over the cliff? That was just for openers. Coming to earth meant death in our place. It was a terrible role Jesus had to accept.

In his book *Promise and Deliverance*, S. G. DeGraaf says that Jesus went up the mountain to pray for strength to remain obedient to God, to accept the suffering that was coming closer. DeGraaf says Christ's prayer was so intense that he became one with the Father and could see the end of his suffering and his coming to glory. Intense prayer made Christ shine with the Father's own light and glory. Because Christ was in perfect harmony with his Father, he was transfigured, filled for the moment with his Father's brilliance.

But at the moment of the transfiguration, his face shining with the glory of God, Jesus also accepted what still remained to be done. He knew that he still had to suffer and die. That's why Peter's idea of three tents was silly. The time for such glory hadn't come.

Peter and the others didn't quite understand—not yet anyway.

127

CONCERN FOR NEIGHBORS

Prayer:

Fill us with your Spirit, Lord, so that helping others becomes second nature to us. Amen.

Read Luke 10:25–37 and Matthew 25:34–40

The parable of the good Samaritan is a favorite because the good guy is so very good. Show me someone who doesn't appreciate this sweet Samaritan, and I'll show you someone who hates dogs and kids.

But the parable preaches a lesson that goes down hard, especially for those of us who consider ourselves Christians. Take a good look at the two characters who let the beaten man lie there: one was a priest, the other an expert in religious law. In other words, both were really big-time religious figures.

Who stopped? Neither of them. Why not? Maybe it was because they were on their way to a Jewish religious ceremony. If so, they needed to be in their Sabbath-best. They both may have assumed the beaten man was dead; they knew that if they touched the body, they would become unclean and would have to go through some extra synagogue purifica-tion. To the priest and the Levite, the ceremony was much more important than tending to the needs of this down-and-outer lying limp alongside the road.

But the Samaritan stopped. He had nothing to gain by helping the poor man. In fact, if the victim was a Jew, the Samaritan had reason to hate him; after all, the Samaritans and the Jews were hardly kissing cousins. But he stopped anyway—even though it cost him something.

What a lovely man this Samaritan was. What scoundrels those hypocrite religious folks were.

See who was wearing the white hat?

But here's the stinger. Who are we? If we had to line ourselves up with either the Samaritan or the Levite and the priest, where would we stand?

Let's put it another way. In Matthew 25, Christ explains how he'll separate the saints from the sinners. "You people go on my right hand," he'll say. "You've helped me, dressed me, and given me food."

But listen to the righteous: "When? We don't remember."

In my opinion that's one of the scariest lines in the Bible. You see, the righteous people are not those who are trying to "do good" by feeding the hungry or helping the poor. The righteous people aren't even thinking of serving Christ when they lend a helping hand. For them, helping comes naturally.

When the Samaritan helped the beaten man, he wasn't thinking about what his friends would think or how, after all, "we really *should* do good once in a while." He saw only that there was need, and without a thought, he helped. He didn't even do it with the idea of pleasing God. He just saw a man who needed help— that's all. It was like instinct.

The scary part of the parable of the good Samaritan is that helping others just came naturally to him—and it should to us too.

We all can be Samaritans, but only with the Holy Spirit directing our lives. Christ's Spirit helps us help, naturally.

128

TOUGH CHOICES

Read Luke 10:38–42

Mark loved basketball and he hated English class. He figured his English teacher was as old as Count Dracula, and he really didn't care about anything she had to say. So he sat in the back with his buddies and whispered about the next basketball game.

One day the teacher got tired of it. "Mark," she said sharply, "you get up here and sit in the front."

Mark looked around, picked up his books, and shuffled up toward the front, really angry. In fact, he bounced his books on the desk she was pointing at, just to show her.

The teacher went back to a poem by William Shakespeare.

"Shall I compare thee to a summer's day?

Thou art more lovely and more temperate:

Rough winds do shake the darling buds of May,

And summer's lease hath all too short a date:"

(Something dumb about love, Mark thought—yecch!)

"Sometimes too hot the eye of heaven shines—"

Then she stopped. "Class," she said, "what does Shakespeare mean by the 'eye of heaven'?"

Now Mark was no dummy. Just because he didn't like poetry didn't mean he couldn't understand such a simple question—the eye of heaven meant the sun, of course. Then it struck him: if he were to answer every one of the teacher's questions, the guys in the back would go crazy. "Can you believe Mark?" they'd say. "What a great show he put on in English!"

So he answered her question—and the next—and the next—and the next—until the teacher deliberately ignored his waving hand.

But something happened. The more he got into the poem, the more he kind of liked it—

especially the last two lines:

"So long as men can breathe or eyes can see,

So long lives this and this gives life to thee."

Mark realized that Shakespeare was telling his readers that his love for this woman would live on forever in the lines of his poetry. Here they were, hundreds of years later, still reading about that woman. Crazy Shakespeare was right!

The next day Mark faced a choice. He could either sit in the back with the rest of the guys and clown around or he could plunk himself down in front and get into Shakespeare's poems. That was the choice.

He stood at the back of the classroom and waited—but only for a second. Then he sat in the back with the guys.

His choice indicated that at this point in his life his friends and basketball meant more to him than poetry. Sitting in the back showed it clearly.

Most of the time our choices demonstrate what we value most. It was true of Martha; that's why Jesus scolded her. And it was true of her sister, Mary. It was true of Mark too.

By the way, today Mark teaches poetry. Believe me—I know.

Prayer:

Lord, help us with the tough choices we have to make. May we always choose to listen to you. In Jesus' name,

Amen.

129

THE PRIVACY OF YOUR OWN MIND

Prayer:

Keep our inner voices clean and strong and ungreedy, Father. Speak to us clearly through your word and Spirit. Amen.

Read Luke 12:13–21

Every one of us has more than one voice. We each have a public voice—the voice other people hear. But we also have a private voice—a voice we alone can hear, a voice that speaks inside our minds.

Michelle and Rachel represented their school in the annual math contest. Michelle put in lots of hours studying for the contest. Rachel barely glanced at the book. But when the contest results were announced, Rachel had beaten Michelle by five points.

"That's not fair!" Michelle's inner voice said. But that's not what Rachel heard her say. All she heard was, "Congratulations, Rachel. You did just great."

Or take the case of Bryan, whose father was complaining about the mess in Bryan's room. "I want you to pick up all the junk off the floor. Then vacuum the whole room, including under your bed," Bryan's father instructed. Bryan could see that his dad was really quite upset.

"It's *my* room. What do you care how dirty it is? It's clean enough for me," said Bryan's quiet voice.

Fortunately for Bryan, all his dad heard was a somewhat reluctant, "All right, I'll clean it up."

Part of growing up is learning to control the bad things that private voice sometimes wants to say. Of course, most of us can never *completely* shut up that inner voice—not in this world anyway. And that's probably a good thing. That private voice isn't all bad. Sometimes it warns us against doing things that are really wrong. We call that warning voice our "conscience."

The rich man in Jesus' parable had a private voice too. But it was a dumb private voice that gave him bad advice. We can listen in on that voice in the parable as the rich man carries on a private conversation with himself.

It seems the rich man had had an even bigger harvest than usual. So he thought to himself, "What shall I do? I have no place to store my crops." Nothing bad about that really. He was just planning ahead. But then the private voice told him to tear down his old barns and build bigger ones.

"Go on, do it," the private voice urged. "Then you'll be able to say to yourself, 'You've got plenty of good things laid up for many years. Take life easy; eat, drink, and be merry.' "

We used to sing a song called "You Cannot Hide from God." This parable makes me think of that song. Of course, Jesus didn't say whether the rich man was trying to hide his private thoughts from God. But we get that impression. And we know that if he tried, he didn't succeed. God hears our inner voice loud and clear.

In Christ's parable, God spoke to the rich man, right in the privacy of his own mind. "You're a fool!" God said. Imagine how shocked we would be if God spoke to us right in the middle of our own private thoughts.

God's message wasn't pleasant. "This very night your life will be demanded from you," he told the rich man. "Then who will get what you have prepared for yourself?"

The parable was Christ's response to a command: "Please tell my brother to give me what is mine!" Perhaps the man had a legitimate complaint. Maybe his brother really owed him money.

But Christ's parable was aimed straight for the man's inner voice. "Be careful you aren't worshiping the almighty dollar," Jesus told him through the parable. "Be on your guard against all kinds of greed."

When our inner voice whispers greedy thoughts to us, let's remember the rich fool.

130

SUNDAY RULES

Read Luke 13:10–17

What's right and what's wrong to do on Sunday? Maybe one of your friends—someone who goes to your church or to a church like yours—is allowed to do all kinds of things on Sunday. She can watch her favorite sport on TV, go out to eat at McDonald's, or even cut the grass.

Maybe at your house you're not allowed to do any of those things on Sunday afternoon. Or maybe *you're* the one who has all the freedom, and your friend doesn't.

Sunday rules are not a new invention. They've been around almost as long as the day itself has. Some early Americans observed what came to be known as "blue laws," named after the blue paper on which a Connecticut man published his version of Sunday rules. In addition to outlawing amusements like "dancing, playing cards, tennis, or cricket," these blue laws also prohibited more general Sunday activities like "excessive playing, shouting, and screaming of children in the streets and highways."

One historian tells of a man who was almost arrested in Connecticut for traveling on Sunday. He was released only after he explained that he had been delayed the day before and was traveling on Sunday so that he could attend his own church in New York. The man? George Washington.

Many of the blue laws prohibited any kind of work on Sunday. For example, one law said, "No one shall travel, cook victuals, make beds, sweep house, cut hair, or shave on the Sabbath day."

While laws during the past half century have not been as strict as those early blue laws, the Sunday rules of forty to fifty years ago would certainly sound restricting to many of us today. Ask your parents about the Sunday rules they were asked to obey when they were younger. You might be surprised at how much things have changed.

What's the point? Jesus made two of them in today's Bible story. First, he showed us that trying to live by an elaborate set of Sunday rules can get you into a real bind—sometimes even a silly bind. But Jesus didn't find the Sabbath laws of the Jewish religious leaders very funny. "You phonies," he told them sternly when they criticized him for healing the crippled woman on the Sabbath. "You work on Sunday yourselves. Don't you free your cattle on the Sabbath and lead them out for a drink of water? Why is it wrong for me to free this woman from her sickness?"

But in warning the Jews not to get themselves wound up tight in Sunday laws and regulations, Jesus was not saying that the Lord's Day should be just another day in the work week. It should be a special, very different day. For Christ, resting from work meant healing, teaching in the temple, doing the work of his heavenly Father—special work for a special day.

Let's face it—some Sunday rules are good and necessary. Else Sunday would soon become just another work day or play day. Your parents generally have good reasons for their Sunday rules. Respect them.

But don't let Sundays become "rule days." Make them special "Lord's Days" by worshiping with God's people in church, by learning more about God, by resting from the things you do all week, and by finding ways to serve God by doing good to people around you.

131

SELF-RIGH-TEOUSNESS

Prayer:

Forgive us, Lord,

for thinking too

much of

ourselves. We

are sinners who

need your

forgiveness.

Thank you for

your forgiving

love. In Jesus'

name,

Amen.

Read Luke 15:11–32

In this famous parable the son who runs away usually gets all the attention—not the brother who works hard for his father. It's understandable. The prodigal son's story is much more interesting. He goes away, spends all his money, runs around with some really seedy people, then ends up slopping hogs. That's where he bottoms out. When he comes home, his father welcomes him with the biggest party the ranch has ever seen. For him life turns around.

By contrast, his brother seems boring. No one would make a movie about the guy—he never does a thing but work on his father's farm. Where's the excitement?

When you look at what surrounds the parable in Luke, you can see Jesus talking again to the Jewish religious leaders—none of whom, very likely, ever went through anything like the prodigal son went through. Christ is talking to people whose lives resemble that of the at-home brother. They are the even-keeled, straight and smooth, obedient, respectful citizens.

It's not hard to feel a little sorry for this home-boy. Every day he slaves away for his father, and what does he get?—nothing. He never gets a ring or a big bash with the plumpest calf as the main course. Poor guy.

And yet, Christ makes him the bad guy. One son is really lost in the story—but it's not the one who's eaten pig meal. Nope. "It's not fair," the good boy says when he hears about his father's big celebration. He's jealous, of course, and a little self-righteous.

It *is* easy to hate self-righteous folks. Everyone does it. I used to work at a state park near my hometown, a village where most of the people were known in the rest of the county for being very

religious, very pious. In the state park, only one or two of us were from that village. The others used to poke fun of the place. When kids from that town would come camping, the others would make special note of it, then watch those kids closely, hoping to catch them doing something wrong. They thought it was great fun to catch a guy from the super-holy town with his hand around a cold bottle of beer.

It's not hard to hate self-righteous people. But were the people from my hometown really self-righteous? Or were they the victims of discrimination based upon their religion? Was their righteousness real, or was it self-righteousness?

Probably a little of both.

But the home-boy in the parable is definitely guilty of self-righteousness. "I never did a thing wrong," he tells his father. Bingo! You really can't trust anyone who claims he's never sinned. The home-boy deserves what he gets. He's self-righteous—there's no doubt about it.

Now here's an interesting twist. If he confesses (like his brother did), he can have his own big feast. What he has to learn and admit (like his brother) is that he too needs forgiveness.

Right now he doesn't believe that. He'd better.

132

BELIEVE IT OR NOT

Prayer:

Dear Lord, keep our faith strong. You've given us yourself and your Word and your Spirit. We have no excuse for not believing. Help us, always, to believe in you. In Jesus' name, Amen.

Read Luke 16:19–31

The rich man makes two requests of Abraham in this parable. First he asks for a touch of cool water. Abraham says no. So the rich man tries again. "I beg you," he says, "to send Lazarus to my father's house to tell them what things are really like here." That's considerate of him. Since he has now experienced the pain of hell, he asks that someone go back and warn the others.

Tons of writers have written the story of what might have taken place if Abraham had sent Lazarus back to earth from heaven. The idea of someone from heaven or hell returning to earth to warn loved ones makes an interesting plot—probably because the world is full of people who really don't know whether they believe in a heaven or a hell.

Christ himself tells us how the story must end. But the variations writers have added to the story have been as numerous as the writers themselves. Let's try our own version.

We'll call the main character Angela. Angela is killed in a car accident. After a few months or years she's permitted to return to earth for a day and chooses to visit her mother. Angela's mother is surprised—to say the least.

She's missed her daughter, of course. But she can't forget Angela's strange behavior during those last months before the accident. She can't forget how Angela ran off and became a Christian, just about ruining her mother's social standing. Such a daughter!

After the initial shock, Angela's mother decides her daughter isn't really dead. Someone other than Angela must be buried in that grave. "Must be a mix-up," she says to herself.

But Angela is persistent. "I've come from heaven to tell you what really comes after death,"

she says.

Her mother's eyes roll. "She's spouting the same old stuff as before—this must be some kind of joke."

"I know the truth, Mother," Angela says. "You must listen to me."

Her mother leaves the room and calls her psychiatrist. She's convinced her eyes and ears are playing tricks on her. She doesn't believe . . .

Like I said earlier, that story has been written countless times, with many different endings and variations. But according to Christ's parable, only one ending is possible.

This dreamed-up story has to end in rejection. You see, believing that Angela has returned from the dead demands faith, doesn't it? Even though Angela stands right there before her, her mother needs to *believe* that the body belongs to her daughter—that her daughter and the things she is talking about exist.

The rich man thinks that were Lazarus to return, his brothers would believe. Abraham says no. They already don't believe Moses and the prophets. Why should they believe someone who claims to have returned from heaven? They've already got all they need for faith. But they've rejected it.

133

LORD OF LIFE AND DEATH

Read John 11:17–44

The Lazarus story straps us in and takes our emotions on a rollercoaster ride. Right away, we discover that a big crowd of folks has come out to Bethany to comfort Mary and Martha. Sadness—motionless as a heavy fog—sits in the air at Bethany.

Martha hurries out to greet Jesus. Her words hold just a faint touch of blame. "If only you had been here," she says. Martha pours out her heart, and her confession really illustrates her faith: "If *you* had been here, we wouldn't be mourning," she says. She has complete confidence that Jesus could have kept her brother alive—if he had been there. But he wasn't.

That same accusation is repeated twice after Martha first says it. Mary says it in verse 32, and even the crowd voices that idea (v. 37). It's an odd thing to say—deep faith couched in backhand blame. It's like saying, "We know things would have been different if you were here—so where were you?"

What does Christ feel? The Bible tells us in two words. Standing there with mourners surrounding him, *Jesus wept*. Very few gospel passages show us a Jesus who is quite so human.

When I was a kid, I learned that verse—"Jesus wept"— as the shortest verse in the Bible. I now know that it's also one of the biggest verses, because it shows us clearly that Jesus the Christ of God was also Jesus the son of Joseph and Mary—Jesus the man.

But, you might be saying, doesn't Jesus know he can raise Lazarus?

Of course he does.

Then why does he cry for a man who is dead?

Because he is human. Because on this occasion, with all the mourners surrounding him, Jesus' own human emotions are going down and up.

"I am the resurrection and the life. He who believes in me will live, even though he dies," Jesus told Martha earlier (v. 25). That's quite a commitment. Most folks who have followed him have seen him turn a light meal into a well-catered feast for five thousand people. But none of them understands this life from death business.

But Christ delivers. He asks to be brought to the tomb itself. There he stands, people mourning around him, his own eyes still full of tears. Christ carries through on his promises. His word is better than gold. He's no hypocrite.

The word *hypocrite* comes from the Greek word for actor: *hupokrites*. Now an actor is fine, as long as he stays on a stage. Off-stage, an actor is a liar, a hypocrite—someone who says one thing and does another. But Jesus is no hypocrite. His deeds are true to his words.

So he stands there at Lazarus' tomb and calls the dead man. And Lazarus stumbles out, still wrapped up tight in burial rags.

The crowd is stunned into silence. Lazarus walks once again before them. Christ, the teacher, the son of a carpenter, is Lord of life and death. "I am the resurrection," he tells them.

And all of them know it. So do we.

134

BIG FAITH FROM LITTLE PEOPLE

Read Mark 10:13–16

My friend gave me an envelope recently, something he had received from a very famous TV evangelist. Inside were a letter and a little plastic pouch full of some yellow stuff that looked like oil.

The letter explained what to do with the special oil. It said that the person who received the oil should first of all write up a DECREE LIST, a kind of prayer list that included all of the needs—"spiritual, physical, financial, and other"—that that person had. The evangelist even included a special form to make it easy.

Then the well-known evangelist wrote this: "Take the anointing oil and anoint your DECREE LIST after you have written your needs on it. Put a drop of oil on it and pray in Jesus' name." No sweat, I thought, chuckling to myself.

Of course, that wasn't all the advice. "When you send your DECREE LIST with your earnest needs written on it [back to the well-known evangelist], sow your largest bill or check in this ministry just as God sowed his 'best seed' in John 3:16 and Malachi 3:10, 11." There's the catch.

Really cute, I thought. Nobody can send out a couple hundred thousand pouches of vegetable oil for free, after all. It's a scam, of course. I figured that this was the way Mr. Evangelist paid for his five-hundred-dollar suits.

Stupid, plain stupid. This friend of mine gave me the letter because he wanted me to see how stupid the whole business was.

My eight-year-old daughter saw me with the pouch of oil. "What's that?" she asked.

I smirked. "You're supposed to put this silly oil on a piece of paper with a list of everything you want and then just send it in to a preacher," I told her. "Just like that—poof!—you'll get everything you ever wanted. Yuk, yuk, yuk."

"Try it," she said, without even smiling.

I rolled my eyes.

"Try it," she said again. "Go ahead and try it."

My daughter's faith is exactly the kind of faith that Christ talks about in today's passage: simple, honest, believing trust. Her father's too smart for such faith. All my years of experience have taught me to be skeptical of such foolishness.

And it's right that we should be. God gives us minds to think, doesn't he? The oil is really silly, isn't it?—well, *isn't* it?

Of course it is. We don't need any well-known TV preacher to focus our prayers; we don't need our DECREE LISTS stamped with his approval. We don't need to splash oil on paper scribbled full of our greatest wishes.

But all of that doesn't change the fact that my daughter's trust is, in principle, right. Jesus himself claimed that such childlike, undoubting faith is absolutely essential.

Jesus fumed at the disciples. It's the plain and simple truth that nothing is more important than childlike faith.

If we don't believe him, we don't have it ourselves.

135

THE GOOD, THE BAD, AND THE CHOSEN

Read Mark 10:17–27

Prayer:

Father, we know that nothing we can ever do will earn us the right to have everlasting life. Thank you that salvation is a gift from you to all who have faith. In Jesus' name, Amen.

Most kids today don't know much about the wild west. A few years ago, kids were brought up on a diet of television Westerns that went down as easily as popcorn and pop. Those kids knew that bad guys wore black hats and dirty handkerchiefs big as pillowcases around their necks. They rode scroungy-looking, dirt-brown horses with no names. And when they laughed, they always sounded dangerous. Most important of all, bad guys were ugly.

The good guys wore white hats and brightly colored shirts so clean you'd guess they were washed during the Tide commercials. Good guys rode only pretty horses—golden palominos, huge white stallions, or beautiful pintos—that always had names and never seemed to care if their masters jumped on them unexpectedly from second-story windows. The good guys were handsome—and they could sing.

All of that was phony, of course, but it made good television. Halfway through the first minute of the show, you knew who to cheer for.

In real life, of course, it's not so easy to tell the good guys from the bad guys.

Take the rich young ruler, for instance. Handsome? Probably. Well-dressed? You bet. Religious? Absolutely.

The first thing he did when he met Christ was get down on his knees. Now that's not the act of a hypocrite. It's the act of someone who wants to do right. This was a good man, a guy with a white hat.

"What must I do to inherit eternal life?" he asked. He honestly wanted to know.

The Bible says Jesus looked at him and loved him—then put him to the acid test. "Go, sell everything you have and give to the poor, and you will have treasure in heaven. Then come, follow me."

Immediately, the Bible says, his face fell, and he went away sad, because he had great wealth. There went a good guy.

It's easy to think that the disciples understood everything—after all, they were the disciples. But when Christ explained how hard it is for a rich man to enter the kingdom of God, the disciples were shocked. And then Jesus let them have it with a famous comparison: "It is easier for a camel to go through a needle's eye than for a rich man to enter the kingdom of God." That's tough all right.

There's another lesson in this little story, and it has to do with white and black hats on good and bad men and women. The rich man figured he could earn salvation. He had, after all, followed *all* the commandments since he was a kid. But Jesus told him he couldn't earn a dime by doing good.

Salvation comes only by grace. No one earns it, because God gives it. You don't know many camels that could slip through a needle's eye? Neither do I. Humanly speaking it's impossible.

But with God all things are possible. He chooses who gets in—black hats and white hats, handsome and ugly. With God's help camels slip through needles' eyes without any problem.

136

JESSE'S ESCAPE (12)

Prayer:

Dear Lord, when we aspire to great things in this world, help us to keep in mind that everything we do happens through your help and for your praise.

Amen.

Read Mark 10:35–45

At the edge of the pool, the sun's warmth laid a quilt over his body. They had quit driving early; his father said he was tired. They stopped at a motel with a pool.

It had been icy between them ever since the trial. They never looked straight at each other. Jesse sprawled out on a chaise lounge at the side of the pool, while his father sat beneath a sun canopy, reading a paper.

The pool was full of kids, jumping in and out, getting rid of all the energy they had stored up traveling. Jesse wondered what it would be like to feel good about things again, to have nothing more to worry about than what kind of motel they'd be stopping at for the night.

A heavyset kid jumped in quickly, holding his nose, and came up thrashing, like it was the happiest day of his life. Nobody saw him. His friends were already in, swimming beneath the water.

But the heavy kid started yelling, his arms beating away at the water. Jesse sat up on his chair, then stood.

The kid was going down. No one seemed to notice. So Jesse dove in and swam underwater, eyes open, watching the kid's body doubling up, slowly losing strength. He grabbed the kid by the hair and pulled him to the surface, but the kid fought, his arms and legs flailing.

Jesse kicked hard in the water, trying to stay on top, but the kid was heavy, his arms waving madly. "Help me," Jesse yelled. And suddenly his father was there to help pull the kid from the pool.

It really was no big thing. The kid had merely stepped off the deep end and been surprised when he didn't touch bottom. In a minute he was fine—just scared.

Jesse's father walked away quickly, passed the chair, and left the paper behind, not looking back. The boy's mother stood thanking Jesse, her arms around her son. But Jesse was worried about his father.

He found him crying, sitting on the bed, his shirt and pants soaked from lifting the boy from the water.

"It wasn't that close," Jesse said. "I don't get it."

His father kept his head in his hands. "I'm sorry," he said. "Jesse, I am really sorry."

"What is it?" Jesse said. He stood there dripping on the rug.

"I didn't believe you. I didn't believe my own son back there in court," his father said. "Don't you see? I was sure that guy was telling the truth."

"I know that," Jesse said. "I know that already."

He had never seen his father that way before, actually crying because he felt really sad about something big—sad about himself, not his son.

"Will you forgive me?" he said. "I mean it."

Jesse stood there next to his father. "I understand, Dad," he said. "I wouldn't have believed myself. I'm the one who needs forgiveness."

The happy yells from the pool came through the open door behind them.

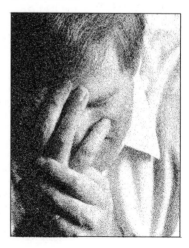

137

UGLY PEOPLE

Read Luke 19:1–10

During the German occupation of the Netherlands (World War II), Dutch people who played along with the hated Nazis were called NSBayers (short for National Socialists—their political party). To say the faithful Dutch people hated the NSBayers would be like saying that sometimes Hitler was slightly naughty. When the Nazis took over the Netherlands, all government officials from the top down were replaced by NSBayers, people who would dance a jig to the jingle of the Nazis' money.

A lady once told me how just before the end of the war a wagon full of NSBayers, on the run from the advancing Canadian army, stopped at their farmhouse in Holland and demanded bacon and eggs. "They sat at our table with their guns beside them! Oh boy—big brave men with guns!" she said. Just the thought of them filled her with disgust—as if all of it had just happened.

Her brother came in and found them there. "Well, now your days are numbered, aren't they?" he said, knowing the Nazis were on the run. Her brother, she said, was cocky.

One of the NSBayers stood immediately. "What's your name and your identity?" he demanded. Her brother took off running.

But during supper, he goofed around with the fugitives' wagon—pulled a few pins here and there so the thing couldn't move too far. Later, the family heard how an ugly bunch of NSBayers were stalled somewhere down the road with a bad wheel.

"Aha! It worked," she remembered the family saying, laughing together. She described the NSBayers this way: "They were scum. They were the ugliest people I have ever met—honestly."

NSBayers may have been the ugliest people in Holland; they were certainly the most unloved jackals around—at least to loyal Dutch citizens. To say they were hated is putting it mildly.

So why all the Dutch history? If you can get a sense of how hated the NSBayers were, maybe you can sense how much the Jews hated that little scummy Zacchaeus. Although his name identified him as a Jew, he was an employee of the Romans, the enemy—a real NSBayer in his time. As a tax collector, he was undoubtedly a dirty politician, a man who squeezed others for every penny he could get, thinking only of good old Number One.

On top of that, he probably was filthy rich. Zacchaeus made big money profiteering on the people he should have loved. It's hard to think of a guy who more soundly deserved hating than this little wealthy wretch, Zacchaeus. He made people want to spit.

That's why Jesus talked to him. And that's the whole story. Jesus spoke to even the ugliest people—particularly the ugliest. That's Jesus for you—and me. Incredible.

138

GET IT?

Read Luke 20:9–19

You can file this story under "Most Embarrassing Moments in My Life." But first, a lousy joke.

What's green and orange and swims in stewed tomatoes?

Come on, take a guess. No? Give up?

Here's the answer: *The New York Times*.

Dumb, you say? Oh, really? Do you get it?

NO? Neither do I. I get *The Chicago Tribune*.

Now the embarrassing part. When that joke was told to me long ago, I didn't want to appear stupid, so I laughed when the guy said, "Do you get it?" "Ha-ha, ha-ha," I said. "Sure, that's great! What a joke!" I was lying, of course—I didn't get it at all. It wasn't even funny without the *Chicago Trib* line. In trying to sound smart, I came off looking like a real dumdum.

Jesus didn't tell jokes often—at least we don't know of many. But he did tell strange little stories called parables. And quite often the same kind of question could have been asked of his listeners: Did you get it?

Sometimes, apparently, they did; sometimes they didn't. Here are a few examples. After telling the crowd the parable of the sower (Mark 4), Jesus simply said, "He who has ears to hear, let him hear." It's a strange statement. It's something like saying, "If you understand—good, if you don't—tough bananas."

Not even the disciples "got" some of the parables. Mark says that often when Christ spoke in parables he would help the disciples "get them" later on, in private. "When he was alone . . . he explained everything" (v. 34).

Once some of the disciples asked Jesus why he kept telling these strange stories even though people didn't always "get them."

He explained why by quoting Isaiah 6:15. "This people's heart has become calloused," he said. Even though they had ears, they wouldn't hear.

Not all of Jesus' stories were difficult to interpret. Some of them went straight to the heart of things. Those were the stories that everybody "got"—really disturbing stories that made his enemies boil. Today's passage is one of those stories. It's apparent that no one in the crowd had any difficulty "getting" this parable. Look at verse 16: "When the people heard this, they said, 'May this never be.' " The people knew immediately that Jesus wasn't talking about some never-never land; they knew he was talking directly to them in the here-and-now. The story was like a finger pushing into their chests.

Look again at verse 19: "The teachers of the law and the chief priests looked for a way to arrest him immediately, because they knew he had spoken this parable against them."

What did he tell them in the vineyard parable? Simply this—that the chief priests and teachers of the law, people who considered themselves keepers of God's vineyard (his people), were plotting to kill this "capstone" (this son of the owner of the vineyard). And that if they did, they too would die. This parable spelled it all out boldly—the plain and simple truth.

Get it? I'll tell you one thing—the ruling Jews sure did.

Prayer:

Father, thank you for sending your only Son. May we never, ever reject him, but always love him with all our hearts. In the Son's name, Amen.

173

139

LOVING

Jewish laws multiplied like rabbits. I may be exaggerating, but my guess is that Sabbath laws alone would go a long way toward filling a book the size of a Sears catalogue. Specific Sabbath laws forbade touching the pits of dates, carrying a large loaf of bread, and walking more than six miles. Solid logic stood behind those laws, I suppose, but it certainly escapes us today. In fact, it probably escaped most of the Jews of Jesus' day too.

Perhaps that's why the young lawyer asked his question— because the laws bewildered him. "Given the fact that we have ninety zillion laws," he might have said, "which is the greatest?"

Christ didn't hesitate for a minute. "Love—," he said. "Love God above all and your neighbor as yourself." That's the biggie. Everything else is a footnote. What good does it do to go to church eleven times on a Sunday if you hate your neighbor? What meaning do thirty-seven prayers a day have if you can't stomach some kids who go to your school? Love, Christ says.

Only four people in the world know this story. When I first heard it, I was told not to write about it. But that was years ago. Today no one will recognize the people involved anyway. So here goes.

Phyllis has three kids, ages four and two and six months. When some people talk about the glories of motherhood, they aren't speaking about two kids in diapers and a third who still has trouble getting to the bathroom on time. Things are hectic in Phyllis's life. Sometimes—since the only people she speaks to are preschoolers—she feels like she's going back to childhood herself. At the end of the day she asks herself what she accomplished. "I did six loads of wash," she says. And after that, she's hard pressed

to come up with anything she thinks significant. It's not easy being the mother of three little kids.

What's more, her husband, Brad, is out of work. He picks up some jobs on the side—painting barns and fixing people's old downspouts—but they make just enough money to keep bread on the table and clean clothes on their kids. They put themselves last, of course.

One Sunday at church a woman named Alma comes up to Phyllis and hands her a check for $100. "You need a new coat," she says. That's all. Then she walks away. Phyllis is absolutely stunned.

Sure, Alma's family has needs too. Her boy would like a two-wheeler. Her baby could use a new dress. Sure, $100 is a lot of money. But this one time, Alma sees a real need in a torn winter coat, and she meets it with love in a beautiful, perfectly-aimed gift.

There have been much bigger gifts, perhaps, but in my mind, it would be hard to find a greater one. Some might say the money should have gone to missionaries. Baloney. Alma's gift fulfills the great commandment like few gifts I know.

Until now, only four people ever knew—four people and God.

Prayer:

Make us good Samaritans, Lord. Help us to respond when you give us love. Make us great givers and worthy receivers. In Jesus' name, Amen.

140

THE GOOD SHEPHERD

Prayer:

Lord, we want you to be our good shepherd. Guide us and lead us. Take control of our lives and protect us from sin and evil. Thank you for loving us. In your name, Amen.

Read John 10:1–15

If I say that a kid named Teri is a real tiger, you all get the picture. Nobody jumps to any silly conclusions about Teri having stripes all over her body, walking on all fours, or snarling at everything that moves. What I mean is clear: Teri loves action and moves quickly, decisively. When I call Teri a tiger, I'm actually giving her a compliment.

The word *tiger*, when used to describe Teri, is called a *metaphor*, a word that originally meant "to carry beyond." Whenever we use metaphors ("Teri is a tiger"), we are carrying meaning beyond the word itself. Teri is more than a tiger.

Jesus himself used metaphors often—"I am the vine, you are the branches," for instance. Other times, he called himself "the light," "the gate," "the way." In today's passage he used a metaphor very familiar to those who listened to him—"the good shepherd." He didn't mean, of course, that he was employed as a shepherd. He carried meaning beyond the word. By calling himself a shepherd, he was telling his listeners that he guides and cares for his people.

Back then his listeners should have understood the metaphor because they were familiar with shepherds. But we've got a problem. Few of us, 2,000 years later, know much about sheep. But we should—in order to understand Jesus.

So jump in the time capsule for a minute. In Jesus' day shepherds drove their herds together at night into one big pen to guard them against wolves. One shepherd stayed with them. In the morning the other sherpherds returned. When Jesus told the people that his sheep knew his voice, he was referring to the morning practice of calling separate herds out of the huge herd circled up for protection at night. The good shepherd knows his sheep, and they know him. They've got a feel for his voice.

If you understand that, you understand more than the Jews did when Jesus first used this metaphor. John says they didn't get it.

Christ saw their confusion and kept on talking. Good shepherds, he said, are not like hired men who don't care about anything but their paychecks. Good shepherds put their lives on the line because they care about their sheep. That's what I'm doing, Jesus said. "I lay down my life for the sheep."

But then he said something else that we need to understand: "No one takes it from me, but I lay it down of my own accord. I have authority. . . ."

Christ's enemies didn't wrestle him to the ground and murder him. Christ sacrificed himself for us. He had the authority to die and rise again.

He is the good shepherd with power to carry even us beyond sin and death.

141

KING OF KINGS

Prayer:

Lord Jesus, you

are the King of

kings and the

Lord of lords!

We praise your

holy name.

Amen.

Read John 12:12–19

Barthius searched frantically for his father, but the streets were jammed with the festival crowd. Somewhere among them was his father, but where? Barthius pushed and struggled through the mob and the dust and the noise. He had to find his father soon—before he saw their own colt in the strange parade moving up the road. He had to find him, tell him how he tried to stop the men who took the colt, but couldn't . . .

The skies seemed almost white in the heat. Sweat curled down the boy's temples and ran down the back of his head as he kept searching. All around him people were chanting about the king of the Jews.

Barthius found his father at a turn in the road, his arms loaded with palm branches.

"Father," he said, panting. "Father, our colt—it is gone. I tried to stop them—" The noise around them was deafening.

"So what is it bothering you?" his father said. "You can see what a great holiday this is for Israel."

Barthius stared, trying to catch his breath. The energy in his father's eyes burned like nothing he had ever seen before.

"Here now, my son—help me here."

Together they laid the branches over the road. For just a minute, Barthius looked down past the stream of people on either side and saw, far down the way, a clump of people around a man on his father's best colt.

"Father, it is our colt he is riding—this man they call Jesus." He tried to explain again, but his father seemed possessed. "I'm trying to tell you—," he said, but his father paid no attention. He was yelling with the crowd and tossing branches wildly.

"It is a great day, my son," his father said, sweeping the sweat from his forehead with the back of his arm. "It is the day of the beginning. We will no longer be slaves to the Romans! You hear me? No longer Jewish slaves. The day of deliverance!"

Barthius stopped at the side of the road and stared down at the men coming towards them. His eyes rested on the still-blurry face of the man riding their colt.

"You think this Jesus is the king?" Barthius asked.

"Everyone says so. They say he can raise people from the dead," his father said. "Surely he can free us from the Romans—"

"Father, he is riding our colt. It is our colt there beneath him—"

His father stared. "Wonderful," he said. "Our own colt, you say? The new king of the Jews riding our colt. How proud we should be, Barthius. Never forget this, my son!"

Barthius stood in silence while the crazed people around him chanted wildly about this man they called king of the Jews.

142

GOOD AND BAD— AGAIN

Read Matthew 21:28–32

There's nothing new in this story. We've heard it before in countless parables and sermonettes: *everybody* needs forgiveness—absolutely everyone, even the big shots.

Why did Jesus keep bringing up this same point? Because so very few of the people he talked to really believed it. It was just too easy for the temple crowd to think they were big-time believers. "Get off our backs, Jesus," they probably said. "We do things right."

The big shots knew only two kinds of people. The first kind—the street women, the conniving tax collectors, the dregs of society—were the bad guys. The second—the people who knew the law backwards and forwards, the rich people with handsome homes, the big shots—were the good guys. It wasn't hard to draw those lines.

But the parable says that's wrong. Some of the prostitutes and tax collectors repented, while some of the big shots never realized they were muddied with sin and deceit. The bad guys listened more intently to Christ's words—and the words of John the Baptist—than the good guys, who just couldn't imagine that they were as dirty inside as Christ kept telling them they were.

Why? Maybe the bad guys had nowhere to go but up. Christ offered them something eternal, and they had nothing to lose by accepting it.

The good guys had a different problem. They were already on the top, sitting pretty in positions of leadership. They had *everything* to lose by getting down on their knees before this character from Nazareth—or so they might have thought.

The town where I live has a volunteer fire department. For years already, it has served the town well. But for a while it faced a serious problem: for some reason, no one ever quit. There's no way some of the old hands could get up and down ladders like they used to, and they just weren't strong enough to lug the heavy hoses. Fact is, they couldn't do the job effectively, and no one knew it better than they did. *But*, no one had ever quit, and to them the idea of being the first to throw in the towel was simply out of the question.

Finally, a couple of the old guys got together and talked about it, then came together to the department and asked to resign. They dared to quit only in a group. The power of tradition was so incredibly strong that no one dared to break it alone, even though it was obvious to everyone that something had to change.

What's the point of all this? No one in the Jewish society of Jesus' day was more rooted in thick tradition than the rulers were. It was almost impossible for them to get out. And yet Christ told them they had to—they had to see that the tradition alone would get them nowhere. They had to see that everyone needs forgiveness through God's only Son.

Good guys and bad guys alike need to bow before Christ. So do we.

143

THE PRACTICE OF PODIATRY

Prayer:

Heavenly

Father, make us

humble. Help us

to see that the

way to please

you is to serve

others. Thank

you for the

example you've

given us in

Jesus. In whose

name we pray,

Amen.

Read John 13:1–17

Athlete's foot is a fungus that grows between your toes and splits the skin. It's not very attractive. Corns, ugly little mounds of dead skin, are caused by shoes that don't fit. They hurt. Bunions form when the big toe is jammed toward the others, pushing the whole joint out of place. They hurt too.

Ingrown toenails curl back into the toe. They're not very pretty. Sometimes they get infected. Ouch. Verruca is an infectious virus that causes warts on the bottom of the foot. Sometimes verruca causes epidemics. Usually a foot doctor—a podiatrist—has to dig verruca warts out. Not much fun.

Let's face it—feet can have a lot of problems. And on top of everything else, they smell.

One of my favorite songs is "Take My Life," a hymn we quite often sing in church. Many of you probably know it. The verses spotlight different parts of our lives and even our bodies—our intellects, our silver and our gold, our voices, and our hearts. We ask God to take all of them and use them for his kingdom.

One verse (the second) always makes me shiver because it seems weird. "Take my feet and let them be/Swift and beautiful for Thee," it says. It's really hard to think of feet as being beautiful. Arms are okay, legs are very nice, even hands can be handsome—but feet just can't be beautiful. Big veins stick out of them all over the place. And when you get older, little red and blue things appear beneath your ankles, like tiny worms. Nope—not at all beautiful.

And yet, here's Christ, stooping lower than his own disciples to wash their dusty feet. Such a job is, of course, usually done by a hired servant. Nobody with any social grace would ever wash feet. And yet, Jesus does it. Why? The first verse says it all: "Having loved his own . . . he now showed them the full extent of his love."

Hurrah for Peter! While all the rest sit there, allowing Jesus to wash their feet, Peter the Rock says, "No way." He isn't going to let Christ stoop that low. He has principles.

Unfortunately, they are the wrong principles. Peter is still operating the way the world operates. He still hasn't allowed his values to be shaped by the gospel of love. He thinks washing feet is a job for slaves. He thinks great people shouldn't wash feet.

Peter is dead wrong. Christ's whole mission on earth turns that idea over directly on its head. Jesus himself has said, "He that is greatest among you, let him be servant of all." In Christ's scheme of things up is down and down is way up. Peter still has to learn that.

So do we.

Christ makes the disciples' feet beautiful before that last supper. In just a few hours he will go to the Garden of Gethsemane. Then he will be betrayed, tried, and crucified.

Then he will rise. His blood will make us beautiful—feet, hearts, and souls. That's how low he stooped to destroy sin and death, to conquer as King.

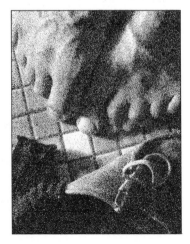

144

THE LORD'S SUPPER

Prayer:

Thank you for our families, Lord, including our church family. Thank you for delivering us from sin and death through Christ, the lamb. Amen.

Read Luke 22:14–23

In the last few years my parents have spent their winters in the Florida sun, more than two days' travel from my family here in Iowa. That's put an end to some of our best family celebrations. My sisters' families and my own used to gather with our parents round the table every Thanksgiving for turkey and cranberries—just like millions of other families do. But getting together now for Thanksgiving is out of the question.

I miss those old Thanksgiving meals, that huge table full of relatives. I miss all the chatter, the laughs, the swapped stories, and my father's prayer—the one that went on so long that the vegetables got cold. There's something indescribably wonderful about eating together and just being together that way. It's a custom, all right, but it's a custom with loads of meaning. That's why I miss it.

The Lord's last supper with his disciples had loads of meaning too—far more than a family reunion does. When Jesus "broke bread" with the disciples, he was participating in the old and rich Jewish tradition of the Passover, a tradition which is carried on even today in Jewish families from Syracuse to Stalingrad. Today, Jewish people call the ceremony the "Seder," but its meaning hasn't changed much; it still celebrates God's deliverance of the Jews from the slavery of the Egyptians.

Christians celebrate the Lord's Supper instead of the Passover. We believe that through his death and resurrection Christ changed that old ceremony into something new. Instead of celebrating Israel's deliverance from Egyptian bondage, we celebrate our own deliverance from the slavery of sin.

In Jesus' day Jews celebrating the Passover drank three cups of wine. The first was the cup of *sanctification*, a reminder of the reverence needed in approaching the holy God.

The second was the cup of *plagues*, meant to create memories—instant replays of the frogs, the rivers of blood, and darkness over all the land.

The final cup, the cup of *redemption* taken after the meal, was the one that Christ changed. God's old covenant with his people was illustrated in the blood of the lamb splashed on Jewish doorposts, the sign that saved covenant believers from death at the hands of an angel that one horrid night in Egypt.

But now, Christ said, my own blood is about to be shed so that you can be free from death eternally. "Take this," he said, "in remembrance of me." Drinking the cup of *redemption* helps us remember that Christ himself is the lamb killed for our deliverance.

As the disciples and Christ gathered around the table for that last supper, their celebration was more than a family reunion. Our Lord's Supper today is more than a family reunion too. But like a family gathering, the supper brings us together to celebrate. And through that supper we become a family—brothers and sisters in the family of God. That's cause for great celebration.

145

THREE-IN-ONE

Prayer:

Send us your

Spirit, dear

Father, just as

you sent the

Spirit to the

disciples after

Jesus ascended

into heaven.

May the Spirit

give us strength

and

understanding.

In Jesus' name,

Amen.

Read John 14:15–27 and 16:7–16

It's hard not to notice that in today's passage Jesus talks about his Father and about the Holy Spirit. Counting Jesus, that's three persons. We usually call them the Trinity.

When we say we believe in the Trinity, we mean we believe in one God who exists in three persons: Father, Son, and Holy Spirit.

One of the most unusual analogies I've ever heard about the Trinity came from a book I read long ago—a book called *Soul on Ice*, by Eldridge Cleaver, a man who, at the time, seemed to hate Christianity.

Cleaver remembered Bible classes when he was a boy. He described how hard the preacher worked at getting the kids to understand the Trinity. Cleaver thought about it for a while and then decided the Trinity was a little like Three-in-One oil. Although the can held only one oil, the company that made it claimed it had three different functions—it could do three different kinds of jobs for you. In the same way, thought Cleaver, while there was only one God, there were different jobs for each member of the Trinity. God the Father created the world and keeps it going, God the Son saves us from sin, and God the Holy Spirit makes us gradually more and more like Jesus.

In today's passage Christ tells his disciples that when he leaves them, God will send the Holy Spirit (a Counselor) to help them with the work Jesus has begun. What does Christ have in mind when he promises the Spirit? Does he mean that his own memory will live in the hearts and minds of the disciples, something like the way the memory of a great person lives on in us?

You know what I mean by that kind of memory. Say someone in the US wants to make a grand speech about freedom. All she has to do is mention Abraham Lincoln, a man who is long dead but whose memory lives on. When Lincoln's name is mentioned, people see instant images of a man who lived and died for freedom. You might say his "spirit" is still with us. If a politician says we ought to be living in the "spirit of Lincoln," everybody knows what he means.

When he talks about the coming of the Spirit, however, Jesus means something much more than "my memory will linger on." Christ is talking about a real Person who is going to come to earth to comfort and guide the disciples—and us. "Unless I go away," Jesus says, "the Counselor will not come to you. If I go, I will send him to you." One thing for sure—Christ is talking about a *real*, divine Person, not just a memory.

But what will this special person, this Counselor, do? Jesus says, "He will bring glory to me. . . . All that belongs to the Father is mine. That is why I said the Spirit will take what is mine and make it known to you." There it is again. The Trinity, I mean. Father, Son, and Spirit. Three Persons, one God. Three-in-One.

Together, Father, Son, and Holy Spirit, have worked and are working today to make this world a brand-new place and to make us new people.

By the way . . . today Cleaver believes in God, the great Three-in-One.

146

AGONY

Prayer:

Lord, thank you for not giving in there in the garden. Thank you for winning the battle for us. In your precious name,

Amen.

Read Luke 22:39–46

People today make a big deal out of sweating. Jogging and pumping iron are not only very "in," they're big business too. If you want to be physically fit, you've got to soak yourself with sweat.

Jesus' sweat was the same kind of stuff, but it came from a completely different source. Jesus wasn't pacing the garden, he wasn't splitting wood, and he wasn't toting boulders. All he was doing was praying. When he left the disciples, he told them to pray for strength against temptation. But his own prayer was so intense and so agonizing that he broke into a sweat—not just the kind that wets the hair at the back of your neck, but the kind that rolls off your face "like great drops of blood."

How can anyone pray that hard? Think of it this way: Jesus Christ fought a war that night in the garden, a war between his human nature and his divine nature. Only a few hours after the last supper, he knelt alone in the garden, knowing very well what kind of awful humiliation and suffering he would face later that very night.

Twice Jesus asked the disciples to pray for strength against temptation. But they nodded off right away. The disciples' mission on this long night in the garden was to be faithful and loyal followers of the Savior. The sound of their snoring said they were miserable losers.

But what kind of temptation was Jesus praying to withstand? Very simply, the powerful temptation to escape from the suffering and the death which he knew were coming. Even though Christ knew the details of his mission on earth right from the start, at this eleventh hour his human nature screamed out in agony. He begged his father to let him escape what he knew he must face.

So a battle was fought that night in the garden: Jesus' human nature raged to stay alive, to continue healing and preaching, to do good. But his divine nature, that part of him which was truly God, knew full well that the only way to succeed at his task of bringing salvation was to go through with the original plan—to be accused and tried, to be mocked, to carry the cross, to be crucified, and, finally, to die.

The great drops of blood poured from his face when everything in him that was human begged to get out of the job facing him that night. We all have the human instinct to live. So did Christ. His own humanity waged war with the will of God the Father.

"Father, if you are willing, take this cup from me," he said. The warfare was fierce and bloody.

But here's the line of final victory: "Yet not my will, but yours be done." Although every inch of his humanity screamed for release, he accepted what had to come. The temptation, and the war, was over.

Who won the big war in the garden? You're right—we did.

147

JESSE'S ESCAPE (13)

Read John 18: 15–27

"Hey, Jess—what you been doing since you been back? Haven't seen you around much." Seth Foster pulled the bottom edge of his tank top out from his shorts and flapped it, fanning his chest beneath. For the past few hours Seth, Jesse, and Butch had been working for Seth's dad, cutting long rectangles of dark green sod that would eventually end up as somebody's new lawn.

"I been around," Jesse said. The truth was he hadn't been. He'd spent more time at home than he ever had before, and he really didn't know why. It wasn't that his parents had grounded him or anything. "Just haven't run into you, I suppose," he said.

Seth scratched his chest. "How 'bout we go out tonight—like we used to? Head on down to the park. We got to hear the whole story of running away. Lots of us want to hear it—don't we, Butch?"

Butch nodded, his head bent over his work.

Jesse hesitated. There was something scary in thinking about hanging around the park like the old days. It was as if he didn't trust himself. Just the thought of the park at night was enough to make his stomach feel tense.

The world was different since he had come back. But nothing had changed for his old friends. They thought he was a big hero for being tough enough to take off the way he did, for being out there on the road alone and giving his parents all that grief.

"What do you say?" Seth said. "No big deal or nothing."

Jesse jerked his knife out from his back pocket, made a straight slash through a row of sod, and finished rolling the ball.

"Something happen to you or something?" Seth asked.

"What do you mean?" said Jesse.

"Well you just never show up anyplace anymore," Seth said.

"Parents nail you down to the floor or what?" The flatbed rocked when he slammed down the sod. "You're a big man around here now, Jesse—ain't that so, Butch?"

Butch looked up from the row he was cutting and nodded.

"That's what kids are saying, Seth?" Jesse said.

"Some. Most kids just don't understand why you never come around anymore. You got a record or something? How come you're always hibernating?" Seth snapped off his headband and rang out the sweat in one fist.

"I been around," Jesse said. "I been around all the time." He stared at the sod knife, seeing his face reflected in miniature. Sometimes it was if he didn't recognize himself, as if even his face wasn't the same, as if he didn't belong in his old bedroom anymore. Six weeks already he'd been back home. But it just wasn't the same.

"Look, Jess—come on down to the park tonight. You don't want everybody thinking you turned into some kind of goody-goody or something." Seth pulled the headband back through his hair. "What do you say?"

Jesse nodded and threw the knife down so the point stuck deeply in the sod.

148

INHERI-TANCE

Prayer:

Dear Lord,

forgive us when

we think too

much about the

things we wear.

Keep reminding

us of our real

treasure: eternal

life with you

and all God's

people. Thank

you for that

inheritance. In

Jesus' name,

Amen.

Read John 19:17–24

Upstairs in our bedroom is an old maroon collarless shirt that I picked up years ago at an antiwar rally in Washington D.C. I never wear it these days, because it's not the kind of shirt thirty-six-year-old men normally wear. It's also hopelessly out of style. I keep it like a relic, I guess.

Styles change. Yesterday kids liked surgeons' shirts and baggy white pants with loops beneath the front pockets. Today my children claim they must have tennis shoes without shoe-strings—"strap shoes," they call them. Fashionable clothes always show their purchase date, even when we snip off the tags. By their shapes and colors, clothes have a way of saying a lot about us and about what we value.

That's true even of Jesus Christ. His clothes tell us something about him. The night he was born his mother wrapped him in "swaddling cloths"—really nothing more than rags. At his death four soldiers, like vultures, divided his garments; then, rather than rip up an undergarment, they cast lots to figure out who would take it home.

What's interesting is that Jesus came into this world with nothing and left with nothing. When he was born, his perfect little body was wrapped in swaddling cloths, and when he died, his very ordinary clothing was taken from him. If he dressed in fashion, it was a fashion all his own.

Some men leave behind monuments. For example, Napolean left behind the incredible mansion at Versailles in France. Andrew Carnegie gave away a fortune to establish libraries all over America. William Shakespeare left poetry and plays that have charmed millions.

All Christ left was a worthless robe and a handsewn under-garment. He certainly left no will—no barns full of produce, no bank account, no real estate holdings. Just the clothes on his back.

The point is crystal clear: Christ's kingdom is not of this world. Just about everything the world treasures—fine clothes, political clout, fame and fortune, easy living—he cared nothing at all about. And the world had no room for his teaching either.

For a while he was fashionable—when he fed thousands with nothing more than a sack lunch, when he healed the sick and raised the dead, when he turned water into wine, when he rode into town on a colt over streets spread with branches and coats.

But most people misunderstood him; even the disciples couldn't always figure out what was going on. His fashion was different.

He died because he had to—it was all part of the plan. And the inheritance he left us is greater than gold and diamonds—much greater.

What his death left us was nothing less than life itself. When we get snarled up in fashions, it's far too easy to forget that simple truth.

149

LOVE AND SHOCK AND JOY

Read John 20:1–18

Mary Magdalene was the perfect candidate to be the first to see Jesus after he rose from the dead. It's hard to imagine anyone—even Peter—who loved Christ more than she did.

How do we know she loved him? First of all, she got up before dawn to go to the tomb. That in itself took commitment.

Second, she had good reason to love him. In other gospels Mary is identified as one who had once been freed of seven evil spirits. This Jesus had brought her peace and hope, meaning and order.

Third, Mary's actions at the tomb showed how almost crazy with devotion she was. Look at the way she begged a fight of the man she mistakenly thought was a gardener.

"Who is it you are looking for?" Christ asked her.

Mary didn't recognize him right away. "Sir," she said—ever so politely, "if you have carried him away, tell me where you have put him." Then she added: "And I will get him."

Wasn't she something? That wasn't a challenge—it was a promise. "I'll get him," she said. "I'll take him right back here." Mary was a woman with commitment, a woman who was willing to stand up to anyone who came between her and the Christ who had freed her from sin.

What seems so strange is that she didn't recognize Jesus right away. Any person that devoted, anyone who had spent as much time around Jesus as she undoubtedly had, should certainly have recognized him immediately.

How could she possibly mistake the face of her friend—even in the early light of dawn?

We have to remember that neither Mary Magdalene nor the disciples really understood that Christ would come back to life the way he did. The idea that Christ might just walk out of the grave hadn't occurred to Mary. She was convinced that someone had taken off with the body for some unknown reason.

Then came the moment of recognition. There stood Mary, challenging the man she thought was the gardener. "I'll take him back," she said, determined.

And Jesus needed to say only one word—"Mary."

(Whenever I read this story, I can't help but remember the passage about the good shepherd. My sheep, Christ said there, know the sound of my voice: all Jesus said was Mary's name, and she recognized him instantly.)

She must have run to him immediately, for he told her not to touch him. She must have wanted to hold him, to be held in turn by the man who had given her life order and hope. But he said no, not right now.

So she returned to the disciples with the news. She delivered the headline: "I have seen the Lord!" What a wonderfully powerful and simple testimony from this woman who loved Jesus Christ. "I have seen the Lord!"

Mary deserved to be the first.

150

THE DOUBTER

Read John 20:24–29

I'm writing this on June 6, 1984. Unless June 6 is your birthday, it may not mean much to you. It's not a holiday. But it *is* a day that many people will never forget.

Forty years ago today, thousands of Allied troops—soldiers from Canada, Poland, Australia, and the United States—fought on the beaches of Normandy for a foothold in Europe. Many of them died in the attempt to wrestle Europe loose from the teeth of the tyrant Hitler.

Elmer Vermeer, a farmer from Pella, Iowa, was one of the two hundred fifty American Rangers who landed early on June 6, 1944, on a beach lined by sheer one-hundred-foot cliffs. "We used rockets to shoot grapnels [giant hooks] with ropes attached and then we climbed the ropes hand over hand," Vermeer recalls. In the long climb, under heavy fire, more than one hundred fifty of his friends were stopped.

It's horrible even to try to imagine, but put yourself there for a minute. All around you thousands of soldiers are fighting and dying, while you're inching up a rope far above the beach. The Nazis are spraying machine-gun bullets, dropping grenades, and rolling huge stones over the cliff; and your friends, many of them, are falling around you.

The only thing you're sure of is that above you your hook is stuck on something. You're blind to what's coming. For all you know, there may be a dozen Nazis at the end of that rope, waiting. Climbing those one-hundred-foot cliffs took incredible faith . . .

Mr. Vermeer fought his way up that rope with the faith that Hitler's tyrannous Nazi regime was more horrible than war itself. He had never met Hitler; few Allied troops knew anything about the concentration camps that mercilessly butchered millions. Undoubtedly, Mr. Vermeer was scared, but his faith in the cause of freedom pulled him up those ropes even though the ripping machine-gun fire overpowered even the roar of the ocean behind him. Such faith is a tremendous thing.

Thomas's faith in Christ wasn't very strong. The disciple didn't believe Christ had come back; he wanted physical proof. He wanted to touch the wounds to make sure this guy was no hoax. He wanted to be certain this was the man he had been following for several years.

Thomas is the sort who would have insisted on proof that Hitler gassed Jews. Then he'd fight.

Christ gave Thomas the proof he claimed he needed. Then he scolded the disciple. "Because you have seen me, you have believed; blessed are those who have not seen and yet have believed."

Visible proof is not available anymore. We'll never be able to touch Jesus' wounds as Thomas did. But we do have the testimony of eyewitnesses, the testimony of the Gospels. Blessed are we if we accept what we've read as true, if our faith remains strong in the living Savior whom the Bible reveals.

The old catechism says that true faith is not only a sure knowledge of the truth of the gospel, but a firm confidence, planted by the Spirit in our hearts, that Christ's death and resurrection give us forgiveness and salvation.

Prayer:

Dear Lord, help us through those times when we have doubts about you. Make our faith strong and sure. In Jesus' name, Amen.

151

PETER THE ROCK

Prayer:

Lord, when we fall like Peter did, pick us up and help us to walk with you, always. Help us to show with our lives that we love you. Amen.

Read John 21:15–22

The three questions Jesus asks Peter in today's passage are important. For one thing, they remind Peter of the three lies he told the night of Jesus' arrest.

But Christ has more on his mind than merely jogging Peter's memory. His questions are real questions. After all, let's not forget Peter knew ahead of time that he was going to deny Christ. Christ told Peter what would happen. But Peter blurted it out three times anyway: "I tell you—I never laid eyes on this character before."

This time Jesus wants real commitment from Peter, so he asks him the same question in three different ways. He begins by phrasing it this way: do you love me more than these other men? Peter had always been the big talker, remember. Maybe Christ is testing him, checking if getting caught in three lies has knocked him down a few pegs.

"You know that I love you," Peter says.

Then Jesus changes the question slightly. "Do you *truly* love me?" he says. I'm told that the Greek word for love which Jesus uses in both questions is a shade different from the word Peter uses. Both words point at really deep affection, but Jesus' word hints at something that lasts year-in, year-out. The same word is used in two of the most famous passages about love in the Bible: John 3:16 and 1 Corinthians 13.

Why doesn't Peter use that word for love? Maybe he's holding back some of the old big talk. Maybe he's mellowed since the night he told Christ there was no way he'd ever deny him.

The third question is a bit different. This time Jesus uses Peter's word for love instead of the big word he had used before. Why? It's like saying, "This is what I heard you say—now is that what you mean?"

Peter shows his faith. "*You* know," he says, because he knows that Jesus knows without even having to ask.

But there's more. Jesus reminds him of his independence when he was younger and tells him a time will come when things won't be so good. Jesus warns him of his death. Then, he says, "Follow me."

Peter's mind has to be spinning. He's very likely haunted by the memory of having lied about Jesus. He's just been tested by the man he once boldly stated was "the Christ of God." And he's been welcomed back: "Follow me," Christ says.

But when he's warned that he will die in an ugly way, Peter trips just a bit—just as he did that time when he was sure he could walk on water. He looks around. "What about him?" Peter asks, pointing at someone else—as if misery wants company.

"What happens to him is none of your business," Jesus says. "Your business is following me."

Peter—this Peter the rock—should give all of us hope. He's no saint. He's no perfect man. He's no Rock of Gibralter. He can be moved. He can sin—and he does. He trips up.

But God forgives him, time after time. And when the final tally is taken, Peter will still be the rock.

Like Peter, we can be strong too—even in our weakness.

152

LORD JESUS, COME QUICKLY

Prayer:

Lord, we know that someday we will meet you face to face, either when we die or when you come again. Thank you that we don't have to be afraid of that day. Make us ready and willing to work for you.

Amen.

Read Acts 1:1–11

O Lord, do not rebuke me in
    your anger
or discipline me in your wrath.
Be merciful to me, Lord,
    for I am faint;
O Lord, heal me, for my bones
    are in agony.
My soul is in anguish.
How long, O Lord, how long?

In these first verses of Psalm 6 David makes it obvious that his pain is really tough—his bones are hurting and his soul is wrenched. All he can say is—"How long, O Lord, how long?"

Millions of Christians repeat David's question every day. They ask it in a variety of circumstances, hundreds of places, and many different languages—but it's still the same question: "O Lord, how long?" Maybe you've heard it another way: "Lord Jesus, come quickly." Or maybe you've used different words altogether. But chances are pretty good that at some moment in your life you, or someone close to you, have felt the same way David felt when he wrote this psalm.

Why would someone who loved God ask this question? Let's look in on Marvin for a minute: Marvin wants his daughter to go to college, wants it more than anything else in the world. But the meatpacking plant he works for isn't making money. One day Marvin gets a notice that the whole shop will close down. He'll be out of a job.

Marvin's worked as a meat-cutter for years, ever since he and Gloria were married. He really has no other skills, and he knows it. He also knows jobs are tight. Finding another job as a meat-cutter is going to be next to impossible.

Marvin's a strong Christian. He knows that prayer can bring miracles. But he's not expecting a miracle this time. He's already told his daughter that he can't afford to send her to college. He feels like he's really let her down. He knows he shouldn't feel so hopeless, but he can't help himself. "I just wish it would all end," he tells himself. "Why can't you just come now, Jesus?" he whispers. It's like a prayer.

Marvin's words express the same idea as "O Lord, how long?" Most Christians ask that question once—some a whole lot more.

The disciples asked David's question at the very moment of Christ's farewell. "When are you going to come again?" they said. "O Lord, how long?" It was a typical question for them too. They'd never quite been able to shake the idea that Christ was going to conquer the Romans and bring about a new and beautiful Jewish state.

Christ answered them in two parts. First, he explained that the time is known only to God. Then he said, "You will receive power and you will be my witnesses." He told the disciples not to set their alarm clocks and then sit around waiting for them to go off. "I'll come in God's good time," he assured them. "But meanwhile, you see to it that my work gets done. There's plenty of it—I know."

The disciples and millions of other Christians aren't wrong to hope for Christ's second coming. But if our wishing stops our working, then we're wasting our time—and God's. And there's lots of work to be done.

"I'll give you power," Jesus said, "but you've got to do the work."

153

FLIP-FLOPS

Read Acts 2:1–13

Most of us have either read about or witnessed really big character changes. We probably haven't seen any ugly frogs turn into handsome princes, but we've heard of changes almost as astounding.

Not many years ago one of the most popular TV series was a really whacky show about a gentle guy who suddenly split right out of shirts and pants by turning green and muscle-bound. Like some sweet monster, he'd rescue pretty girls or beat the tar out of ugly villains. That show was so popular that you can still buy "The Incredible Hulk" comic books, even though the series has been scratched for a long time.

Some of you may not like to hear this, but I know parents who claim that their kids went through strange changes when they got to their early teens. None of them burst out of their clothes and emerged as green monsters, of course, but they changed just the same. Kids who used to be free and easy—always talkative, always joking around—suddenly became moody and started moping around a lot. If they spoke at all, they just grunted. Some of those symptoms, I'd guess, come from the dreaded disease called adolescence.

I remember once hearing a young man preach in the church of his boyhood. It was a good sermon, and he was a good preacher. Afterwards, older folks were talking about it—how it was odd to hear that guy preaching because he had done a lot of rotten things as a teenager. Apparently, he hadn't just been "naughty," but a whole lot worse. Now he was telling other people how to live.

One man in the congregation said he couldn't even listen to the sermon because his mind was still poisoned by all the trouble the guy had caused. That's sad, but understandable. It's often difficult to believe that such major character changes are real.

The disciples went through one incredible character change when the Holy Spirit entered their lives. Before Pentecost they were scared. Christ was gone now, and being a Christian was hardly a popular occupation. So the disciples locked themselves up behind doors and sat around whispering, always scared.

Suddenly the Holy Spirit was there. He came with noise and with little tongues of fire, and he reached into each of their hearts and voices. Right away they unlocked the door, went outside, and started speaking to hundreds of Jews, in dozens of different languages.

Christ said he'd send this Spirit, and he did. And this Spirit really shook things up. He turned Jerusalem into a new Tower of Babel. At the tower many languages had confused the people; at Jerusalem many languages brought them together in one new Christian faith.

It was all the work of this Counselor Jesus said he'd send. He did what he said he would. He sent the Spirit.

And if you think the Spirit can't still pull off some incredible changes, you just ask that preacher—the one with the past some people find so hard to forget. He'll testify.

154

THE LEAPER

Prayer:

Heavenly Father, when we count up all the blessings you've given us, we've got reasons to jump for joy too—just like the beggar. All praise to your name!

Amen.

Read Acts 3:1–16

Last night at a ball game I saw a spunky fifth-grade kid who recently broke her leg. Dressed in shorts, she was hobbling around on crutches, her broken leg encased in a white cast scribbled up with her friends' names.

I thought I'd have a little fun. "Hey," I said, "you got to get some sun on this leg—the other one's much tanner than this one." I tapped the cast with my knuckles.

She tried to smile but didn't quite succeed. "Very funny," she said.

Later when I remembered the details of her accident, I could guess why she had trouble smiling about it. The break itself was really severe. The kid spent weeks in the hospital in traction, forced to lie in just one position. That's tough for anybody, but it's especially rough if you're a spunky kid.

What's more, her leg will stay in that cast for a long time. Atrophy—the gradual wasting away of muscles and tendons that aren't being used—will set in. And there's nothing this girl can do to stop it from happening. When the cast finally comes off, the leg will look gray and puny. She'll have to work hard, exercising, if she expects to get around as quickly as she did before the break.

That kind of reconditioning has been done before. In fact, there are some super stories about athletes whose legs survived much worse problems. Glenn Cunningham, one of the first really great milers, burned his legs in a house fire and was told by doctors that he'd never walk well again. They were wrong. But Cunningham had to work hard for a long time to prove them wrong.

If you think the miracle in today's passage is the beggar's walking, you're only half right. There's more. Read verse 8: "He jumped to his feet and began to walk. Then he went with them into the temple courts, walking and jumping, and praising God." The other half of the miracle is that the beggar *jumps*. It's likely he hadn't used his legs for years, if ever (the Bible says he was crippled from birth). But Peter tells him to get up and walk, and boom!—he not only walks but also jumps around as if it were the opening day of the Olympics.

Now Peter could have made headlines with this feat—just as Christ could have done with his miracles. But when Peter and John talk to the people who can't believe what's happened, they scold them. That's right, they scold the people. "You killed Jesus," they say. "You gave him up to be murdered. Yet it's this man's faith in Jesus that gives him the strength to be jumping around the temple." Peter and John remember what Christ told them at his ascension about being busy with his work. They don't want headlines; they want believers.

And they've already got one— the guy who's running around and jumping like a track star. He *believes*, and because of his belief he's been cured completely. He's got instant muscles again. And all the thanks, he knows, goes to God.

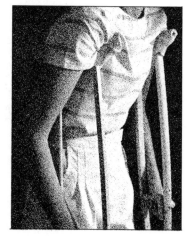

155

MARTYRS AND MADMEN

Prayer:

Lord, our faith
is small when
compared to
martyrs like
Stephen. But
with your Spirit
we too can love
others, even our
enemies. Help
us to look to
you for strength.
In Jesus' name,
Amen.

Read Acts 6:8–15 and 7:54–60

Some people claim that terrorism is the greatest threat facing civilization. As long as lunatics are willing to die in order to kill the enemy, no one is really safe.

Not long ago a mad terrorist drove a truck through steel gates and plowed into a compound of sleeping American soldiers. When the explosives in the truck detonated, he and more than two hundred troops died. Why would a man sacrifice himself like that?

The story of Stephen might give us some clues. Stephen, as most of us already know, is considered the first martyr because he was the first believer to give up his life for his belief in Christ.

What exactly are martyrs? They are persons who—like Stephen—are absolutely and eternally committed to their belief. Verse 8 says Stephen was a man full of God's grace and power. Verse 15 claims that in the face of lies and false accusations, Stephen's face lit up "like the face of an angel." Martyrs, Stephen's story reveals, are so committed to their cause that they become unconscious of danger.

Even when things got hot, Stephen's face showed nothing but peace. When he blamed the courts for killing the only righteous Man, "they were furious and gnashed their teeth." Stephen merely looked to heaven and saw Jesus.

Martyrs, both Stephen and the terrorists, commit themselves so totally to their gods that they fear nothing, not even death.

BUT don't ever get the idea that Stephen is even closely related to mad bombers, suicidal pilots, or hijackers with pockets full of nitroglycerine. There's one huge difference.

At the moment of his stoning, Stephen, like Christ before him, prayed for his persecutors, asked God to forgive them.

The madman who drove his truck into the marine compound in Beirut obviously had no such forgiveness in mind. His head full of hate, he gritted his teeth and smiled at the idea of the hated Americans dying along with him. His religion convinced him that his enemies must die. He hated them so much that he was willing to blow himself off the face of the earth to destroy them.

Not so with Christ. Not so with Stephen. The difference between a Christian martyr and a satanic madman is all summed up in one small word—*love*, the greatest of the commandments.

And that's the gospel truth.

156

JESSE'S ESCAPE (14)

Read Acts 8:26–40

"I think I'm going to die if I don't cool off," Seth said. He was sitting cross-legged on the grass, smoking. "What I need is watermelon."

They usually met somewhere in the park just east of downtown. The police hated kids hanging around there—but they kept showing up anyway.

"Where you going to get watermelon? Still too early in the season," Butch said. Jesse nodded.

Seth leaned back on his hands. "I know a jerk who's got them. Starts the plants in his basement way back in February."

"Let's do it," someone said. "Where are we going?"

Seth stared at Jesse. "Bronson," he said, "Mr. Ed Bronson."

Jesse shook his head. Bronson was the teacher who had gotten him in trouble just before he took off on his motorcycle.

"You mean Bronson the teacher?" Butch asked.

"Same jerk," Seth said. "You ought to love this, Jesse."

Stealing watermelon was a big sport later on in the summer. Usually, in the darkness they could rifle someone's garden in just a few minutes and eat melons until they were stuffed.

Jesse had no choice. If he said he wouldn't take Bronson on, all the guys would say Jesse wasn't the same guy anymore.

Only a kitchen light burned through a drawn window shade at the back of Bronson's house.

The boys crept along behind the garbage cans and got down on all fours when they came to the rose bushes. Even in the moonlight Jesse could see that Seth was right about the melons. They humped up from the leaves like giant turtle shells.

"Get us a good one, Jess—," Seth said.

He knew it was wrong, but he did it anyway—came out from behind the hedge and tiptoed into the melon patch.

"Now stomp the garden, Jess— go on!"

Jesse heard the others laughing. He felt terrible. "What for?" he whispered.

"Cause Bronson's a jerk," Seth said. "You know that."

The garden was set in perfect rows, grass clippings spread like a quilt through the plants. "No way," he said. Grabbing the melon was one thing, but stomping the Bronsons' garden was something else.

Seth suddenly stood there beside him. "Like this—," he said. He kicked over the wire cage around the tomatoes and jumped on the potato plants.

"Cut it out, Seth," Jesse said.

"Give me a hand," Seth said. "Come on, you goody-goody."

Jesse burned inside. It was all aimed at him—the whole plan was aimed at him, and he knew it. Almost without thinking, he raised the melon and flung it at Seth. The melon caught him smack in the stomach, bowling him back through a row of sweet corn until he fell on his backside.

Suddenly the lights went on in the Bronsons' backyard, and all seven guys scattered, running hard.

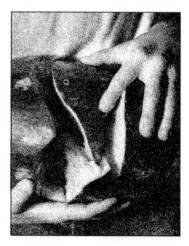

Prayer:

Lord, thank you for men like Philip who could walk up to a stranger and talk about you. Forgive us for sometimes hiding our Christianity. Help us to show—by our actions and our words—that we love you. Amen.

192

157

PAUL, THE TURNCOAT

Read Acts 9:1–19

The way the high priest glared, I was afraid he would have me killed—and for nothing more than telling the truth. I told him everything that had happened on the road to Damascus.

"Some very bright light?" he sneered, pointing up to the ceiling. "Maybe it was the sun's reflection? Maybe lightning?"

I didn't know what to say. One doesn't tell the high priest that he is dead wrong.

"And some speaking, some noise?" He stood there and folded both arms across his chest, staring above my head.

"It was nothing like I have ever seen or heard. It was—I think it was—unnatural—"

He laughed out loud. "So people say it was the voice of Jesus, do they? Saul goes crazy on the way to Damascus, and you want me to think it was a dead man who spoke to him?"

I held to the arms of the chair. "I don't know, sir. It is no more clear to me today than it was the day it happened."

He dropped his arms and walked away, keeping his back to me. "So tell me then, what about Saul's three blind days and this strange Christian man visiting—is all of that the truth?"

"High priest, your servants led him all the way to Damascus, as if the light itself had burned up his eyes. He *was* a blind man, I swear it. He ate nothing for three days—"

"—He was full of terror about his blindness, nothing more!"

"That wasn't it, sir. He was at peace. You know Saul. You've seen him war with the Christians. This blind man was not Saul—he was quiet, as if he had become a new man."

The high priest turned toward me again. "It's not that I believe the stories, you understand. It's not that I think a dead man can speak. What upsets me is losing Saul. You know how he is—how he hated them. It's an insufferable loss."

And we sat in stillness while the high priest's eyes swept over the floor, as if there he might find some answer.

"And the old man?" he said.

"We didn't know who he was. He said he knew what happened to Saul. We were scared, sir. He looked to be a holy man, so we let him in. We were afraid of what had happened to our friend."

"And what exactly did this man do?"

I didn't want to tell him. I hated to tell him, because I thought he would go into a rage. I didn't know what he would do.

"Well—what happened?"

"He baptized Saul—like the rest of Jesus' followers, and—

"Then what?—go on—"

"—And then Saul could see." The high priest turned away quickly. "I swear, sir. I don't understand, but he could see."

The high priest sat back slowly in his chair, breathed deeply. "Well, you tell me, then—what must I think of all of this? You were there through all of it, all of this mystery."

I wanted to leave the room—so badly I wanted to leave the room. "I'm sorry, sir, but I think Saul is lost. He has gone over to heresy." It was very hard to tell him, so very hard.

158

ADJUSTING TO THE NEW WAY

Prayer:

Thank you, Father, that your gift of salvation is given to all who believe, no matter what their nationality or skin color. May your gospel, your good news, make us all one in your Son, Jesus Christ. Amen.

Read Acts 11:1–18

It won't be long now before a big change occurs in your life: you'll be moving from junior high to high school. Sometimes the big change happens at grade 9, sometimes at grade 10. Either way, it can mean getting used to lots of new things.

What kinds of things? Well, take kids for openers. Because many high schools draw on several junior highs, all of a sudden there'll be two or three or five times as many kids running through the halls. It can be kind of scary (or exciting!) to see so many new faces every day.

Some of those new faces will belong to a whole flock of teachers, all of whom, rumor has it, hand out homework in amounts you never dared think about in junior high.

Then there are those brand-new subjects—things like geometry and Spanish and computer programming—all designed, or so you've heard, to terrorize the timid freshman coming through the door for the first time. Just figuring out your schedule and finding your classes can be a real challenge for the first couple of days.

Of course, just about everybody eventually adjusts to the big change. "It's no big deal," you'll be telling people who ask how you like the new school. Still, any really big change usually makes us kind of nervous until we get used to the new way.

Adults find it hard to adjust to big changes too. A friend of mine told me his father was really ornery for a whole year after he moved to a smaller home to retire. "I can't find anything!" he kept saying. "Back home at least I knew where to look."

How about Peter? Of Christ's hand-picked disciples, he had to be one of the best and the brightest. Jesus had promised Peter that he was the rock on which the church would be built. Peter was as quick as a whip, but even Peter couldn't adjust to Christ's way of thinking. For centuries the Israelites alone had been the "chosen people." The great I AM was simply the God of the Jewish people.

But not anymore, Christ said in the dream.

Peter should have picked that idea up from Christ's own words, but some ideas get buried so deep inside a person's head, it takes something like dynamite to get at them. Christ sent a vision, took Peter by the shoulders, and turned him around to see things in a new way.

The dream showed Peter that Christ's promises aren't just for the Jews; that instead, the gospel belongs to everybody—"Red and yellow, black and white, they are precious in his sight." Once Peter saw the vision, he was struck colorblind. He knew the Lord is king over everything and everybody—who cares what color or nationality!

And the dream came to him in the nick of time. The moment it ended, three men, non-Jews, stood before him, asking about the gospel. Had Peter not seen the vision, he might never have talked to them. He had always assumed, after all, that other kinds of people had other kinds of gods. The dream came to convince him that the old way, Jews-only, was dead and buried. Christ himself had destroyed the old way of looking at things; the temple veil was torn in two at the moment of his death.

Some lessons don't come easily, not even to Peter.

159

JAILBREAK

Read Acts 12:1–19

Early in 1980, a man named Christopher John Boyce, 27 years old, escaped from Lompoc Penitentiary in California. Robert Lindsey, a journalist who once wrote a book about Boyce, claimed that the escape didn't surprise him. Lindsey said Boyce hated prison life.

Boyce was smart, very smart. In order to escape, he sculpted a papier-mâché dummy that looked just like him and left it in his cell so the jailers would think he was still there. Then he hid in a drainage tunnel at a blind spot beneath a tower manned by guards ordered to shoot first and ask questions later.

With a ladder Boyce made himself, he scaled a chain-link fence, snipped alarm cables and razor-sharp wire coils at the prison's perimeter, then took off into uninhabited countryside with nothing more than a pair of running shoes and his prison uniform. He made it. He had it figured out exactly right.

The escape of Christopher Boyce would make a great TV drama. Boyce himself is almost a hero—a really sensitive guy who is smart enough to outwit men hired to shoot on sight. He's a man willing to die for his freedom. It's easy to like a guy like Boyce, and it's easy to view the jailers as dangerous slobs who stand between him and freedom.

It's also easy to ignore what Boyce is—a spy. He's a man who sold highly classified documents to the Russians. There's nothing heroic or noble about selling out to the Soviets—but his sneaking away so intelligently makes people forget about his crimes. That's the problem with most jailbreak stories—the bad guys turn into heroes.

But not so with Peter. Peter didn't spend months, or even weeks, planning his escape. He didn't even know it was going to happen. An angel showed up one night and steered him right out of prison. The Bible says Peter thought he was dreaming. He didn't believe what was happening until he found himself on a street outside the prison gates.

Boyce had the whole escape route figured out; Peter didn't have a clue what was going on until it was over. Of course, that's not the only difference. Boyce was a criminal; Peter was imprisoned innocently for doing exactly what Jesus, his Lord, had commanded him to do.

So who gets the glory? In Boyce's case, he does. He pulled it off. Whatever glory comes to a man who sells out his country comes to Boyce. He's a smart criminal.

Not Peter. Peter gets no glory whatsoever. Don't misunderstand—Peter was a smart man. But God gets the glory for this jailbreak, because God himself pulled it off.

As smart as Boyce was, his plan was nothing at all next to God's plan. Peter's escape was designed by the master planner. And once Peter was on the street, he understood. "Now I know," Peter said on his way to Mary's house, "that the Lord sent his angel."

160

ROLLING WITH THE PUNCHES

Read Acts 14:1–20

There was never a dull moment on the missionary trail. Inside of twenty verses in today's passage, Paul and Barnabas zip in and out of three different situations, just barely escaping with their lives.

Two qualifications for the job of missionary were probably pretty standard. Christ himself had stated them: love God above all and your neighbor as yourself. But after that, I can't help but think that somewhere on the list might have been the ability to roll with the punches. Things happened fast out there in the field.

First, Iconium. Following their usual pattern, Paul and Barnabas visited the synagogue. The Jewish synagogue was the perfect place to preach because any male was permitted to speak there. Paul and Barnabas preached salvation through Christ's death and resurrection, and while some believed, others got testy and finally downright hostile. So when they heard of a plot to have them stoned to death, Paul and Barnabas secretly slipped out of town and started preaching in the country.

At Lystra it was a completely different story. Here, Paul healed a cripple—something he had done before, of course. But the people went crazy thinking that the missionaries were gods. The people's mythology taught them that at certain times gods took human form, came down to earth, and performed superhuman feats. Paul's miracle fit into that pattern perfectly. Therefore, to the Lystrans, Paul was a god. A pagan priest hauled in animals to sacrifice to these wonder-workers. But Paul and Barnabas would have none of it.

Think about it. They could have eaten up all this glory, but instead they ran outside, tore up their clothes, and yelled that the good people of Lystra had it all wrong. "We aren't who you think we are!" they screamed.

The Bible says that despite all the apostles' noisy claims, the people insisted on making sacrifices to them. Strange folks.

Then all of a sudden some of the angry folks from Iconium joined the crowd. It didn't take long for them to convince the Lystrans that Paul and Barnabas deserved to die. Soon the bunch that minutes before wanted to worship Paul stoned him and left him for dead.

But this wasn't Paul's time to die. His friends picked him up, treated his wounds, and took him back to the city.

You'd think that after all of that Paul would have wanted some rest and relaxation, maybe a couple sunny weeks off in a southern resort town. But the Bible says the next day he and Barnabas were off again, back at it.

If you think it was easy being a Christian after Christ's resurrection, these twenty verses alone should be enough to convince you that there was never a dull moment.

Only the Holy Spirit could give these men the strength to go on and on and on, when they hadn't the slightest idea what they would find just around the corner—love or hate.

161

CONVER-SION

Prayer:

Father in

heaven, thank

you for your

power to change

people's lives.

Thank you for

sending Jesus to

save us from

our sins. In his

name,

Amen.

Read Acts 16:16–34

Being converted can be a scary business—it changes your life. Just look at this jailer.

When Paul and Silas were hauled in, he took them, beaten and bloody, and did exactly what the judge commanded him to do—dragged them into an inner cell and slapped locks around their feet. These men had been flogged severely; he could have just let them lie there in peace for a while. It must have been obvious that they were in no shape for a jailbreak.

But he had his orders. He was a man of the law.

Then two things happened. First, Paul and Silas gathered an audience with their praying and singing. The jailer must have expected two guys who'd just been whipped to be more than a little upset about it. But these two lay there and sang. It had to be a shock to see them happy, their backs caked with dried blood.

But that was only the beginning. God sent an earthquake that pulled off a miracle. Not only did it rattle the place up a little, but it broke open the doors and shook the chains right off the prisoners.

Now remember—this jailer was a man of the law. For him, doing his job right was a matter of honor. If the prisoners walked out, he knew it would look as if he'd failed. So he drew his sword, ready to end it all. He took it personally.

But Paul told him something amazing: all the prisoners were present and accounted for. "Hold on," he said. "Put that thing away."

Astonished, the jailer was converted—right there on the spot. "Sirs," he said, "what must I do to be saved?"

And then the jailer became a completely different guy. Once he accepted Paul's simple offer, he took the men into his house, cleaned them up, and fed them supper. In a way, he broke the law he had considered so important not more than an hour before—so important that he was ready to kill himself with his own sword. Now God was giving orders in his life.

Real conversion changes a person much more than getting a new haircut or losing a pile of excess weight does. It really changes your insides and makes you act differently—like the jailer did. After the earthquake he was a new person. In him, all the laws had been changed. From this point on he would take his orders from God Almighty.

162

MIRACLES— BIG AND LITTLE

Read Acts 23:12–34

Some miracles are really showy. When men and women, blind from birth, can suddenly see—that's dramatic. When a man who hasn't walked for years suddenly jumps high enough to dunk a basketball—that's worth headlines.

We've all heard of miracles happening around us. A man with cancer walks into the doctor's office, takes a few tests, and finds that all the bad cells have vanished. The doctor—who's supposed to know it all—says it's got to be a miracle. He's so stunned he can't say anything else.

Or, a woman, suddenly given superhuman strength, lifts her car off a child who had been pinned beneath. A tornado destroys a home, but leaves the family sitting beneath, roofless but safe. When such things happen, we call them miracles—even today.

But not all miracles make such a big splash. I remember two guys who were among the naughtiest kids I ever knew. If I could tell you some of the things they did, I would—but I can't. Just think the worst. Maybe the only commandment they didn't break was "thou shalt not kill." They snapped all the rest like frozen twigs. I always figured these guys would end up in jail somehow— that's how bad they were.

A few years ago I found out that one of them was a member of the school board in a Christian school. The other was spending his free time leading a church youth group.

I don't know if there were ever miracles in those guys' lives— some booming moment like the flash Paul saw on the road to Damascus. Somehow I suspect that nothing quite that dramatic ever happened. The miracle of their lives was probably simple: over the years they were gradually converted into people who believed.

Today's passage tells about a miracle too—even though we don't usually think of it that way. God planted a young spy among the Jewish leaders, and the spy heard the plot to get rid of Paul.

Paul found out and got word to the chief captain, who responded by calling up five hundred troops to protect Paul as he left town. Hated by the Jews for what he was saying about Christ, Paul suddenly was given a big-time escort. Those plotters who swore not to eat until Paul was dead had to either break the oath or wrinkle up and die.

God's plot for Paul's life was greater than the plot cooked up by his enemies. Someday Paul would have to die, but right now God used nothing less than Roman law to protect him. It was a miracle.

Maybe Paul was remembering that great trip out of town when he wrote "all things work together for good to those who love God and are called according to his purpose."

That promise in itself is a big miracle. It rarely makes the headlines, but it's a miracle all the same.

163

EARS THAT CAN HEAR

Read Acts 27:27–44

The waves reared above them like open hands, then slapped over their heads.

"The bottom—I felt the bottom," Claudius yelled to his friend. "It's there!"

The pounding of the waves was deafening. Claudius saw only the sweep of wet hair as his friend tried to motion with his head.

He stood for a moment on the sand, the water chest-high beneath the breaker's ridges, before a wave shoved him back into the foam. For life itself, he held to the slick timber.

Neither of the men had the strength to walk once they reached the shoreline. In the spray of the sea they lay, arms outstretched, over the cool sand.

Morning came slowly through the grays of the storm. The angered surf softened into waves that curled over the shoreline sand. Claudius pulled himself up. "Barthis," he said, jarring his friend's shoulder. "We're alive!"

Barthis rolled on his side and itched sand from his eyes. "Never again will I ship with that centurion," he said. "He's a madman. He almost killed us."

"We're alive, Barthis," Claudius said. "We're alive."

Barthis dug his fingers into the sand and flung a handful into the waves. "Why did he listen to that man? We could have escaped in a lifeboat long ago. But Paul said 'stay,' and the lunatic centurion believed him."

"We're alive anyway," Claudius said.

"But who else? Two of us—out of almost three hundred. And all because the centurion listened to that Christian, Paul—" Barthis stood slowly on the sand and stretched the strips of clothing out from his body. "You tell me what will happen when all the prisoners are gone—what will be said of us? They will say that we let them go. *I* wanted to kill them. Remember? 'Kill the prisoners,' I yelled in the middle of that storm. But, no! The centurion would have no part of it—and all because he wanted that Christian, Paul, alive." Barthis kicked at the sand.

Suddenly the two men heard a sound behind them—voices, familiar voices, from dozens of people. "We're not alone," Claudius said. "We're *not* the only ones who made it. Look—"

"I will kill that centurion if I see him."

"Maybe he saved our lives, Barthis. Maybe he is right about this man named Paul."

Claudius waved his hands high up over his head to get the attention of the others. He kept telling himself the good news. He kept pinching his chest to remind himself that he was alive. They had done exactly what this Paul had commanded, and they were alive! That's what was stuck in his head. Thank God, they were alive!

Prayer:

Great God, you were with Paul wherever he went—even in a storm on the high seas. Thank you for your promise to always be with us too. Help us to hear your voice above the storm. In Jesus' name, Amen.

200

164

SECTS

Prayer:

Lord, sometimes

it's hard for us

to see that we

are different

from all the

people who

wander up and

down the aisles

of shopping

malls. Help us

to see ourselves

as Christians,

your own

unique people.

Amen.

Read Acts 28:17–30

Most of you probably have heard people talk about "sects" at one time or another. Among Christian people sects are a popular topic—maybe because there are so many of them around.

If I told you a friend of mine belonged to a sect, you'd probably picture her hoeing a row of beans on some plantation commune, her head wrapped up in a red babushka. Or maybe you'd imagine her selling flowers on a street corner, or chanting, or swaying in chorus with a whole bunch of weirdoes wearing ponytails.

Or maybe you'd think she was a Moonie, that she and her boyfriend were among the two thousand couples married in one mass ceremony in New York's Madison Square Garden.

At any rate, you'd probably assume she was doing something strange.

To Christians, the word *sect* doesn't have a particularly sweet ring—and it's not hard to see why. A few years ago the leader of a sect, the Rev. Jim Jones, commanded hundreds of his loyal followers to drink punch laced with poison. The mass suicide occurred just hours after he had murdered some people who had come to his South American commune to investigate what was going on. Rev. Jones used Christianity to get people excited about following him. Jones's sect made all Christians look bad.

And yet in today's passage Paul and his buddies are called a "sect"—a small religious group which some persuasive individual has led astray from traditional beliefs and practices. In Christianity's early days, the church was considered a sect, a group of strange people who broke away from the traditional teachings of Judaism.

When you think about it, it's really not so difficult to understand why people called Christianity a "sect." Just look at the strange things Christians did. The whole time Paul was under house arrest in Rome, chained to a guard, he continued to preach the gospel, discuss Christianity, and debate with unbelievers. If you had been there, you'd have thought he was strange too.

What's more, outside the prison, Christians—followers of this gospel Paul taught—were being persecuted for preaching about Jesus Christ, a man who got himself crucified. If you weren't a Christian back then, if you read about Paul, the jailbird preacher, if you heard strange characters yelling about Jesus over the streets of the city—you'd probably think the whole world had gone berserk. "What crazy people these Christians are," you might have said. "What a strange sect."

Although the Bible doesn't tell us the end of Paul's story, church tradition claims that he was eventually sentenced to death—not because of the charges brought against him, but because he was a Christian, a member of a sect people thought the world would be better off without.

165

IRON-PUMPER

Prayer:

Lord, thank you
for Romans 5.
Help us to feel
your grace in
whatever
situation we
face. Thank you
for your love
that never quits.
In Jesus' name,
Amen.

It was dark in the church basement. The only light in the room came from a spotlight above my head. It helped me read, but cast a veil over the audience. I read a short story I had written, a complicated one. After it was through, it took a little explaining to convince them that my story was, in fact, a Christian's story.

When it was over, I was no more than out of the basement door when a guy grabbed my arm. "Remember me?" he said.

I didn't. He was about my height, but thin and tired-looking. His dark hair was cut very short.

"I'm Herb—remember? We used to live in the same apartment at college?"

"Herb," I said, "sure, Herb. Sure, sure, of course." The guy didn't look at all like Herb. Herb was a weight lifter, arms hung with muscles like thick ropes, a waist super-thin, and shoulders like a middle guard. Herb was the kind of guy who didn't have a neck—that's how big he looked.

This wasn't the Herb I knew.

"That story?—you're just fooling around," he said. "Why do you have to be so tricky—just tell the gospel straight out," he told me. It was like a scolding. He wasn't really angry or anything, but he meant every word he said, I could tell. "Just tell people about Christ's love—don't jazz it up so much."

"You think so, huh?" I said. I still couldn't get over how skinny he was. His shoulders were absolutely gone. "Herb," I said, "still pumping iron?"

He laughed, something like a snort really. "I got cancer," he said. "You didn't know?"

How could I? It was more than ten years since we had shared the same apartment. I didn't know. My mind went suddenly dark and empty. I tried to find something to say—"Too bad," maybe. Or how

about "I'll pray for you"? Nothing sounded right. Cancer had dried up all Herb's muscles. Maybe he was dying.

"It's the greatest thing that's ever happened to me," he said. "It's made me see things straight, perfectly straight."

Then I knew why he was bugging me about my cute writing. "Tell it straight out," he had said. "Don't jazz it up."

He used to bulge out of T-shirts with his big, sausage arms. Now there was nothing there. But he told me cancer was the best thing that had ever happened to him.

It makes sense to me now, after reading one of the most comforting chapters in the Bible—even suffering brings hope and comfort to those who are in Christ. Cancer took one huge weight lifter and shrunk him into a skinny sheath of a guy, but at the same time it pumped him full of joy in his own salvation. God showed him what was important, left his life as uncluttered as an empty gym so he could see the truth.

Even the worst of times can be the best of times. That's the idea of Romans 5. Even with cancer warring against your body, you can have peace with the Prince himself.

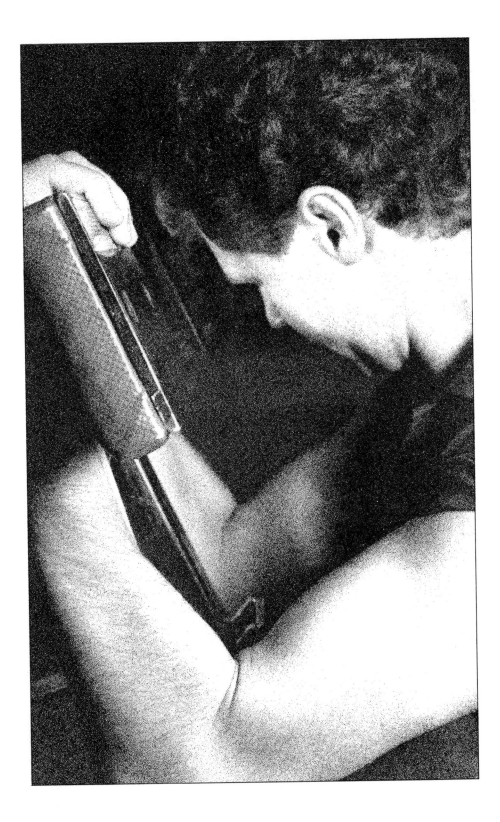

166

JESSE'S ESCAPE (15)

Prayer:

When the time comes for us to take a stand, Lord, please give us courage and conviction. Thank you for your promise to always be there. Amen.

Read Romans 8:31–39

After doing two blocks in a hard sprint, Jesse realized that Bronson couldn't be chasing every one of them. He heard no footsteps cracking the gravel behind him, so he stopped at the end of the alley, just out of the spread of the streetlight, and looked back. No one was following him—not even any of the guys. He dropped his hands to his knees and tried to regain his breath.

The neighborhood seemed very quiet. Houses stood like huge, motionless boxcars in the half darkness. The only sound came from the buzz of cars on a busy street several blocks away.

Jesse didn't know who he was. That was his problem, he thought. Something had happened on his cycle, something he couldn't get yet—something so big he could see it only in outline, like tall backyard trees against the stars in the sky.

That farmer, Arlen, took two bales and slapped them together into one open spot, made the two things fit together perfectly. It was something like that. What he had to do was fit this new guy—this guy that saw everything differently now—with the old one—the guy with the friends. Those two characters had to fit into one body somehow. That's what he thought. He couldn't just walk away from the old guys who'd been his friends. Somehow he couldn't run away again. He had to go back and tell them the truth.

For a minute he hated himself for growing up, for changing. He wished he could turn around and go back to Seth and Butch, be the guy he used to be—good old Jesse the troublemaker, the smart guy. He wished he could go back to Bronson's garden and smash it all, wreck the whole business and laugh about it. But he knew he couldn't. It was out of the question. He knew it was wrong, and he couldn't do it.

There was something sweet about the silence all around him, about being alone with himself. It would be easy to let the world go by without him. He could bury himself—walk back home and stay there forever, away from all his old buddies. But that would be wrong too, and he knew it. Somehow he had to go back— maybe not tonight, but he had to go back. And he knew now that he could do it alone.

This time Jesse didn't say any "amens" when he prayed, because this wasn't like the prayers he had heard when he was a kid. He leaned up against a pole, put his face in his hands, and prayed. He asked God to make him strong enough to go back and face his buddies, to go back and tell them he was different now.

That's all—it was just that simple, but this time his prayer came deep from the darkness inside of him, came up searching for the light.

And when he pulled himself back up and started walking, he just had to laugh, because he knew—he just knew—that God was there listening. And he knew that on his way back to the park he wouldn't be alone.

167

SPRINTERS AND WEIGHT-MEN

Read 1 Corinthians 9:24–27

My mother wasn't the first person to notice that I wasn't blessed with great speed. I knew it long before she did. One day she watched the neighborhood kids having a track meet in our backyard, and she saw me, huffing and puffing, and coming in last. "Why do you let Tom beat you?" she asked later, over lunch. "He's two years younger than you are."

Even as a boy my friend Tom had skinny, little ankles and calves as round and hard as fists. He had legs like a thoroughbred horse— all lean muscle. He could run— boy, could he run! When he got to high school, he ran sprints and beat just about everybody around.

When I was in high school, I was on the track team too—all four years. But I never ran one race. I was a "weightman." We were called "weightmen" because we threw "the weights"—a discus and a shotput. But we were also men of great weight. Any two of us weighed more than a whole relay team of sprinters.

When the weightmen used to run, the sprinters would laugh their heads off, because most of us ran like half-dead mules in slow motion. "Boom, boom, boom"— one foot over the other.

The coach loved to make jokes. "You weightmen run well," he said, "but you run too long in one spot." Ha-ha. Very funny. "Hey, Jim—if you're going to run, take that piano off your back." Yuk, yuk. Everybody had fun with the big blob weight-men. We didn't have skinny legs like the sprinters—we had thunder thighs. "Boom, boom, boom."

Paul knew that the Corinthians loved track and field. They held big athletic festivals right there in the city. So when Paul wrote to them, he used language they would understand.

Paul also knew why people train to run. When a Corinthian sprinter broke the tape at the finish line, he was given a round of applause and a little wreath of pines to wear like a crown. That was it. No medals, no ribbons, just a couple twigs full of pine needles and a couple minutes of glory. Doesn't sound like much, does it? Two weeks and the needles would get yellow.

So Paul told the Corinthian sprinters that running the long race of life in praise of God will get you a prize that won't lose its needles.

Somewhere—I'm not even sure where—I've got a drawer full of ribbons and medals from sports. Unlike pine needles, they'll last a long time. But they aren't that big of a deal to me anymore. When it comes right down to it, they're a lot like those pine needles the Corinthians wore.

If you want the big prize, Paul said, train to be one of God's sprinters. If you win, you'll have something really great.

And yet there's a difference. God's gold medal is really a gift. It's not something you earn, even by working up a bucketful of sweat. God gives the blue ribbon of salvation to all who train in his service.

Christ's gift of salvation makes all those who run the race—even those with thunder thighs—into thoroughbred champions.

168

LOVING YOUR NEIGHBOR

Prayer:

Lord God, make us humble enough to put others first. Make us strong enough to give in when we should. Help us not to cause others to stumble because of our words or actions. In Jesus' name, Amen.

Read 1 Corinthians 10:23–33

Some good Christians are teetotalers. They think that all liquor—from beer to wine to whiskey—is evil. Other, equally good Christians like a glass of wine with a meal. Put those two types of good Christians together, and there might be trouble.

Some Christians don't have TVs; other Christians watch their sets every night. Some Christians play bingo; others think gambling is a sin. Some Christians smoke; others think tobacco is Satan's weed.

I have a friend who used to teach at a school where smoking was thought to be absolutely sinful. This guy is one of the best Christians I know—but he smokes a little. When he taught at that school, he carried his cigarettes around tucked in his sock.

What happens when two really strong Christians disagree about what is and what is not a sin—a cigar, a movie, a dance, or Sunday brunch at a restaurant?

Paul had a line on that kind of problem at Corinth. In that city people sometimes ate meat from animals slaughtered in a religious sacrifice. Some Christians wouldn't eat that food; they felt that eating such meat was like being part of the pagan religion.

So what happened when a Christian went to his neighbor's for dinner and discovered he was serving sacrificed meat? Paul told the Christians in Corinth not to get huffy about it. If your host doesn't make a big deal out of it, he said, don't go raising a stink—just be cool and eat hearty.

But what, the Corinthian Christians asked, if the host announces that he's proud his lamb chops come from a sacrificed animal? In that case, said Paul, stay away from the meat—just take an extra helping of coleslaw. Why? Because if you eat that chop, you'll make him think

he should be proud of his silly meat. You'll make him believe his own dumb ideas. So stay away from the meat, the apostle said, for your neighbor's sake.

All these table manners came from Christ's example, of course. Remember how he washed the disciples' dirty feet? Paul says it in verse 24: "nobody should seek his own good, but the good of others." Put your neighbor first.

Paul's opening line is unbelievable: "everything is permissible." That's freedom all right. But he also says that everything is *not* beneficial. There are times when we should say no.

And finally, here's the big rule: whatever you do—anytime, anywhere—be sure you're doing it to bring glory to God. Keep God first always.

Sometimes you may have to hold yourself back. Sometimes you may have to bend over backwards . . . but then Christ's days on earth were spent doing pretty much the same thing.

169

"THE GREATEST OF THESE"

Read 1 Corinthians 13

Once upon a time a man who could really turn on an audience filled assembly halls and churches wherever he went. People sat on hardwood benches and stared at him, entranced. When the speech was over, many went out crying, claiming that their lives were changed forever. The man was a phenomenon. Thousands obeyed him; those who didn't, he despised.

Once upon a time a writer spent years studying the world she lived in, then wrote a shelf full of books about how things were and how they might be. Thousands read her books, and later her newspaper columns, because she seemed to have a crystal ball. If she said there would be war or peace, there was. She lived alone in a mountain cabin and refused to see any guests.

Once upon a time a scientist worked his entire lifetime to find a cure for a crippling disease. He was so devoted to his task that he cared very little for his wife, and his children never knew him. When the man was almost sixty, he found the cure which had eluded him for so long. His story appeared in all the leading magazines. Soon an inoculation was developed; the disease he fought against was conquered. He received a medal of honor.

Once upon a time a preacher who read the Bible very carefully decided to start his own church, convinced that all other preachers were dead wrong about their doctrine. Often, right in the middle of worship services, he would thunder against those who didn't believe exactly what he preached. Sometimes he would weep, right up on the pulpit. Everywhere he looked he found enemies. All of them, he claimed, were children of Satan.

Every single one of these "once-upon-a-time" people were headliners. Every one of them was really gifted with talent and power. Every one did great things. But every one fell short.

Love, Paul says, is "the greatest of these." Big talk, big money, big brains, big zeal—all are second-fiddle to the kindness, the humility, and the sweet honesty of selfless love.

The Pharisee and the high priest saw a beaten man in the ditch. They thought about helping him, but they were busy—they had big things to do. The Samaritan never thought—not even for a moment. He just acted—out of love.

Faith is important, hope is necessary, but love is something else all together, Paul says. Love—loving others as Christ has loved us—is "the greatest of these."

170

DEATH AND LIFE

Read 1 Corinthians 15:12–26

I have a scrapbook that holds absolutely everything there is to know about a man named Edgar Hartman. He was a great uncle of mine, but I never knew him.

Edgar grew up in a Wisconsin village. When he was in his early twenties, he went off to war in France. It was 1918, just a few months before the end of what people called "the war to end all wars." Edgar fought only a few short weeks before he was killed by German artillery.

My scrapbook contains Edgar's baby picture, a portrait of Edgar with his grade-school graduating class, four snapshots of him decked out in his military uniform, and a picture of the white cross that marks his grave in France. It also contains some letters sent to Europe by his sister, my grandma, after she hadn't heard from him for weeks. Each letter is marked with a return-to-sender stamp. None were delivered.

Also in the scrapbook is a notice from the government, telling the family of Edgar's death, and a handwritten letter from a friend who saw Edgar die in the trenches. On the last page is a handsome certificate with fancy script writing, announcing that Edgar died for his country.

Today, everything there is to know about Edgar Hartman fits between two covers of a scrapbook. His sister, mother, and father are long gone from the earth. No one alive remembers Edgar Hartman. This book is all that remains—one man's whole life between two covers.

In a way it's scary to page through that scrapbook. It's as if I'm holding a grave. And it reminds me that someday I, like Edgar, will be completely gone from the face of the earth. So will my wife, my children, and all of you who are reading this right now. Maybe someday some nephew or granddaughter will have the pictures of our lives in a scrapbook.

No one even remembers Edgar Hartman. There's something scary about that too. It's pretty easy to be afraid of dying.

In today's passage Paul gets a little angry with some Corinthians who question the resurrection from the dead. If the dead are not raised, then Christ hasn't been raised either, Paul tells them. And if Christ did not rise, then you're all dead in sin. That's a reason to be scared.

It's pretty easy to be afraid of dying, but if you believe that Christ himself walked out of the grave, then death isn't anything to get worked up about. His resurrection brings eternal life to all who believe in him. His resurrection makes death itself turn belly-up.

And when Christ comes again with life, my Uncle Edgar will be much more than a scrapbook. He'll pop right up, as will all of God's sleeping children, because Christ has already nailed down the lid on death's coffin. That's what Paul says.

171

Prayer:

Father in

heaven, help us

to be loving and

forgiving

toward others,

as you are

toward us. In

Jesus' name,

Amen.

Read Galatians 6:1–10

Jani and Donna were buddies. They lived two blocks from each other, and ever since second grade, they'd stood at the same bus stop, boarded the same bus, and attended the same school. They couldn't count the times they'd slept overnight at each other's houses. They even went to the same church.

One Saturday afternoon the two girls headed to the mall to meet a bunch of their friends. It was March and the storefronts were full of summer clothes. Jani said she wanted to try on some blouses, so she and Donna hit a bunch of different shops. Jani found this really wild, orange and white striped top with a low scoop neck.

Donna whistled when she stepped out of the dressing room with it on. "Why don't you buy it?" she asked.

"I don't have enough money," Jani told her, turning in front of the mirror.

Donna checked out the slacks at the back of the store until Jani came out of the dressing room. "It's way too much money anyway—my mother'd kill me," Jani said.

On their way out of the store, the girls passed a rack of tank tops. "Check out this one," Donna said, but Jani was in a big hurry all of a sudden.

The girls were no more than twenty feet out of the store when a guy in a sport coat grabbed Jani's arm. "I'm sorry, Miss—but you'll have to come with me," he said.

"What for?" Jani asked, pulling her arm away.

"I think you know why," he said. He grabbed her arm again, this time managing to hang on.

"What's going on?" Donna said. "Let go of her."

"You're under arrest, Miss," the guy said to Jani.

Minutes later Donna heard the man accuse Jani of shoplifting—of walking right out of the store with that expensive blouse under her clothes. Donna didn't believe it at first—not until she saw Jani cry as she followed the man back into the store.

Donna sat on a bench in the mall with her head in her hands. She just couldn't believe it. She would never have guessed Jani would do it—never. It was such a dumb thing to do, such a bad thing. Donna didn't know what to think of her best friend. She just knew that she didn't want to see Jani. She was scared to death of trying to find the right way to talk to her very best friend.

The apostle Paul could have helped Donna. He told the Galatians to try their best to act like Christ himself would act with a friend who's in trouble. He would have told Donna the same thing. He would have encouraged her to be truthful with Jani, but in a gentle way. "Restore that person gently," Paul said.

"Try to do what Christ did—carry each other's burdens," Paul told the Galatians. "Forgive them. Love them."

Nobody ever said it was easy, but Christ showed the world it was right.

172

JESSE'S ESCAPE (16)

Read Philippians 2:5–11

They spotted him as he crossed the street to the park.

"Hey, Jesse," someone said. "Bronson get you?"

"Never saw him," Jesse said.

About fifteen kids stood or sat around in a circle.

"I don't think he ever came out of the house," Butch said. "He won't see his garden until he sits down for breakfast." The others laughed.

Seth sat there drinking a can of pop and glaring. "How come you didn't help me stomp it, Jesse?" he said.

The laughing died in a flash. The gang waited, eyes trained on Jesse.

"It wasn't necessary—all you wanted was a melon," Jesse said. "It was dumb and it was wrong."

Seth spit on the grass. "Something's wrong with you, Jesse. You ain't the same guy we used to know. We can't trust you anymore—now that you're going to start teaching Sunday School—"

Five or six of the kids laughed.

"I've been saying that I think you're a chump now, Jesse." He was building up for a fight. Jesse knew he was pushing him hard. "Nobody here needs somebody telling us what's right and what's wrong."

"Maybe you're right, Seth," Jesse said. "Maybe I don't belong here. Maybe you hit it right on the head."

"Dumb accident scrambled your brains." Seth pushed himself up to his feet and looked over both shoulders to make sure people got his funny joke.

"Leave him alone, Seth," Butch said.

Jesse shook his head. "I'm *not* the same guy I used to be. I was almost dead. Maybe you see things different once you almost been dead."

Seth was angry. "I think we're going to make a new person out of you, Jesse." He raised the can and flung pop all over Jesse, all over the front of his shirt. "I baptize you as one big jerk," he said.

Butch grabbed Seth's arm. "Nobody here's laughing at your jokes," he said. "Leave Jess alone."

"I'm sorry it's got to be this way," Jesse said. "But I've changed. Lots of things are more important than they were. Somehow God's got me trying to love other people. I know it sounds weird—"

Seth jerked away from Butch. "Guy's a jerk—bounced on his head on that cycle of his," he said, "and has never recovered."

When he walked away, several others walked with him.

"That took guts," Butch said, "a lot of guts."

Jesse nodded. He knew he was done running now. Tonight he'd start praying for Seth and the others. Tomorrow would take more strength and more courage.

"So what happened anyway when you ran away?" Butch said.

Jesse sat down in the cool grass, pulled off his sticky shirt and laid it next to him. It would be a long story.

173

THE BIG DAY

Read 1 Thessalonians 4:13–18

Chances are not many of us spent much time today thinking about Christ's second coming. We're all busy—with work, with meetings, with school, with babysitting, with church, and with a dozen other things. We're all too busy to sit back and think that someday the whole silly world will shut down tight when Christ comes again.

But some Christians do spend a lot of time thinking about the second coming. A man named Hal Lindsey has written a number of books in the last few years, most of them having to do with what theologians call "eschatology," or the study of the last days of the world. Lindsey claims that if we read some parts of the Bible very carefully, we will see that the last day is not far off.

Lindsey may well be right, of course. But he may well be wrong too. The Bible says more than once that we won't know exactly when that day will be. It will come "like a thief in the night."

Mr. Lindsey isn't the first to try to pinpoint God's timetable. Lots of others have tried it too. My grandpa used to tell me about some people who went up on a mountain one special Tuesday because they expected to see Jesus Christ riding down to earth in a golden chariot. There they sat, all day and all night, but it didn't happen. Must have been a long trip home for those folks.

In today's passage Paul talks about Christ's second coming. Paul was worried because some of the new Thessalonian Christians seemed to have an old idea of death—that it was really the end of things. Now any Christian who feels that way is bound to get a little sad; after all, if death is the end, we don't have heaven to look forward to. And that's exactly what some Thessalonians thought. They thought that only the people who were alive when Jesus came would be taken to glory. And they didn't care to be left behind.

So Paul explained things by using the word *sleep.* He wanted the Thessalonians to think of death as going to sleep.

Not long ago our son fell out of bed in the middle of the night. My wife and I both woke up in a flash, and David started bawling his head off. So we tucked him back in, told him everything was all right, and in a couple of minutes he was sound asleep again.

The next morning I asked him if he hurt himself. He looked up from his toast and stared. He didn't remember a thing. He sleeps like a rock.

Someday every one of us will sleep like a rock. But then that big day will come and all God's people will snap awake—zap! just like that. Your parents won't even need a cup of coffee.

Death, said Paul to the Thessalonians, is really being "asleep in Jesus." Don't worry, he said. When the big alarm goes off, you'll all be wide awake.

174

ALL-STARS

Read Hebrews 11:1–16

I'm no racing fan, but I went to an Indianapolis 500 museum once, years ago. I got a big kick out of that museum. It was full of old junk: oil cans, helmets, tires, and a bunch of old-time racing cars, fat and round as a summer sausage riding on a pair of spindly bicycle wheels. The place was like an Indy hall of fame—lots of big pictures of famous drivers and spectacular crashes.

I've never been to Cooperstown, New York, but you can be sure that if I ever get there, I'll take in the Baseball Hall of Fame. I love baseball. For me, just seeing Babe Ruth's bat would be a thrill. Being right there next to Willie Mays' tube socks would be something I'd never forget.

Nearly every sport has a hall of fame—probably because that type of museum makes a lot of money off tourists. Somewhere, I'm sure, there's a golfing hall of fame, and, even though I wouldn't cross a street to see it, I suppose there's a bowling hall of fame too. For all I know, there's probably a buffalo chip throwers' hall of fame out West, and a hog callers' museum down South. People like heroes. We've all got them.

Hebrews 11 is a famous chapter in the Bible; you might think of it as a believers' hall of fame. In fact, it's fun to think of designing a hall of fame to go with Hebrews 11. We'd call one room "The Abraham Room." But what would we put in it?

First, we'd have to hang a big picture somewhere; then maybe a couple of Abraham's suitcases as a reminder of the time he picked up and left his big ranch because God told him he had to.

It'd be great if we had a sound track of Abraham and Sarah laughing when God told them about having a son. We could hook it up to a little button with a sign telling people to push it if they wanted to hear some silly chuckling.

If the faith hall of fame were a big place, maybe we could even include a big tent with a sign over it—"Abraham and Sarah slept here."

What's great about museums is the way they help you feel like you're part of history. If we could stand right there in Abraham's tent, most of us would probably feel a lot closer to the man who received God's big promise.

Faith's hall of fame would probably be a moneymaker too. But, intriguing as it sounds, it might not be such a good idea. Abraham, Enoch, Abel, and Noah—all these characters are part of the list because they believed without "proof." They didn't need a museum to tell them that the great I AM exists. Faith was enough for them. That's why they're in Hebrews 11.

"Faith is being sure of what we hope for," says the first verse, "and certain of what we do not see."

Faith's hall of fame features none of the world's all-stars. It includes God's heroes. These heroes turned their backs on the world's promises and followed a dream God gave them. That's faith. That's why reading Hebrews 11 is a thrill for believers.

These folks are heroes, real heroes. They've already got their hall of fame right now in another country—a heavenly one.

175

SNOTTI-NESS

Read James 2:1–13

Kids break all God's commandments, I'm sure, just like adults do. Wait a minute, you say—how about committing adultery? Okay, I'll grant you that not many kids commit adultery.

Well, how about "you shall not kill"? Not many kids are murderers either, right?

Sometimes I wonder. Sometimes I think that kids can be absolutely murderous on each other, even when they're very young. Take Jeff, for example. He's only six. He's got an eye problem that makes his eyes flutter. He'll grow out of it, but right now it's a problem, The kids on his block just about bug him to death about it. They say all kinds of mean things.

In junior high things don't change much. In junior high kids start ganging up in cliques that put other kids down just by keeping them out. Kids can be terribly snotty. *Snotty* is an odd word, but you probably all know what it means. It has to do with the nose. Snotty kids are usually the ones who walk around with theirs peaked.

Snotty kids form cliques for specific reasons. Sometimes it has to do with what a person wears—all of Sandy's friends wear two earrings in each ear, for instance. Sometimes it has to do with other things—Jack's buddies are all jocks. If you don't have doubly-pierced ears or you can't dribble a ball between your legs, you just don't get in. Sorry.

It can almost kill kids to feel out of it. And that's a kind of murder.

The book of James tells us that real faith shows itself—clearly—in the lives of those who have it. If it doesn't, James says, then it's not real faith. If you claim to be in God's family, then you'd better act like it.

The world is full of cliques—rich people, white people, beautiful people, athletic people, powerful people. But God's kingdom includes all those who believe—rich and poor, red and yellow, black and white, clumsy kids, and even beggars. And if Christian kids like only those who look or act or smell or think like they do, James says they aren't Christians at all.

That's really tough stuff, isn't it? Some people aren't easy to love. Some kids aren't very handsome or pretty. Some dress in out-of-date clothes. Some can't laugh at jokes. Some are dumb.

Makes no difference, says James. There's no room for any snottiness in the life of a Christian—old or young. Sorry.

Prayer:

Help us, Father in heaven, to love others, whoever they are. Teach us not to give in to the hype of the world in which we live. In Jesus' name,

Amen.

176

THE LITTLE BEAST

Prayer:

Forgive us, Lord,

for saying

things we don't

mean or things

that hurt others.

Teach us to

control our

tongues and our

thoughts. In

Jesus' name,

Amen.

Read James 3:1–12

Some people dislike dogs. Others really hate cats. But there's probably no animal that upsets people the way snakes do. Snakes can turn some people so completely inside out that they go into a stark-raving panic. My wife's one of them. If there's a snake on TV, she leaves the room—zip! she's gone.

Maybe it's their slithery-ness. Maybe it's their greasy-looking skin, or the way their bodies seem to ride through the grass on invisible legs. Maybe it's their pointy heads, or their absolute silence. Or maybe it's their tongues—flitting in and out of their closed jaws like a quiet whiplash.

I think of a snake's tongue when I read verse 8: "It is a restless evil, full of deadly poison." But James isn't talking about a water moccasin here; he's talking about us—plain old flesh-and-blood humans. Monster humans with snakes' tongues? It sounds like a horror movie.

But the horror in the passage doesn't come from the idea that a human being might be born with a fleshy tongue shaped like a forked stick. What's scary about these verses is that each of us already has a monster organ in our mouth. James says the tongue is like a fire that can burn down an entire forest. Too often, he says, our tongues steer us into trouble.

Think of it this way. Karen likes Sam, and it's no secret. One day she sees Sam talking to Ann, who at that exact moment becomes her ex-friend. "I'll never talk to her again," Karen says to all her friends, "never—mark my word."

Total silence between the two girls grows into three long weeks, even though Ann says she never had her eyes on Sam anyway. She even apologizes—through a mutual friend.

One weekend there's a concert in a nearby city, and Ann's mom says she'll take the girls. Somebody else—not Ann—calls Karen and tells her that she's invited too. But Karen is one stubborn cookie. She remembers what she said in front of all her friends. "I'm sorry," she says; "I'm busy." She puts down the phone and goes to her room and cries.

Sometimes our tongues make commitments that we'd rather not live with later on. We put ourselves on the line—maybe because we're really upset or angry or just plain dumb—and we feel that we've got to live up to whatever idiot thing we've said.

That's what James warns us about. The gift of speech is one fine thing, he says, but unless we keep a close watch on what we say, we can get ourselves into big trouble over and over again. Our tongues, like every other part of us, are affected by the naughtiness that's in us from our birth. One moment we can sing hymns; an hour later we can sit in a circle and put down our friends. All sorts of sweet things and all sorts of trash come from the same tongue.

Tame that beast, James says, or else it will control you.

177

JOHN'S TESTIMONY

Read 1 John 4:7–21

When the kids had lit the candles, the lights were turned out. A bearded preacher held a thick, golden candle in one hand and read from the Bible. Strange shapes danced along the windows of the shelter house. On the ceiling, reflections from twenty yellow flames shifted in and out in living patterns, as if there were some unsettled breezes blowing across the kids sitting cross-legged on blankets and sleeping bags strewn over the floor.

When the preacher was finished, the kids sang soft hymns and chants—"Kum-ba-yah, my Lord, kum-ba-yah." In the quiet darkness their faces glowed like masks in the candlelight. "Someone's crying, Lord, kum-ba-yah."

Then the preacher waited in silence. No one moved. He kneeled and prayed for the Holy Spirit to come into their hearts. In one corner, a kid sobbed so gently he could barely be heard.

When the prayer was over, the others waited, motionless, many of them with their heads down.

"Would anyone like to testify what Christ means to them?" the preacher asked, his voice low and deep and sweet . . .

Some of you may have been through that kind of thing. I have—many times. I understand why the preacher wanted kids to testify about their faith. He wanted them to make a public commitment to Christ. That's good. It's difficult to imagine how anyone— a kid or an adult—can claim to be a Christian if she or he won't confess, out loud and in public, that Christ is King.

But even though I understand why testimonies are good, I never liked being a part of the ritual— the dark silence, the candles' glow, the chanting, and all the gushy emotions.

It's not that I'm against

testimonies. I love John's testimony in this letter. "If anyone says, 'I love God,' yet hates his brother," John says, "he is a liar." John should know. There was a time he hated; now he loves. That's his testimony.

Luke (chapter 9) tells us how an entire Samaritan village told Jesus' messengers that they wanted no part of this Jesus business. Tell him to stay away, they said.

John and James boiled in anger at the Samaritans. "You want us to call in angels and burn the whole place to the ground?" they asked Christ. That's how angry they were. But Jesus rebuked them, Luke says. It doesn't take a genius to guess what Christ told them about love.

Today's passage shows that John has learned some things about loving others. John doesn't talk about air raids anymore—no more fiery destruction. "Whoever does not love does not know God," he says, "because God is love." It's just that simple with him now, because he knows. And it doesn't take candlelight to get it out of him.

178

JOHN'S DREAM

Read Revelation 12

Revelation is a strange book. The Old Testament is filled with stories and songs and prophecies. The Gospels tell the story of the Messiah who was promised in the old stories. The letters of the apostles tell Christians how to be believers.

But Revelation is something else completely.

If we want to make any sense at all out of this odd book, we have to understand that it is a dream, a vision. The Bible is full of dreams, but none of them go on quite as long as John's long dream in Revelation.

Dreams aren't like stories. Abraham *actually* left all his land to follow God's direction. David *really* killed a big guy named Goliath. And the Israelites were *in fact* thrown out of the land that God had promised them. Those things happened.

John's dream actually happened too, but we should read it like a vision, not a story. Otherwise, it makes absolutely no sense. It's really a bunch of symbols.

For instance, the woman "clothed with the sun" isn't really a woman at all. She represents the church, or God's people. And the wild seven-headed dragon represents Satan. He stands waiting for the woman to give birth to a child, who is Christ, God's Son who became human to save us from our sins. But when the child goes back to be with God, the woman runs off and hides in the desert for 1260 days, waiting for the child to return.

Twelve hundred and sixty days, or a little less than four years, have long since passed—and still Christ hasn't come. The number is a symbol of an unknown amount of time between Christ's ascension and his return.

Then comes the war in heaven between Satan and his troops and God's overpowering might. John says that the dragon and all his sidekicks got thrown down to earth in one mighty flip. In verses 10–13, that big victory is celebrated in a song. But there's a warning too, a warning that Satan will be tough to beat on earth. It's a warning for the woman, for God's people. We've got to be on constant guard against the power of the devil.

Revelation's story isn't a new one. The whole Bible has already shown us how the big wars will end. God's people get in trouble, but God never breaks his promise to be faithful. He stands by his word, even when his people don't always live up to their promises.

The book of Revelation may be John's really strange dream—but the story behind it isn't new. We've been reading the same thing all along.

Prayer:

Thank you, Father, for showing us again that you will always be with your people and that you will defeat Satan and evil. We praise you for your faithfulness and your power. Amen.

179

A NEW HEAVEN AND NEW EARTH

Read Revelation 21:1–8

By this time you know that the Bible is full of stories and ideas, songs and prayers. Between its covers you will find whole books full of laws and commandments, and enough history to keep a teacher lecturing for years. The Bible's a scrapbook of colorful characters, from villains like Ahab and Jezebel, and scoundrels like Judas, to heroes like Joshua, the mighty soldier, and Rahab, whose life flip-flopped when she simply believed the rumors she had heard about the great I AM. The Bible tells of more unusual things than *Believe It or Not*: mules that talk, paraplegics that jump, and a big-mouth giant flattened by a pebble whipped at him by a little guy who should have been tending sheep in the back forty.

And yet, sometimes we wish the Bible told us more.

For instance, it doesn't color us a picture of what the new heaven and the new earth will be like. Will there be streets of gold and pearly gates? No one knows. Will all of us suddenly be turned into one mass choir? No one knows. Will there be bicycles there? Baseball games? Bananas? Nice soft beds? No one knows.

So all we can do is imagine. I'm sure my son couldn't think of a heaven without some kind of *Star Wars* toys. My wife is sure she won't have to plan dinners anymore, and I'd like to believe that I'll have the time and ability to write a great novel.

Likely as not, we're all wrong.

We could be shocked. For instance, maybe we'll see mass murderers there. I know that seems impossible, but nothing is beyond the power of the I AM. All of us will be changed; maybe I'll actually enjoy painting the house. Maybe my daughter will just love to sit down and practice piano. Maybe that guy behind me in church, the guy who sings like a tortured bull, will turn into a concert tenor.

John's vision helps us to see something at least. The new heaven and the new earth will be beautiful, he says: no crying, no pain, no death, no mourning. And here again is God's promise: "They [God's own] will be his people, and God himself will be with them and be their God." That's the promise given to Abraham. That's the promise millions have ignored from way back in biblical history up through today. But finally, after Christ's return, God will be with us—living just next door and sitting at our tables.

God's faithful people really don't need to know a whole lot more than that to keep them happy. The thought of God right here—seeable and touchable—is enough to help us pray for that day. And it should be enough to keep us faithful until he comes again.

180

RIVERS OF LIFE

Prayer:

Lord God, thank you for your Word. Keep us faithful to it and to you. Make us strong and loving Christians, we pray. Forgive our sins and our doubts. Thank you for your great love. In Jesus' name, Amen.

Read Revelation 22:1–7

The desert can be a beautiful place. The giant saguaro cacti, their towering arms reaching up twenty feet or more above the ground, wear flowered crowns in the early spring. But even in mid-summer's heat, the sandy, soft tones of a desert horizon can be peaceful and lovely.

The desert also can be deadly. Without water, people don't do as well as the cacti. In a matter of hours, extreme desert heat draws moisture from our bodies and drains our strength to zero.

Phoenix, Arizona, is a big city built right in the desert. Although more than a million people live in the surrounding area, there isn't enough water to keep them alive. So the city pumps in whole rivers of water from the mountains. No one can live without water. Mountain water keeps the city alive and growing.

Old Jerusalem is like Phoenix. Even in the Old Testament, Jerusalem's residents knew that if there was one problem with their city, it was the lack of a river. Isaiah predicted that "the glorious Lord shall be to us a place of broad rivers and streams" (33:21). God's people were always conscious of this one flaw: Jerusalem, like Phoenix, needed a river of living water.

John's vision of the New Jerusalem refers back to the old problem. "Then the angel showed me the river of the water of life, as clear as crystal, flowing from the throne of God and of the Lamb down the middle of the great street of the city." In John's mind, the new Jerusalem won't have a single weakness. As great as the old city was, the new one will be perfect, its river of life bringing fruit to the city's trees.

The curse of the garden will be erased, the trees' leaves bringing healing where for thousands of years there was nothing but brokenness and suffering. Darkness will be gone, John says, and all of God's people will live in the perfect light of God's face as he dwells right there in the new city.

And there's more. John says we'll all be branded somehow with God's name over our foreheads. It's hard to imagine such a thing as being beautiful—a whole bunch of folks with tattoos. But you can be sure that the Father will find a way to make it pretty. And you can be sure that we'll love it.

This is the end—and the beginning. We've been through the whole book—from Adam's first bite into the forbidden apple to John's glorious dream. We've seen the Word made into human form when Christ came way down to our level to pick up all our sins and take them off our backs. We've heard his commandment to love, his warning to those who don't, or won't. We've watched a young church struggle to grow, powered by the Spirit. And we've seen John's vision of the end—which is actually the beginning.

"It's all true," the angel tells John.

Rivers of living water will turn our earth back into the beautiful, thistle-free garden it once was and change all of us into peaceful neighbors full of praise. God himself will live with us.

"Lord Jesus, come quickly."